Augustine's Prayerful Ascent

Augustine's Prayerful Ascent: An Essay on the Literary Form of the *Confessions*

✠

Robert McMahon

The University of Georgia Press ✠ *Athens and London*

© 1989 by the University of Georgia Press
Athens, Georgia 30602   All rights reserved
Set in 10/13 Trump Mediaeval
The paper in this book meets the guidelines for permanence
and durability of the Committee on Production Guidelines for
Book Longevity of the Council on Library Resources.
Printed in the United States of America

93 92 91 90 89   5   4   3   2   1

Library of Congress Cataloging in Publication Data
McMahon, Robert, 1950–
Augustine's prayerful ascent: an essay on the literary form of the
Confessions / Robert McMahon.
p. cm.   Bibliography: p.   Includes index.
ISBN 0-8203-1126-X (alk. paper)
1. Augustine, Saint, Bishop of Hippo. Confessiones.
2. Augustine, Saint, Bishop of Hippo. 3. Christian saints—Algeria—
Hippo—Biography. 4. Hippo (Algeria)—Biography. 5. Literary form.
I. Title.
BR65.A62M42 1989
242—dc19   88-27893   CIP

The author gratefully acknowledges permission to reprint excerpts
from *The Confessions of St. Augustine*, translated by John K. Ryan.
Copyright © 1960 by Doubleday, a division of Bantam, Doubleday,
Dell Publishing Group, Inc. Reprinted by permission of the
publisher.

British Library Cataloging in Publication Data available

To my wife, Kim Orr,
opera tua, totum hoc placitum non dissiluit

Contents

Acknowledgments

One pleasure in completing a work like this lies in the opportunity to thank the friends along the years who have enabled it. "Suole a riguardar giovare altrui," Dante writes, yet it is pleasant not only to look back but to express gratitude.

I first encountered Augustine's genius in classes taught by Vincent H. Learnihan and Harry J. Carroll, Jr., at Pomona College two decades ago. Their example as teachers, men of learning, and craftsmen of words led me to this profession and remains for me the standard of humane scholarship.

But I have been fortunate in my teachers. I first became interested in the problem of the *Confessions'* unity while studying Dante's *Commedia* with Robert M. Durling. Professor Durling has shared his thinking on Augustine with me over many years. Even when my own ideas diverged from his, he has remained as generous and amiable a teacher as ever. It is easier for me to declare where our ideas differ than to discover how deeply my work emerges from his.

The thesis argued here first saw the light in a rambling paper I wrote while in graduate school. Several learned friends charitably undertook to read and discuss it with me: Robert M. Durling, Ronald L. Martinez, Myra Uhlfelder, Victoria Kirkham, Fr. Robert Russell, O.S.A., and Frederick Van Fleteren. I remain grateful for their advice but, even more, for the belief they expressed in the value of my thinking, raw as it was.

While writing the present *Essay,* I have enjoyed the sustaining intellectual companionship of many here at Louisiana State University, but especially of Jim Babin, Jesse Gellrich, Michelle Gellrich, and Irv Resnick. Jesse Gellrich also read an earlier draft of the first two chapters and offered searching and helpful criticism. They have all been, at different times and in different ways, an affable, inquiring, and constructive audience for my efforts. One could not ask for finer colleagues.

I am grateful to the Council on Research at Louisiana State University for a Summer Research Grant that enabled me to complete the manuscript and to Gloria H. Henderson, who typed all my drafts with enduring good cheer. I also wish to express my thanks to the publishers of Doubleday-Image books for permission to quote from John K. Ryan's fine translation, *The Confessions of St. Augustine,* throughout this book.

Last, but never least, the dedication expresses my profoundest thanks. It says too little, but what could say enough?

Introduction

Questions regarding the formal coherence of Augustine's *Confessions* have been variously posed and still more variously answered.[1] Most frequently, they address the "unity" of the work. Some scholars hold that the *Confessions* has none. Pierre Courcelle and John J. O'Meara, for example, find Augustine pursuing a number of disparate projects in the volume: the confession of his past (books 1–9) and of his present (10), followed by an exposition of the first chapter of Genesis (11–13).[2] These projects, their arguments imply, are juxtaposed rather than coherently united in the volume; the subject matter of each is so different that only Augustine's title and his intention to "confess" hold them together.

For some, the "confessional" aim of the work is itself sufficient to give it "unity." Augustine uses the words *confiteri* and *confessio* throughout the volume to acknowledge his sins, praise God, and profess his faith.[3] A. Solignac finds in the *Confessions* "a unity more *interior* than logical: a unity of spirit and intention more than a coherent and progressive order of developments," and he quotes Paul Louis Landsberg for support: "The supreme unity of the *Confessions* is in the confession."[4]

Though the centrality of *confessio* to the work is universally recognized, other scholars have continued to seek for a more compelling principle of unity. Some have attended to a theme or cluster of themes treated recurrently in the volume. John C. Cooper, for example, cites numerous passages where Augustine explores the relations between eternity and time, while Ralph Flores examines Augustine's representation and use of reading and speech.[5] Some have traced a thematic progress through the parts of the work. Landsberg, followed by J. M. Le Blond, finds a principle of unity in Augustine's treatment of time: Books 1–9 concern his past and rely on *memoria*, book 10 explores his present and requires the writer's *contuitus*, while books 11–13 concern his future and exercise *expectatio*.[6] Some scholars have looked to other works by Augustine for a structural-thematic model adequate to the *Confessions*. Georg Pfligersdorffer, for instance, appeals to the *De beata vita* for his scheme: the journey to truth (books 1–9), announcing its exposition (10), and then presenting it (11–13).[7]

This rough taxonomy of approaches to the "unity of the *Confessions*" hardly begins to describe the variety of solutions to the problem. Of the many proposed, each has its adherents and its critics; each points, albeit in different ways, to important aspects of the work. Indeed, Agostino Trapé, after summarizing more than twenty such solutions, offers this shrewd comment: "From this rapid review the alert reader will be persuaded not only of the extraordinary complexity of Augustine's masterpiece which, like all great masterpieces, offers many diverse aspects to the consideration of readers, but also of the risk one runs in transforming a single idea—however valid, however present in the work— into a fundamental principle of its whole structure."[8]

A useful distinction in this debate is offered by Luc Verheijen in his paper "The *Confessions*: Two Grids of Composition and of Reading."[9] Verheijen distinguishes the question of the "unity" of the work from whether it embodies a coherent "plan." He points out a number of themes and modes of expression that run throughout the *Confessions*, all of which give the work "unity." However, this derives from a "unity of soul" in a single author, a man with persistent concerns and habits of expression. Augustine's "homogeneous gaze" unites the various parts of the work. By no means does such unity imply that the *Confessions* is coherently planned. Verheijen finds no such "plan" in the volume and argues that the "unity" imparted by Augustine's "homogeneous gaze" of mind proves far more important than any plan could be.

In the present book, in contrast, I argue that the *Confessions* is a coherently planned work. I endeavor to describe that plan and to set forth its governing principles. However, I do not deny the experience of "planlessness" that readers so often feel in studying the *Confessions*. Rather, I argue that such planlessness proves part of Augustine's plan. And yet the title of this book points not to the "plan" but to the "literary form" of the *Confessions*.

The word "plan" suggests an architect's drawing, the delineation of a structure subsequently to be built, while "form" points to an experience of order that may emerge through time and not simply in space. In the first chapter, I discuss the temporal unfolding of the *Confessions* as the fundamental principle of its self-presentation. I argue that the text presents itself as the written record of an *oral* prayer, unfolding in an ongoing present which our reading recreates. The *Confessions*, thus, is not so much a written text as a speaking text, not so much a product as the record of a process: the speaker's dynamic encounter with God recreated in the present of our reading. The speaker's *inquisitio veritatis* presents itself as unrehearsed, and so it moves circuitously and sometimes wanders into digressions. As a prayer, however, it proves equally responsive to the spur of grace; hence, its sudden leaps of thought and resolution of perplexing difficulties. For all its planlessness, its writer-speaker repeatedly avers that God is guiding his prayer. These principles in the self-presentation of the *Confessions* are fundamental to its literary *form* in a way that the word "plan" does not adequately suggest.

"Literary form" appears in the title of this book so as to suggest its formalist approach to the *Confessions*. To define that approach negatively: this work does not concern itself primarily with the history of Augustine's life or thought, or with the truth or validity of the positions he avows. Historical, philosophical, and theological questions, of course, are crucial to understanding the work, and the present book is informed by scholarship on them. But it does not explicitly address those issues. Defined in positive terms, this book approaches the *Confessions* "intrinsically": as a literary work that engages its audience in particular ways, possesses a variety of internal patterns, and proceeds in a narrative movement. I attempt to examine the work's self-presentation, to interpret certain recurrent patterns of imagery and theme, and to reveal the formal principles underlying the progressive unfolding of the work. This formalist approach to the *Confessions* is not ahistorical, however, even though it refuses to consider historical questions. I define the literary form of the work in terms deriving from the Christian-Platonist antique literary culture in which Augustine wrote. Such an approach might well be termed historico-formalist.

Perhaps an example may serve to illustrate the difference between a "historical" and a "literary" approach to the *Confessions*. When Peter Brown records Augustine's conversion in his biography, he quotes copiously from book 8, chapters 6–12, Augustine's own record of the event.[10] Brown thus uses the *Confessions* as a reliable source for historical knowledge. He does not concern himself with the other conversion stories recorded in book 8 or with their complex interrelations. These, however, prove central to Robert M. Durling's literary examination of the text. His treatment certainly bears on questions of history, but does not pursue them.[11]

To be sure, the "historical" and the "literary" approaches need not stand in isolation from each other, and in teaching and studying the *Confessions*, I would argue, they should not. Scholarship, however, tends to privilege one set of concerns over the other.[12] This seems unavoidable, since our publications respond less to the complexity of the work than to the problems we define for ourselves.

Hence, my approach to the *Confessions* proves formalist only in this book, and even here, not rigorously so in a theoretical sense. First, any formalist reading of Augustine must be informed by historical research, and I hope that this one may inform it as well. Second, I understand "literary form" as always addressed to an audience. Hence, such form is never "purely formalist," never merely an object for aesthetic contemplation in the Coleridgean sense. Literary form, rather, embodies a kind of "symbolic action," in Kenneth Burke's phrase; it involves strategies that work upon readers to persuade them of the viability or vitality, at the very least, of the literary work.[13] And the *Confessions*, surely, seeks to do more: to persuade its readers to believe in its truths, its Truth, or at least the principles of its search for truth. The strategies by which Augustine thus engages and persuades his readers prove central to the literary form treated in this book.

This formalist begging of the historical question requires me to distinguish, in literary terms, between the young Augustine and Augustine the writer. Some such distinction has always been made de facto in scholarship: between the young Augustine, whose acts are recorded in books 1–9, and Augustine the bishop-writer, whose "voice" records his past. However, since this book treats the *Confessions* in literary terms, it follows the conventions of literary criticism and records the deeds of the young Augustine in the present tense, rather than the past. This is not a common practice in literary study on the work, though I believe it should be. Even though I recognize the importance of the volume to our knowledge of Augustine's life before his conversion, I do not probe the work for historical understanding here as, for example, John O'Meara and Peter Brown have done.[14] Hence, this book adheres to the conventions of literary interpretation. It thereby avoids the past tense in recording the events of the work and so attempts to avoid historical statements for which it has no warrant, given the nature of its project.

I begin the project, in chapter 1, by discussing the self-presentation of the *Confessions*. Much of the work's repetitiousness within books and chapters, its tendency to digression and sudden shifts of direction, and much of its seeming planlessness begin to appear "natural" when the text is viewed as the *record* of an unrehearsed and relatively spontaneous *oral* prayer. Such a view departs somewhat from scholarly tradition and opens up a new perspective in reading the work. Augustine's "voice" in the text, the tone of his speaking, becomes as worthy of attention as subject matter, themes, vocabulary, and so on.

This understanding of the *Confessions* requires me to posit a distinction between Augustine the author and Augustine the speaker. The distinction is purely heuristic, of course: they are the same Augustine, but they are located in different dimensions with regard to the work. Augustine the author has composed, shaped, and revised the work so as to present convincingly the unrehearsed, spontaneous, and often wandering prayer of Augustine the speaker. Augustine the author stands, as it were, outside the work: he has shaped Augustine the speaker's prayerful encounter with God, a drama recorded in and through the text. The premise of the *Confessions* is that God, not Augustine the speaker, is guiding the course of the prayer. The speaker has not planned his *Confessions*; hence, their "obvious" lack of plan. Whatever latent design may be discovered in the volume as a whole, thus, purports to be providentially created, according to this premise. Since I must treat this premise critically, I attribute the latent design of the work to Augustine the author.

In chapter 2, I use this distinction to examine the conclusion of the work, the allegory on Genesis in book 13. I argue that the allegory presents itself as radically different from the treatment of Genesis 1 in books 11 and 12. The subject of the allegory, its style, tone, pace, the density of its scriptural allusions, its difficult texture: all imply that the allegory is "inspired" by unusual grace. In those twenty-seven chapters, Augustine the speaker asserts extraordinary insight into Genesis: he has examined God's will in the things recorded there

(13.34.49). As Solignac has observed, Augustine's allegory embraces the scope of all Creation "in its material reality and its spiritual significance, that is to say, as a figure of the Church and the spiritual Universe of the saints." It also encompasses the scope of all time, from the creative *fiat* to the "sabbath of eternal life" (13.36.51) after the Last Day.[15] Hence, Augustine discovers all of Scripture, from Genesis to Revelation, in its very first chapter. He also finds the sweep of human history in the text on its origin, and the meaning of history as well: salvation through the Church. The extraordinary scope and sweep of this hermeneutic vision argues it as "divinely inspired," and the text states this explicitly. The allegory, thus, provides a fitting conclusion to Augustine's *inquisitio veritatis*. Given suddenly to Augustine the speaker by grace, according to the premise of the work, this conclusion has been carefully planned by Augustine the author. It constitutes a kind of summation of Scripture and so provides a paradigm for the plan of the whole *Confessions*.

That plan is set forth in detail in the following two chapters. Chapter 3 explores the relations between the allegory in book 13 and books 1–9. Augustine discriminates nine divine acts in the week of Creation; his allegory on these proves parallel to the nine books of his autobiography. Act by allegorical act and book by autobiographical book, chapter 3 traces detailed parallels in their progress, central themes, and controlling metaphors. According to the premise of the *Confessions*, these parallels lie beyond the ken of Augustine the speaker: as he prays his way through the record of his past, he cannot possibly foresee the "divinely inspired" conclusion to his prayer. But just as God guides the wanderings of the young Augustine to conversion, so does he guide Augustine the speaker's wandering *Confessions* to a good end. The principle governing the young Augustine's history, thus, is precisely that which governs the literary form recording it: the content and the form of Augustine's conversion story are precisely aligned, given the premise of the *Confessions*.

The parallels between the autobiography and the allegory imply Augustine the author's bold self-understanding. God's creating the young Augustine as a Christian, in books 1–9, recapitulates God's creation of the Church in the allegory on universal Creation, in book 13. Augustine's autobiography, thus, parallels the astonishing scope and sweep of the allegory, albeit in a different mode. Augustine's creation as a Christian proves a microcosm for the scope, sweep, and meaning of all Creation and its history, as envisioned in book 13. Scholars have often pointed to the "universality" of the *Confessions* and of the Augustine they present. Solignac defines Augustine's "universal value" as "a universality which is not only that of a *type* of existence, but indeed that of a destiny understood in the history of universal Redemption."[16] The detailed parallels between the autobiography and the allegory in book 13 give this perception a new emphasis. Clearly, Augustine in the *Confessions* envisions himself in the universe, and the universe in himself, more profoundly, more literally and figuratively, than scholars have hitherto imagined.

Chapter 4 examines the paradigmatic analogy between the allegory and books 10–12. The *Confessions* turns, in book 10, "from a *narrative of memories* to the *principles of Memory*," in Kenneth Burke's phrase.[17] Hence, I follow this "turn to principles" and reexamine the allegory for an underlying structure, a governing principle, that also informs books 10–12. As a principle of the allegory, it also governs books 1–9 at a deep level.

That principle is the "return to origins," culminating in a "return to the Origin." Solignac has observed that the allegory in book 13 encompasses all time, for a Christian, from the Creation to the peace of the "sabbath that will have no evening" (13.35.50): "The cycle of time is, in that way, dialectically perfected: time is opened for us out of eternity by the *fiat* of the Creator and it is closed in the eternity of the heavenly rest, without ceasing to be governed by the transcendence of the divine eternity."[18] Time emerges from and is concluded in God's eternity: its progress culminates in a return to its Origin. This Christian understanding of time and history is revealed by the structure of Scripture: the Bible begins with Genesis and closes with a vision of "a new heaven and a new earth" (Rev. 21:1). Augustine's allegory encompasses the sweep of time, from eternity to eternity, and the movement of Scripture, from Creation to new creation. "Return to the Origin" is the principle governing the narrative structure of all of these.

The first part of chapter 4 establishes this principle in the allegory and reviews its multiple resonances in Augustine's thinking. As is well known, "return to the Origin" is the principle governing the Neoplatonist Upward Way. As such, it possesses metaphysical, ontological, moral, and epistemological implications. As John Freccero has shown, "return to the Origin" also describes Augustine's theories of history, of biblical allegory, of conversion and conversion narrative, and of communication in language.[19] It is a principle at the heart of Augustine's thought.

The second part of chapter 4 applies this principle to the *Confessions*, first with regard to books 10–12. Kenneth Burke has argued that books 10–12 trace "the kind of dialectical progression that is traditionally, in Neo-Platonist thought, called the Upward Way."[20] Book 10 largely concerns the principle of Memory; book 11 inquires into the nature of time; and book 12 dwells on God's sempiternal "heaven of heaven." Here, clearly, is a progression upward on a "return to origins." Time is a principle anterior to memory, just as God's sempiternal heaven proves anterior to time. Chapter 4 goes on to outline the progress of books 10–12 as a return to origins in much greater detail. Subsequently, the principle is applied to the narrative structure of books 1–9. The young Augustine's journey to conversion progresses as a return to the Origin, and the autobiography concludes with the death of Monica: the return of Augustine's origin to her Origin.

By the end of chapter 4, the thesis of this book is articulated in its details. Chapter 5 introduces the theological term "recapitulation" as a slightly different way to describe "return to the Origin." With this term, I recapitulate the whole argument so as to provide a concise and comprehensive statement on the unity and scope of the literary form of Augustine's *Confessions*. Having thus described that form "intrinsically," I hazard some thoughts on how Augustine envisioned the form to function for himself and his readers. Speculative as this attempt is, it seems demanded by Augustine's explicit concern, in the work, with his own motives for writing, and his readers' for reading, his *Confessions*.

To define the formal, unifying, principle of the *Confessions* as the "return to origins" places the work in a long, important, yet select tradition. For Augustine's masterpiece does not simply articulate, here and there, Christian-Platonist ideas: it embodies Platonist principles in its very narrative structure. Among Plato's dialogues, it has been argued that the *Phaedrus* and the *Republic* each unfold as an "ascent to principles," following the Upward Way.[21] Among Augustine's successors, Dante's *Commedia* is perhaps the most obvious example of a narrative that both articulates and embodies Christian-Platonist principles.[22] But the tradition certainly includes Boethius's *Consolation of Philosophy* as well as Kenneth Burke's *The Rhetoric of Religion: Studies in Logology.*[23] Each of these works proves a rich combination of narrative practice and literary theory. Each articulates the philosophical principles informing its own plot structure. Augustine's explicit meditations on the principles of memory and time following upon his autobiography clearly reflect upon his narrative in complex ways. In short, the *Confessions* is central to our tradition of Platonist literary form. And that tradition includes at least one rather un-Platonist work that nonetheless traces a narrative progress toward its own origins, where it discusses its theoretical principles: Proust's *A la recherche du temps perdu.*

What emerges from my analysis is a vision of formal coherence in the *Confessions* much like that in Dante's *Commedia*. Each work traces a three-part return to origins; each recapitulates the principles of the universe it envisions. One crucial difference between Dante's journey and Augustine's deserves careful notice, however. Dante presents his ascent as a providentially governed pilgrimage completed in the past and recreated in his poem. The ascent of Augustine—of Augustine the writer-speaker—takes place in the course of his ongoing prayer. It, too, is presented as providentially governed. But the formal coherence of that governing is by no means as readily apparent in the *Confessions* as in the *Commedia*. The return to origins is a fully coherent principle in the temporal unfolding of Augustine the speaker's dialogue with God, yet it has been carefully occulted by Augustine the author. The *Confessions* thus embodies, in its literary form, the dialectic all Christians experience between the obvious disorders in our history and God's providential ordering of all things. The ongoing, often wandering dialogue between the speaker and his God reproduces the dialectic between temporal events, with all their vagaries, and the eternal master plan in which they unfold. Here is a bold literary strategy indeed. I try to show how fully Augustine has planned and executed it.

To argue as I do for the "unity" of a literary work perhaps seems a rear-guard project in the wake of our several poststructuralisms. Dialogical criticism, for example, would urge us to treat "lack of unity" in the *Confessions* as positive, revealing musical dissonances in Augustine's polyphonic execution of the work. Equally, though in a different mode, the Derridean critique of Platonism cautions us against any attempt to portray the "unity" of a complex field, for such representation necessarily represses crucial différances. A Derridean might argue that "lack of unity" in the *Confessions* reveals Augustine's ambivalent awareness of these repressions in his Platonist conceptions of language, cosmic order, and so on. Deconstructionist approaches to certain aspects of the work have, in fact, been articulated by Margaret W. Ferguson and Eugene Vance.[24] Unfortunately, their work has won few followers and remains outside the mainstream of Augustine scholarship.

As valuable as deconstructionist and dialogical approaches to the *Confessions* can be, simply to celebrate the work's dissonant variety would prove ahistorical in at least two ways. First, Augustine himself stood squarely in the Platonist tradition and prized "unity" as an ideal—psychological, spiritual, ecclesiastical. "Lack of unity" in his masterpiece, therefore, remains a genuine scholarly problem. The formal coherence of the *Confessions*, it seems to me, needs to be demonstrated before the work can be fruitfully deconstructed and dialogized. Second, Augustine studies today stand at a juncture very different from that of literary studies in America. The latter have been turning away from "New Critical" formalist interpretation for well over a decade; recently, they have embraced a reconceived historicist criticism. Augustine studies, on the other hand, have long been thoroughly historicist in their methods and aims. "Heteroglossia" is a new term in literary studies for what Augustine scholars have long been exploring in highly sophisticated ways. In other words, formalist interpretation of the *Confessions* works antithetically against the dominant modes of scholarship in Augustine studies, just as historicist criticism is now doing in literary studies. The formalist project of the present book aligns itself, paradoxically enough, with an avant-garde in the study of antique Christian letters. It aims to bring Augustine scholarship and literary criticism more closely together, for perhaps no great work of literature has received so little close literary interpretation as the *Confessions*.

The problem explored here enjoys a prodigious history of scholarship. I do not review it in detail in these pages and I respond to it but selectively, for several reasons. First, the thesis I offer either disagrees or proves not directly compatible with most of it. To attempt to refute other views would have created a tedious and acrimonious work, one hardly in accord with the charity Augustine hoped for in his readers. It seems to me sufficient to argue my own thesis as carefully as possible and allow refutations to be read between the lines by those familiar with the *status questionis*.

I have also refused to contest other solutions to this problem because many different "right understandings" of formal coherence in the *Confessions* are not only possible but inevitable. No single view need be, or can be, right in any absolute sense. Dante's *Commedia*, for example, can be understood as representing a journey with three guides or as one recorded over three *cantiche*. These two descriptions divide the poem in very different ways and involve different visions of its literary form. Yet both are clearly correct within their own terms. The formal coherence of the *Confessions* may similarly be described in different ways, all of them "correct," each with its limitations. The best descriptions, it seems to me, comprehend the work more completely than others. They reveal the *Confessions* as an even more beautiful, more coherent and compelling work than it has hitherto seemed.

Several scholarly works have been crucial to the development of my thesis and I treat these at some length. In each case, I have sought to clarify the ground of difference between their thinking and mine, but, even more, I have sought to chart analogous or compatible solutions to the problem. Wherever possible, I have sought to ally my insights with those of others. For this reason, the present work is not entitled *The Literary Form of the Confessions* but *An Essay* on that subject. A kind of intellectual aesthetic functions in the various solutions to the problem: what one mind finds coherent and beautiful, well-ordered and satisfying, does not necessarily strike another as such. Throughout this book, I have sought to incorporate the works of other scholars into my own thesis, always presented as more comprehensive than theirs. Needless to say, my own vision of the *Confessions'* unity seems to me more intellectually satisfying than, for example, R. D. Crouse's, to which it proves broadly similar. Yet I do not pretend that Crouse will agree with such an assessment. Is this scholarly and dispassionate judgment on my part, or mere devotion to the product of my labors? I cannot say. The heart of a scholar is an abyss, and even the spirit of the scholar that is in him cannot plumb it.

Hence, the pages that follow do not deny the history of scholarship on this question even where they ignore it. I do not pretend in this book to argue the single absolutely right understanding of formal coherence in the *Confessions*, even though I endeavor to comprehend the whole volume in its discussion. That endeavor is not a modest one, no more than the *Confessions* itself. I am confident that it will find a variety of critics, yet hopeful that it may contribute something to our understanding—and so, to the continuing life—of Augustine's masterpiece.

Augustine's Prayerful Ascent

1 ✦ The Self-Presentation of the *Confessions*

Augustine's *Confessions* is a prayer. Perhaps no other quality of the work is so immediately obvious. This long volume, from its very first words to its very last, takes place as a dialogue with God. Peter Brown notes Augustine's originality in making prayer the literary form of so long a work.[1] He terms the volume a "lively conversation" with God and insists that "Just as a dialogue builds up a lasting impression of the speakers, so Augustine and his God emerge vividly in the prayer of the *Confessions*."[2] Similarly, Solignac calls the work "a long dialogue with God" and argues that God is present throughout as an "invisible Interlocutor": "a speechless character who is nonetheless an essential character, whose regard, subtly perceived in the interior of the soul, sustains the search, approves and disapproves solutions, maintains a lively attention even to the final conclusion." God remains active through the whole of Augustine's encounter with him in the *Confessions*, according to Solignac: "Throughout these thirteen books, Augustine *allows himself to be taught by God*."[3]

G. Bouissou further defines this position in his approach to Augustine's style. He argues that certain sudden shifts of style in the work should be seen as God's responses to Augustine's prayer in and through that prayer. He describes the *Confessions* as a "dialogue in one voice" because "only Augustine speaks—or rather, we only hear his voice—but from his language, his feelings, the tone of his discourse, and in a certain way the reactions of his countenance, we sense the divine replies."[4] Bouissou goes on to cite several passages that illustrate his point. More recently, José Oroz Reta argues this same understanding of the *Confessions* as a prayer, calling the work "a colloquy with the Lord who seeks to instruct us."[5]

In this longstanding view of the work, the prevailing terms treat of an encounter in and through speech: dialogue, conversation, voice, response, and so on. Yet this view has always existed alongside another which moves in an opposite direction: the *Confessions* is a written text, revised and shaped into its present form by Augustine. And not only shaped, but badly shaped. "We all know that Augustine composes badly," writes Christine Mohrmann, reporting a scholarly commonplace.[6] John O'Meara agrees with this principle and finds the *Confessions* typical of Augustine's ineptness in planning a book.[7] O'Meara is but one among many great scholars who find Augustine's masterpiece "badly composed."[8]

Yet what genuine conversation has ever been "composed" at all? A dialogue is never composed, properly speaking: it emerges through the interaction of two interlocutors. In genuine dialogue, neither party dominates or controls the discussion. Rather, both contribute vectors of intentionality whose force and direction change at various times, and the dialogue proceeds according to their dynamic interplay. In this way, the encounter seems to take on a life of its own, formed by the unique and shifting confluence of two contributors.

Perhaps, therefore, the "poor composition" of the *Confessions* does not reflect Augustine's ineptness but his skill: his skill in composing a text that represents a genuine dialogue. Scholars have often noted how compelling is Augustine's prayer in the work, how vivid and sincere it appears. Augustine, perhaps, has composed his prayer to be convincing not only in its texture but in its structure: with the disjointed parts and unexplained transitions that inevitably appear in a long conversation. The work's literary form as a prayerful conversation with God demands a certain incoherence as part of its coherence. The plan of such a genre requires the work to appear poorly planned.

To assay this hypothesis, I propose to explore the *Confessions'* self-presentation as a "dialogue with God" and to consider its implications as a literary form. Though the work is widely recognized to be a prayer, scholars have rarely pursued the consequences of that understanding. Historians tend to read books 1–9 as though they formed a finished historical narrative, while philosophers and theologians examine various texts as though they were part of a finished treatise. These approaches to the work are valid within certain limits, to be sure. But they tend to neglect the temporal dimension of Augustine's prayer as a progressively unfolding "dialogue with God." I argue that such neglect has created problems—and false problems—for our understanding of the *Confessions*.

Let us then examine the prayer of the *Confessions* as a literary form.[9] How does the volume present itself to us as a prayer? Its title declares the work a prayer before it is even opened. Once opened, its very first chapter immediately dramatizes itself as addressed to the Christian God:

> You are great, O Lord, and greatly to be praised: great is your power and to your wisdom there is no limit. And man, who is a part of your creation, wishes to praise you, man who bears within himself his mortality, who bears about within himself testimony to his sin and testimony that you resist the proud. Yet man, this part of your creation, wishes to praise you. You arouse him to take joy in praising you, for you have made us for yourself, and our heart is restless until it rests in you. Lord, grant me to know and understand which is first, to call upon you or to praise you, and also which is first, to know you or to call upon you? But how does one who does not know you call upon you? For one who does not know you might call upon another instead of you. Or must you rather be called upon so that you may be known? Yet how shall they call upon him in whom they have not believed? Or how shall they believe without a preacher? And they shall praise the Lord that seek him, for they that seek him find him, and finding him they shall praise him. Lord, let me seek you by calling upon you, and let me call upon you by believing in you, for you have been preached to us. Lord, my faith calls upon you, that faith which you have given to me, which you have breathed into me by the incarnation of your Son, through the ministry of your preacher.[10]

In these few lines, the Lord and Creator of the universe is directly addressed more than thirty times and referred to in the third person five times. Readers are immediately aware that the *Confessions* is addressed to God as though by a speaking voice. The work begins by quoting from a traditional prayer, Psalm 144:3. The whole passage portrays a speaker praying to God, asking him questions and working toward answers, seeking aid in his *inquisitio veritatis*. The first-time reader has no hint as yet of Christian autobiography or scriptural exposition. Though the matter of the text will change often, and the manner too, the writing already is establishing its generic mode: a prayer presented as though being spoken to God in the present, where the writer is engaged in seeking the truth under divine guidance.

That the *Confessions* presents itself as *being spoken in the present* has not hitherto been noticed, as far as I know. The point is worthy of attention. A dialogue recorded in a text ordinarily presents itself as taking place in and during the time of reading or speaking it. *Othello*, for example, always takes place in the "now" of reading or performing. Even a play offered as a memory of the past, like Tennessee Williams's *The Glass Menagerie*, occurs in and as the ongoing present of memory. Since the *Confessions* presents itself as a dialogue with God, it too takes place in the ongoing present of our reading, which recreates Augustine's speaking. Its very title implies that it is *spoken in dialogue*. *Confessio* derives from *con* + *fateri*: it implies an utterance being spoken (*fateri, fari*) with (*con*) another. Augustine is not recalling his *Confessions*, as he does recall his past. Rather, the volume presents him speaking to God "now" and his past is *being recalled* in the present of confessing.

Further, the genre of the *Confessions* implies God's responsive engagement with what the speaker is saying. The work presents itself as a prayer, and hence it asks its readers to be alert for evidence of God's responses to that prayer, in and through its own movements. The genre of the *Confessions* represents a relationship, a dynamic interplay, between the speaker-writer and his God. That dynamic has two poles, and the current is represented as flowing in both *directions*.

God's responsiveness to Augustine's ongoing prayer is dramatized early in book 1. Chapters 2 and 3 are largely made up of questions regarding God's presence and immensity in relation to the sensible, physical world. The inquiry is posed in terms of "bodies": by what analogies can God be said to "be in" or to fill the world? Chapter 3 concludes with four brief, crisply phrased questions. Chapter 4 begins with four more brief questions, before the prose turns suddenly into praise:

> But since all things cannot contain you in your entirety, do they then contain a part of you, and do all things simultaneously contain the same part? Or do single things contain single parts, greater things containing greater parts and smaller things smaller parts? Is one part of you greater, therefore, and another smaller? Or are you entire in all places, and does no one thing contain you in your entirety?
>
> IV. What, then, is my God? What, I ask, unless the Lord God? Who is Lord but the Lord? Or who is God but our God?
>
> Most high, most good, most mighty, most almighty, most merciful and most just, most hidden and most present, most beautiful and most strong, stable and incomprehensible, unchanging yet changing all things, never new and never old, yet renewing all things, leading proud men into senility, although they know it not, ever active and ever at rest, gathering

in yet needing nothing, supporting, fulfilling, and protecting things; creating, nourishing, and perfecting them; searching them out, although nothing is lacking to you. (1.3.3–1.4.4)

The shift in tone, style, and matter could not be more striking. From brief questions in a patient, searching inquiry, the writing moves to a breathless string of oxymoronic assertions, addressing and praising the transcendent God. Both inquiry and praise take place in the ongoing present of Augustine's prayer. The shift from one to the other seems to occur in the second question of chapter 4. *Rogo* ("I ask") signals a movement from real questions to rhetorical ones.[11] The following two questions quote Psalm 17:32 and stand, in effect, as assertions. The text then bursts into an encomium in the high style.[12]

I suggest that the prayer of the *Confessions* asks us to understand this shift as enabled by God's grace. This abrupt and radical change in style and tone, Augustine's text implies, is God's responding through the writer to his own questions. That response does not really answer the questions of chapters 2 and 3. Rather, it reveals their images to be completely inadequate to God: phrased in terms of physical space and bodies, the questions misconceive the transcendent Spirit of the Creator.

Chapter 4 then continues its encomium, moving to the praise of God's redeeming love. At the beginning of chapter 5, the writing returns to inquiry, again phrased in brief questions that grope their way toward answers. The subject has changed from metaphysics to morals, in line with the shift in the encomium just noted. The new change in tone implies that the surge of God's responding grace has passed, now that it has led the writer to new questions.

It is difficult to raise the issue of God's responding to Augustine's prayer in and through the process of his writing. One sounds either credulously pious toward the text or utterly skeptical of Augustine as a manipulator of his readers. I hope to avoid both extremes. Yet a literary approach to the *Confessions* must take seriously the work's self-presentation: a written text that represents a voice speaking in prayer to God. The genre Augustine has chosen, therefore, requires us to be alert for, and to acknowledge, the effects of prayer in what the text asks us to see as God's responses. As in all prayer not resulting in mystical visions or voices, those responses are registered in the "movements of spirit" of the prayer itself. The person of prayer comes to a new realization, or resolves a problem, or arrives at a new perspective "through grace." Augustine presents the *inquisitio* of the *Confessions* as guided by God, and he dramatizes that process at the beginning of the work.

But not only there, to be sure. Perhaps a clearer illustration may be found in book 11, the inquiry into the nature of time. That inquiry begins in chapter 14 and arrives at its final answer in chapter 28. In those fifteen chapters, the writer prays for guidance three different times, in chapters 9, 22, and 25. Each time the inquiry, which had gone aground on some difficulty, is liberated, enabled to move forward. In the text, the writer presents himself as undertaking the *inquisitio at* and *in* the time of writing book 11.

The verbs that narrate his search are in the present tense. In the prayer of chapter 25, for example, the writer directly acknowledges his continuing ignorance in the present: "Et confiteor tibi, domine, ignorore me adhuc, quid sit tempus" ("I confess to you, O Lord, that I still do not know what time is"). And the prayer concludes with his belief that God's grace will grant him understanding in the future: "domine, deus meus, inluminabis meas tenebras" ("O Lord, my God, you will illumine my ignorance"). We are asked to imagine—we are led to feel—that with each prayer God's grace comes down and so enables the writer to answer his questions, resolve their difficulties, and continue to proceed toward the truth.

This self-presentation of the inquiry as taking place at and in the time of Augustine's speaking-writing has never, so far as I know, seemed a problem to scholars. The historian reading for history, the philosopher examining philosophy, perhaps tend to view the implications of genre as an aspect of the manner, and not the matter, of the *Confessions*. Given their aims, they may be right to do so. But they thereby approach the work as though it were a treatise. Patently, it does not present itself as one.

The point bears some consideration. The *De doctrina Christiana*, begun about the same time as the *Confessions*, provides a useful comparison. First of all, the *De doctrina* does not present itself as addressed, either to God, to a particular recipient, or to the reader in general. It does not, therefore, imitate a speaking voice. Nor does it present a mind inquiring after truth, developing its self-awareness of its positions in the course of the work. Rather, the writer commands the principles of a subject which he wishes to transmit to students. He has a plan for this course of instruction, and executes it. He raises each topic explicitly and, for the most part, informs the reader when he is bringing that topic to a close. The writer is master of his own mind. He articulates principles he has already discovered, positions he has already arrived at. The *De doctrina Christiana* is a treatise and declares itself such by its self-presentation, not to speak of its title.

The *Confessions* is not a treatise, though it might have been one. The philosophical expositions and the scriptural exegesis might have been presented as "finished statements" of the writer's ideas. Inadequate positions could still have been raised, examined, and dismissed. All or nearly all of the "matter" of the last four books could have been stated just as clearly in the form of a treatise as in that of *confessio*. Perhaps only the allegorical exposition in book 13 would need much reworking: the intense frequency of scriptural quotations in some chapters verges on the dithyrambic.

Similarly, the autobiography of books 1–9 might easily have been written as a coherent narrative with moral and theological commentary, without the element of "prayer." Indeed, given the literary models Augustine had before him, this is the sort of volume one might have expected. Autobiographies do not usually present themselves as spoken to another. Even biographies of saints do not address God in prayer throughout. In writing a biography of himself, of course, Augustine does not want to seem his own hagiographer, and the confessional tone of his book avoids that danger. Yet he could have mounted the same moral criticism against himself, and the same theological reflection on past actions, in a narrative-and-treatise form. This would have protected his account from the charge of autohagiography. Augustine could have told the same story, the same reflections, in more or less the "same" way, without addressing it to God as a *confessio*, as a prayer.

What would have been lost thereby? Or rather, what does Augustine gain by presenting his autobiography, philosophical reflections, and scriptural exegesis as prayer and search, addressed to God and under his guidance?

Merely posing that question renews awareness of how the *Confessions* creates sympathy with its writer and his search. We are caught up in the fervor and intimacy of his address to God. The imitation of a voice speaking in the present engages our feelings as the formal tone of a treatise cannot. Listening, as it were, to that voice engaged in the most deeply personal of Christian encounters, we are moved by its movements. We are involved in its questions and in its search for truth. We feel, in a way no treatise or distanced narrative can achieve, the intellectual and moral honesty of the writer thus "speaking" in prayer.

Students of the *Confessions* have often recorded such responses to the writing, historians and philosophers preeminent among them. The writer's voice "speaking" in prayer in an ongoing present involves the reader in the seeming immediacy and spontaneity of an encounter with God. We take Augustine's part in the prayerful drama of the voice we read: its prayerful and searching progress, its exultation in grace-given discovery.

Accordingly, it is not inappropriate to say that the prayer of the *Confessions* incorporates fundamentally dramatic qualities. The volume is not merely a narrative and a treatise, a prepared history with philosophical disquisition. One can read the *Confessions* only by taking the part of its speaker. One cannot read the volume without taking up, in one's own first person, Augustine's *inquisitio veritatis*. One cannot read it without addressing God, whether one believes in God or not. The ongoing present of Augustine's speaking-writing unfolds in the ongoing present of our reading. More precisely, our reading *recreates* Augustine's prayer in our own times and places. Willy-nilly, every reader of the *Confessions* perforce impersonates—takes on the persona of—Augustine.

This is a profound and original literary strategy. Reading any narrative entails a certain imaginative participation in the events recorded and the voice recording them. Reading a drama heightens this participation, while diffusing it through several characters, different points of view. The *Confessions*, as a work "spoken to God" by Augustine alone, achieves that heightening without the diffusion. The reader does not simply "hear" Christianity: he "speaks" it. It is difficult to gauge the persuasive effect this has on a reader, but over the course of the volume, it must be considerable.

The *Confessions*, in short, presents itself as spoken in the present. Augustine's prose-voice works to convince us of its genuinely being spoken, and the prayer of the volume engages us in the ongoing address to God. The writing makes us feel the immediacy of Augustine's concerns, the urgency in his searching, his readiness to pursue the dialogue with God wherever it leads.

Like all genuine dialogue, it does not develop according to some rigid, preconceived plan. Though the *Confessions* traces the course of Augustine's life up to the death of Monica and scrutinizes the text of Genesis 1 more or less verse by verse, it does so with frequent shifts and unexpected moves. In his prayerful dialogue with God, the writer is moved now to narrate some past act, now to meditate upon it, to speak at length of Alypius here and of Monica there, to accuse himself and to praise God by sudden turns. Such turns are part of every genuine dialogue. Neither party alone completely controls its course.

This dynamic, I suggest, provides part of the rationale for any "lack of plan" in the *Confessions*. All readers of the volume experience its sudden and unexplained shifts in tone and mode. The book leaps from one part (or project) to another without transitions that explicitly clarify their relations. Hence, John O'Meara observes that Augustine "combines all these various parts rather awkwardly, merely placing them one after the other. The result is a badly composed book."[13] Those scholars, like myself, who attempt to reveal a controlling plan, necessarily appeal to some notion of latent design. The text does not declare its coherence. Its lack of explicit coherence suggests a writer who is not in complete control of the movements of his writing. The *Confessions*, however, does not content itself merely with suggesting this failure. At several points, and in different ways, the writing dramatizes for us that its writer is not in complete control of his material or of the movement of his thoughts.

Augustine's text declares such lack of control explicitly as the writer meditates upon the death of his young friend in book 4. Chapter 4 describes their friendship, the friend's fatal illness, sudden baptism, and his death. It concludes by describing the young Augustine's unbearable grief and the "sweet" solace of his tears.

In chapter 5, Augustine addresses God in the present of writing and inquires, "Whence is it, then, that sweet fruit is plucked from life's bitterness, from mourning and weeping, from sighing and lamenting?" (4.5.10). He recalls his grief in the past tense only to renew his present questioning, which arrives at no answer. And then, at the beginning of chapter 6, he suddenly reflects on what he has been doing: "Quid autem ista loquor? Non enim tempus quaerendi nunc est, sed confitendi tibi" ("Why do I speak of these things? For now is not the time for questioning but for confessing to you," 4.6.11).

This remark explicitly declares the previous chapter to have been a digression. It marks chapter 5 as inappropriate to the writer's current project, and yet the chapter remains within the text. What does the presence of this declared anomaly signify?

When a writer composing a work discovers he has been straying from his original plan, he normally exercises one of two options. He can revise that plan or excise the digression. In the latter course, the digression will itself wander into a footnote, a new project, an appendix, the file cabinet, or the wastebasket. In that case, it proves indeed a digression, off the course originally planned. Sometimes, however, the seeming "digression" reveals itself germane to the project at hand, and the project is partially reconceived in order to integrate the new discoveries.

Augustine's text does neither of these. To be more precise, it declares that it does *not* do both. Chapter 5 is marked as improper to the writer's *confessio* and yet it remains in the text. Though one might observe its thematic importance to book 4 and to other parts of the volume, the writer clearly finds it "out of place" and yet he leaves it in place. The text—this text, at least—declares itself to be unrevised.

The reason for this explicit "lack of revision" is clear: Augustine is not "really" writing but *speaking*: "Quid autem ista loquor?" The text takes seriously its self-presentation as a prayer spoken to God. Speech cannot be revised; it can be retracted only by addition. Augustine's digression cannot be erased because it is already "spoken." The confessional voice can only define what is now past as a digression.

To be sure, I do not wish to argue that the *Confessions* is an unrevised work. Rather, since it represents a prayer *being spoken* to God in the present of writing-reading, the volume *presents itself* as an unrevised work. Indeed, the premise of its being spoken implies that it is unrevisable. This aspect of the *Confessions* has not been noticed, so far as I have been able to discover. Perhaps one reason is that only a perfect literalist would be mad enough to think it genuinely unrevised.

Perhaps another reason lies in the assumption we moderns bring to the printed word. Literary culture is so thoroughly textual for us that we can easily forget how fundamentally oral the ancients perceived literature to be.[14] We tend to read silently to ourselves, but all reading in Augustine's day, *pace* Saint Ambrose (*Conf.* 6.3.3), was reading aloud. Augustine's contemporaries would have felt the voice of the *Confessions* more deeply than most moderns, for his contemporaries would literally have heard the work they read. More than ourselves, they would have encountered the work as a process of speech being spoken in the present. For the *Confessions* does not waver from presenting itself as an ongoing prayer: even the narrative of Augustine's past is carefully and repeatedly placed in the speaker's continuing dialogue with God. What such a dialogue implies for the literary form of the work may be seen in yet another passage where the writer remarks upon a digression.

In chapter 6 of book 9, Augustine describes his baptism. He concludes by recalling that he burst into tears of joy while listening to the hymns and canticles sung at the service. In chapter 7, he then turns to describing the introduction of hymn singing into the Church of Milan, and the discovery of the uncorrupted bodies of Saints Gervase and Protase. These events occurred about the time when the Arian mother of a boy-emperor was threatening persecution. A miraculous cure at the bier of the martyrs in Ambrose's cathedral created such popular excitement that the empress stayed her hand. The writer brings this narrative to a close with a joyful "Gratias tibi, deus meus!" ("Thanks be to you, my God!") Suddenly he turns to comment on his writing: "Unde et quo duxisti recordationem meam, ut haec etiam confiterer tibi, quae magna oblitus praeterieram?" ("Whence and whither have you led my recollection so that I confess also these things to you, mighty deeds that I had almost passed over in forgetfulness?" 9.7.16).

Here again, the text dramatizes the writer's lack of full control over the writing. Since, however, the writing offers itself as ongoing speech in the present, this lack of control is understandable. Perhaps for that reason, the passage goes largely unremarked by scholars.

And yet the text is remarkable. It asks us to see the speaker-writer's lack of control not as a failure but as responsiveness to God's guidance. The text asserts that the previous narrative is indeed a digression. Nevertheless, it remains in the text, brought there, the writer feels, by God's grace informing and assisting his *confessio*.

God's vector in the dynamic interplay of the prayerful dialogue here leaves its trace in the writer's surprised reflection on the course of his writing.

We are meant by this to understand that the *Confessions* is not, simply and purely, Augustine's own book. The speaker-writer here asserts that God has a hand in its formation, just as he has a hand in the direction of all unrehearsed, meditative, searching prayers. Augustine implies an analogy between the course of his life and the course of his book about his life: as God guided him through his youthful *errores,* so he guides the writer through the digressions of his present prayer. However the steps or the words may wander, God's grace calls, prods, guides them forward. This is a central theme of the *Confessions.* The book does not simply describe God's acting in Augustine's past. Its literary form as a spoken *confessio* embodies God's acting in his present prayer, in his ongoing search for the truth. The text explicitly draws our attention to the "evidence of grace" in its very composition.

Further, as a prayer being spoken in the present, the *Confessions* offers itself as uttered in the order of its self-presentation, from book 1, chapter 1, to book 13, chapter 38, chapter by chapter and word by word. It unfolds in the present of reading in the same order it unfolds in the speaker's ongoing dialogue with God. This point is hardly problematic: literary works ordinarily present themselves to be read in a certain temporal order. The *Confessions,* however, presents itself as *originally occurring* in that order. Thus its process of speech, full of swift turns and long digressions as it is, dramatizes the spiritual dynamic of Augustine's prayer through its verbal movements, and their sequence (or lack of it) is meant to be significant. I am not, to be sure, arguing that Augustine really wrote the *Confessions* in the order that the volume presents. The stages of its composition in history lie beyond our ken.[15] Rather, Augustine composed the work—shaped and revised it—so as to *dramatize* the prayerful search for truth, to represent it vividly and convincingly.

Once this literary form of the *Confessions* is taken seriously, a heuristic problem arises. It can be seen in the postulated difference between the order of the book's self-presentation and the stages of its composition in history. The writing dramatically presents an ongoing *confessio,* an unrevised process of speech. Yet, the historical Augustine undoubtedly conceived, composed, revised, and contrived the volume with many changes of wording in the process. It seems that we must postulate, purely for heuristic purposes, a distinction between the voice that the *Confessions* presents to us and the author who wrote the volume.

The voice and the author are, of course, the same Augustine, but in different roles, different functions. For example, book 11 presents a voice working through various conceptions of the nature of time. Are we to believe that the historical Augustine began writing book 11 without having already arrived at the conclusions to which the voice in the writing leads us? It is possible. It seems more likely, however, that book 11 dramatizes in the writing a search that the historical Augustine had already completed. Augustine the author recreates this past *inquisitio* in the present voice of Augustine the speaker.

A striking example of discovery in the volume may serve to illustrate this further. In book 11 the speaker understands Genesis 1:1 to assert that God creates the world in Christ: "In hoc principio, deus, fecisti caelum et terram in verbo tuo, in filio tuo, in virtute tua, in sapientia tua miro modo dicens et miro modo faciens" ("In this beginning, O God, you made heaven and earth in your Word, in your Son, in your Power, in your Wisdom, in your Truth, speaking in a wondrous way and working in a wondrous way," 11.9.11). For the next sixty chapters, the speaker explores and interrogates the text in detail. Then in book 13, he records a new discovery:

> Behold, there appears to me [Ecce apparet mihi] in a dark manner the Trinity, which is you, my God, since you, the Father, in the Beginning [in principio] of our Wisdom, because he is your Wisdom, born of you, equal to you, and coeternal with you, that is, in your Son, you made heaven and earth. Many things have we said of the heaven of heavens, and of the earth invisible and without form, and of the deep, darksome according to the inconstant downflow of its spiritual formlessness, unless it had been converted to him, from whom was life of some kind, and by his illumination made a beauteous life and became his heaven of heaven, which afterwards was made between the water and the water. By the name of God, who made these things, I now understood [tenebam iam] the Father, and by the name of the Beginning the Son, in whom he made them. *And believing my God to be the Trinity, as I did believe [sicut credebam], I searched [quaerebam] into his holy words, and behold [ecce], your Spirit was borne above the waters. Behold [Ecce], the Trinity, my God, Father, and Son, and Holy Spirit, creator of all creation!* (13.5.6, my italics)

This chapter dramatizes the speaker's discovery of the Trinity in Genesis 1 with three "Behold's" (Ecce). The speaker makes the discovery in the present (ecce apparet mihi) and records the process by which he has come to this realization, summarizing the exegetical conclusions of books 11 and 12. Having already discerned the Father as "God," in Genesis 1:1, and the Son, named as "the Beginning," Augustine the speaker insists that he *went on to search* for some record of the Holy Spirit. The writing asserts that he discovers it "only now." In other words, through all of books 11 and 12, the speaker has not looked ahead to Genesis 1:2b, nor has he ever thought about the first verses of Scripture in this way before.

One cannot imagine this to have been true of Augustine the author. Rather, he dramatizes in the speaking voice of his *Confessions* a process of search and discovery that he has already completed. He dramatizes it in a particular way, through a contrived order, to accomplish certain ends. That the historical Augustine made these discoveries and wrote about them is obvious. And, to be sure, he made them in and through his life of prayer. That he made them in the same way he dramatizes them we have no reason to believe. Yet this anomaly has never been felt as a problem before.

The distinction between Augustine as speaker and as author is crucial for this study of the *Confessions*. For the premise of the volume is that God is guiding the speaker's prayerful narration, meditation, and exposition. The speaker has perhaps a certain general plan in mind, at least near the beginning of books 1 and 11: to confess the story of his life and to meditate "upon the wonderful things" of God's law (11.2.3). And yet the dynamic of his encounter with God keeps leading him into extended reflection upon his past and upon the biblical text. The speaker never entirely knows what he is about to get into, for he is being led by God to discovery through prayer. Therefore, he can tell God and his readers what he plans to narrate next: at the beginning of book 2, for example, he promises to recall his "past foulness and carnal corruptions" (Recordari volo transactas foeditates meas et carnales corruptiones, 2.1.1). But the speaker cannot, in the manner of a treatise, apprise God that he intends to meditate on pride as the "root of all sin" (2.6.13) because he does not know this ahead of time. The dynamic of his prayer, as we have seen, leads him in unforeseen and unforeseeable directions.

Hence, whatever plan may be discovered in the *Confessions* is meant to be seen as created through the dynamic interaction of Augustine the speaker and God. The speaker does not plan the detailed course of the volume: it emerges through God's guidance. Clearly, the speaker does not trace a smooth, even journey. Unlike Dante's pilgrim, he does not enjoy the advantage of a series of knowledgeable guides. He must find his own way, but the way emerges in and through prayer and with God's grace. Augustine the author, of course, contrived whatever plan may be discovered in the *Confessions*, latent though it be. And the author, having conceived this plan, also occulted it in the various wanderings of the "present" meditations of Augustine the speaker.

The distinction is heuristically necessary, yet it by no means implies bad faith on Augustine's part. The latent design of the volume certainly arose through his prayerful meditation and probably evolved as a coherent plan through the process of composing his *Confessions*. Augustine the speaker and Augustine the author are the same Augustine, but in different roles located in different temporal dimensions. The author has shaped a literary work that recreates, as the speaker's ongoing *confessio* in the present, a search already completed in theory, if not in fact. The self-presentation of the volume implies that its latent design is formed not by Augustine the author but by the Providence that guides the speaker's prayer, the speaker's life. Just as the young Augustine's errant path to conversion was providentially guided, as the speaker of the *Confessions* believes, so does God's grace guide the often wandering *confessio* to the discovery of his truth. This is the fundamental premise of the *Confessions*— indeed, of all Christian life and prayer. If a coherent plan be found for the volume, the premise implies, it is "put there" by God's action upon and in the speaker's ongoing prayer.

The "lack of plan" in the *Confessions*, I have been suggesting, is part of Augustine the author's plan in creating the work. As far as the work itself is concerned, in terms of its self-presentation, this "author" does not exist. The Augustine whom the *Confessions* presents is a speaker-writer in the present, endeavoring to "do truth" that he may "come into the light" "in corde meo coram te in confessione, in stilo autem meo coram multis testibus" ("in my heart before you in confession, in my pen, however, before many witnesses," 10.1.1). Augustine the author, however, plans this planlessness in order to dramatize the speaker's ongoing, often wandering search in prayerful encounter with God. As far as the *Confessions* in itself is concerned, any coherent plan discovered there, as in the young Augustine's life, is created by God's providential grace. In these terms, God plans the volume, not Augustine the speaker. Augustine the author is a heuristic and theoretical fiction, necessary to explain the volume as shaped, revised, planned.

Such a novel distinction ought to be more than simply plausible. Insofar as it is valid, it should be able to shed light on certain long-standing scholarly disagreements. Neglect of this distinction, in other words, may have created problems which the ideas developed in this chapter can clarify. I hope to show that the heuristic distinction between Augustine as author and as speaker is fundamental to consideration of the *Confessions*. When it is not made, obscurities emerge which subsequently disappear in its light. Two illustrations should suffice.

The first concerns book 2. Augustine's analysis of his motives for stealing the pears contains, as scholars have noted, an inconsistency. He narrates the theft in chapter 4, begins to meditate upon it in chapter 5. In chapter 6 he concludes that the theft had no rational motive in terms of desire for some good but was purely the perverse act of his prideful will. Yet Augustine continues to reflect upon that sin and upon sin in general, and he comes to a radically different conclusion in chapter 9. There, he asserts that he would not have committed the sin by himself, alone. Augustine concludes that his motive was indeed the pursuit of a rational good: the desire for friendship, the love of the love of others.[16]

The negative and irrational motive asserted in chapter 6 cannot be squared, logically, with the positive, rational desire for love asserted in chapter 9. Scholars have usually dealt with this inconsistency by privileging one or the other of these views.[17] Yet the inconsistency itself only proves a problem because scholars approach the *Confessions* with certain assumptions. They assume that Augustine is the author of a finished product, that he knows his own mind on the issues he treats, and that he intends to convey, in the manner of a treatise, a coherent doctrine. All these assumptions ignore the self-presentation of the *Confessions*.

The logical inconsistency in book 2 is no longer a problem when the volume is understood to represent the confessional *process* of Augustine the *speaker*. The views of chapters 6 and 9 are two moments in an ongoing self-examination. We are meant to understand the former as a stage to the latter. The motive expressed in chapter 6 emerges as limited and false, while that of chapter 9 proves true, or at least closer to the truth.

The process by which the speaker arrives at his new understanding of that motive deserves careful attention. In the first sentence of chapter 8, the speaker still holds to the motive understood in chapter 6. Yet because that motive is irrational, he continues to interrogate it: "What fruit had I, so wretched a boy, from those deeds which I now blush to recall, especially from that theft in which I loved the theft itself, and nothing else? For the theft itself was nothing, and by that very fact I was all the more miserable" (2.8.16). Directly, the speaker realizes that "alone, by myself, I would not have done it." Hence, "I loved there the companionship of those with whom I did it." Yet even at the end of that chapter, the speaker has not fully plumbed this insight. He asserts that his pleasure (*voluptas*) lay not in the pears but in the sin itself (*in ipso facinore*), to which the companionship of others brought him (*faciebat*).

Consider, however, the movements of the speaker's thoughts in chapter 9: how he works his way toward a new understanding and how the text registers his discovery.

> What was my state of mind [*affectus animi*]? Truly and clearly, it was most base, and woe was it to me who had it. Yet what was it? Who understands his sins? It was like a thing for laughter, which reached down as it were into our hearts, that we were tricking those who did not know what we were doing and would most strenuously resent it. Why, then, did even the fact that I did not do it alone give me pleasure? Is it because no one can laugh readily when he is alone? No one indeed does laugh readily when alone, but sometimes when no one else is present, laughter does overcome individuals alone if something very funny affects their senses or strikes their minds. *But that deed I would not have done alone; alone I would never have done it.*
>
> *Behold, the living record of my soul lies before you, my God. By myself I would not have committed that theft* in which what pleased me was not what I stole but the fact that I stole. This would have pleased me not at all if I had done it alone; *nor by myself, would I have done it at all.* O friendship too unfriendly! (2.9.17, my italics).

The speaker begins by interrogating himself and his sin. He associates the sin with malicious laughter, and then laughter with a group. He questions the latter idea but then asserts, twice in one sentence, that the group of "friends" was essential to his having committed the act. His tone is now radically altered. Four times in five sentences he dwells on that thought, sounding its depths at last. At the center of this pattern, the speaker records his surprise and gratitude at what is revealed to him: "Behold, the living record of my soul lies before you, my God." This implies that the dynamic encounter between the speaker and God in prayer leads Augustine to understand his real motive for the sin. Sin though it was, his motive was rational. It possessed positive and potentially redeeming elements. We are meant to understand that God, to whom Augustine's soul is always open, guides the speaker to this revelation about himself.

In sum, the logical inconsistency between the views of chapters 6 and 9 remains. But it is no longer a problem. Logic is atemporal, but the *Confessions* records the *progress* of a speaker's understanding. Failure to distinguish between Augustine as speaker and Augustine as author, between the *Confessions* as miming a process and as being a product, creates a false problem.

The second illustration concerns a dispute between Pierre Courcelle and John O'Meara about Augustine's declared project in books 11–13. Courcelle argues that Augustine plans to present "a detailed exposition of Christian doctrine, based on the whole of Scripture, from the beginning of Genesis."[18] His position is largely founded on passages near the beginning of book 11. Augustine avers that "for a long time I have burned to meditate upon your law" and that "on nothing else would I want those hours to flow away which I find free" (11.2.2). Shortly thereafter, he prays to undertake a meditation on all of Scripture: "Let me confess to you [*confitear tibi*] whatsoever I shall find in your books, and let me hear the voice of praise, and drink you in, and consider the wonderful things of your law [*mirabilia de lege tua*] from that beginning, wherein you made heaven and earth, even to an everlasting kingdom together with you in your holy city" (11.2.3). Courcelle's case is a strong one. Augustine uses the verb (*confitear*) whose etymon provides the title of his book. He openly declares his wish to "consider" in these *Confessions*, the *mirabilia* of Scripture from Genesis through Revelation. Such a massive project would surely include, it seems reasonable to suppose, "a detailed exposition of Christian doctrine."

At the end of book 12, Augustine notes the astonishingly slow pace of his exposition:

Behold, O Lord my God, I beseech you, how many things we have written concerning these few words, how many! What strength of ours, what tracts of time would suffice to treat all your books in this manner? Permit me, then, in these words more briefly to confess to you, and to choose some single true, certain, and good meaning which you shall inspire [*et eligere unum aliquid quod tu inspiraveris verum, certum, et bonum*], even though many should occur, where many can occur, in this faith of my confession, that if I should say that which your minister intended [*quod sensit minister tuus*] I will say what is right and best. For this should I strive, and if I do not attain to it, I would still say that which your Truth willed by his words to say to me, which also spoke to him what it willed [*quod si adsecutus non fuero, id tamen dicam, quod mihi per eius verba tua veritas dicere voluerit, quae illi quoque dixit quod voluit*]. (12.32.43)

Here, Augustine prays that God will help him modify, though not substantially change, his project. Rather than "confess to you whatever I shall find in your books" (11.2.3), Augustine prays that God will inspire him (*tu inspiraveris*) to choose some "single true, certain, and good meaning." His intention still seems to be "to treat all your books," though not "in this manner," in that of slow and wide-ranging exposition. Augustine still hopes to plumb "that which your Truth willed by his words to say to me," and God's truth authors all of Scripture, through the words of different "ministers." In this passage, Augustine recognizes that he must limit the detail in his exegesis, though he continues to imply that its scope remains the whole of Scripture.

Courcelle's case, in short, is founded on several texts. Augustine first proposes a project which he then undertakes, and at the end of book 12 he comments on the project and modifies it. O'Meara's opposing argument, in contrast, is based most strongly on Augustine's sanity and good sense. "One cannot easily believe that he ever intended at any stage to give in the *Confessions* a detailed exposition of Christian doctrine based on Scripture," O'Meara insists. And the reason is obvious. Such a task "would take even Augustine a lifetime and very many books." Since Augustine is obviously a rational man,

it is "in the highest degree incredible" that he would attempt to conclude his volume with an exposition of all of Scripture.[19]

One cannot but agree with O'Meara on this score, just as one
cannot dispute Courcelle's textual evidence for his own position. Augustine is a reasonable man, and yet he proposes and undertakes an
impossible project. How can this anomaly be resolved?

The disagreement arises through failure to distinguish Augustine
the speaker from Augustine the author. Courcelle is considering the
former, O'Meara the latter. Both argue correctly. Augustine the
speaker insists more than once that he hopes to examine all of Scripture in order to confess what God's truth wills to say to him (11.2.3
and 12.32.43). Augustine the author knows that this is an impossible
task. The speaker, moved by the ardor of his prayer and by God's
grace, decides to essay an impossible project. And though the speaker
redefines the project after two lengthy books, he reaffirms its scope at
the same time. This Augustine, as we have seen, is not in complete
control of his speaking-writing, because it is occurring in the present
of an ongoing *inquisitio*. He confesses "whatsoever I shall find in
your books" according to the heat or perplexity of the moment.

Augustine the author, in contrast, has shaped the course of this
confessional exegesis as he composed and revised the work. Unlike
the speaker, the author knows his own mind because he has had time
to change it. He has fashioned the last three books of the *Confessions*
in a particular order, with certain styles, to achieve certain ends. Augustine the author has created Augustine the speaker, a figure who
undertakes, pursues, and reaffirms an impossible project.

Yet why should Augustine "do this to himself"? Some answers to
this lie in the catechetical aims of the *Confessions*. The author has
created a speaker enthusiastic for the study of Scripture. Eager for
truth, the speaker probes with questions the biblical text, searching
prayerfully. The author thus dramatically realizes and illustrates a
virtuous mode of Christian reading and meditation. His speaker's desire to search out all the truth in God's Book is exemplary, even if the
attempt to plumb it verse by verse, from Genesis through Revelation,
is a bit daft.

Yet Augustine the author has shaped the speaker's exegetical ambitions for other reasons as well. The speaker's desire to plumb the
truth of the whole Bible does not go unfulfilled in the *Confessions*.
But his ambition, like so much else in the volume, is realized in a

manner unforeseen by him at the beginning of book 11, or even at the end of book 12. Assuredly, Augustine the author has planned it so, in order to bring his work to a fitting and dramatic end. And in that end he has placed the beginning, the principles, of the work: the paradigm for its structure. How the author ends the volume, and in what ways that conclusion proves fitting, are central to the literary form of the *Confessions*.

2 ✦ The Conclusion of the *Confessions*

The *Confessions* ends in a most remarkable way. Augustine completes his exposition of Genesis 1 with an allegorical flourish and closes on his expectation of the seventh day "without an evening" (13.36.51), the sabbath of eternal rest in God. The allegorical exposition is frequently dizzying, but the last four short chapters on God's eternal peace bring the volume to a satisfying close. The *cor inquietum* of the *Confessions'* first chapter arrives, after a long *inquisitio*, at a vision of its eternal *quies* in God.

Though the close of the volume may be satisfying, the allegory in which it is set proves perplexing as a conclusion to the discussion in previous books. Why does the *Confessions* end as it does? Augustine begins to meditate on Genesis in book 11, chapter 3. By chapter 11 of book 13—seventy-two chapters later—he has gone no further than the third verse of Genesis 1. In that chapter he seems about to embark on yet another digression, as he begins to consider the mystery of the Trinity. Yet in chapter 12 Augustine begins to treat Genesis 1 as an allegory for the creation of the Church. Twenty-three chapters later, the exposition is completed. Within twenty-seven chapters all told, the volume is concluded.

How are we to interpret this radical change of pace?[1] Are we to imagine that Augustine grew tired of his project and so brought it to a swift conclusion? Perhaps this change of pace is not meaningful. Many writers treating the unity of the *Confessions* do not even advert to the sudden speed of Augustine's exposition. Ralph Flores, for example, treats the modes of reading and speech represented in the work; he rightly finds its concluding allegory "a celebration of God's eloquence as nothing less than the world's creation."[2] The "unity of the *Confessions*" is customarily conceived in such a structural-thematic and atemporal manner, and this tends to obviate concern with the temporality of the work's unfolding.[3] Perhaps the radical change of pace in book 13 is not meaningful and simply proves another instance of Augustine's inability to plan the work. To pose questions about how the allegory of book 13 concludes the *Confessions* has proved embarrassing to a great writer and thinker who, according to his finest modern students, "composes badly."[4] Such questions have seemed to point to anomalies in Augustine's understanding, or lack of understanding, of how to conclude his masterpiece.

I should like to argue, however, that these anomalies lie not in Augustine's understanding of the *Confessions* but in our own. Specifically, they lie in our failure to distinguish Augustine the speaker from Augustine the author. I hope to show how attention to the process of the volume, to the progress of the voice speaking in the present, resolves these difficulties. The radical change that comes over the speaker in chapter 12 of book 13 inaugurates a coherent and wholly fitting conclusion to books 11–13. All of it has been carefully planned by Augustine the author.

Scholars customarily treat books 11–13 as a self-contained unit within the *Confessions*. What unifies these three books is their exegesis on the Hexameron. This view apprehends the text as though it were a treatise on Genesis 1, composed, revised, and planned by Augustine the author. It is often noted that Augustine, in book 13, shifts from commentary *ad litteram* to allegorical exposition in chapter 12. He begins to interpret Genesis 1 as an allegory of God's creating the Church. Solignac shows how this allegory operates on all the traditionally defined spiritual levels: *allegoria, moralis,* and *anagogia*.[5] F. Cayré argues that these chapters prove the "crown of the work" because they present "a true spiritual doctrine": "a superior synthesis" of teaching on "the perfect life of Christians fully submissive to the Holy Spirit."[6] Clearly, the depth of this spiritual exegesis is something new in books 11–13. Yet why this decisive change should lead Augustine to accelerate and complete his treatment of Genesis 1 needs to be examined.

I suggest that this problem can be treated most coherently in terms of Augustine the speaker. So much in his prayerful exegesis is suddenly new. He discovers a new subject, the Church, a focus (at last) for the multiple meanings of Scripture. He sets forth his exposition in a new tone and a new style. In addition, he begins his examination of Genesis all over again, from the first verse. All this newness represents God's grace informing Augustine the speaker with extraordinary insight and energy. We are meant to understand that this renewal through grace enables him, swiftly and with sublime assurance, to complete his exposition and conclude his *Confessions*.

Consider the change in the speaker as the text moves from chapter 11 to chapter 12. From pondering the Persons of the Trinity, he returns to his exegesis and even to the first verse of Genesis. He now focuses on the Church as revealed allegorically in the Creation account. And his voice takes on a new assurance as he asserts meanings rather than tentatively inquires after them. The style of his utterance changes too, as he quotes from Scripture with dizzying frequency.

> But whether there is a Trinity in God, because of these three acts, or whether these acts are in each Person, so that all three belong to each person; or whether both hold, so that the Self-same exists immutably by its great and plenteous unity, in some marvelous way both simple and multiple, with an infinite end in and for itself, whereby it is, and is known to itself, and suffices to itself—who could conceive such things with any ease? Who could state them in any manner? Who could rashly pronounce thereon in any way?
>
> XII. Proceed with your confession, O my faith. Say to your Lord God: Holy, holy, holy, O Lord my God. In your name we were baptized, O Father, and Son, and Holy Spirit. In your name we baptize, O Father, and Son, and Holy Spirit.
>
> For also among us, in his Christ, has God made heaven and earth, the spiritual and carnal parts of his Church. And before it received the form of doctrine, our earth was invisible and without order, and we were covered over by the darkness of ignorance, for you have corrected man for his iniquity, and your judgments are a great deep. But because your Spirit was borne over the water, your mercy did not abandon our misery, and you said, "Be light made. Do penance. The kingdom of heaven is at hand. Do penance. Be light made." Since our soul was troubled within us, we remembered you, O Lord, from the land of Jordan, and from the mountain equal to you but made small in our behalf. Our darkness displeased us, and we were converted to you, and light was made. Behold, we were heretofore darkness, but now light in the Lord.

I quote the text at such length in order to show how it dramatizes the radical change in the speaker's tone. Chapter 11 illustrates the voice of one engaged in an *inquisitio veritatis*. Like the voice of books 11 and 12, Augustine the speaker reasons carefully and repeats himself as though to clarify his position in his own mind. He goes on to pose further questions regarding the trinitarian analogy he discovers. Patiently setting these forth, he seems about to embark on a more sustained inquiry into the nature of the Trinity.

Suddenly, chapter 12 begins with a command and a ringing, threefold invocation of the Trinity. Augustine returns to the text of Genesis in swift response to the command to "Proceed with your confession, O my faith." No longer does he question the text, worry over its possible meanings, or pray for God's guidance in resolving cruxes. He expounds authoritatively. He asserts meanings, as though he feels no need to argue for them. And what he asserts is by no means obvious, far less obvious than some of the literal meanings for "heaven and earth" set forth so laboriously in book 12. For seventy-two chapters, from book 11, chapter 3, to book 13, chapter 11, the speaker proposes meanings and prays that God may dispose them, according to his truth. In book 13, chapter 12, however, Augustine confidently propounds an obscure and often difficult allegory for Genesis 1. He asks few questions. He seems to have all the answers at his command.

Augustine suddenly commands a completely new view of his text. He interprets God's creating heaven and earth *in principio* as the creation, in Christ, of the spiritual and carnal parts of the Church. This becomes the new subject of his allegorical exposition as he proceeds, with surprising swiftness, to expound all of Genesis 1 in its light.

All of Genesis 1. Though he has spent more than two books laboring on the first three verses, Augustine begins his exposition anew. He returns to the very first verse and defines the subject of his new allegorical exegesis. Over the rest of chapters 12–14, he reinterprets verses 2–3 in terms of the Church. Augustine writes as though his entire exposition *ad litteram*, so carefully searched into through books 11–12, were irrelevant to his new subject, his new certainty.

The speaker of the *Confessions* is, suddenly, a changed man. We are meant to believe, I suggest, that God's grace surges within his prayer in a radically new way. He no longer questions patiently and prays for guidance because he no longer needs to. He possesses a vibrant, new conviction about the text. We are meant to understand that God's Spirit is suddenly alive within him in an extraordinary way. Augustine the speaker is inspired. Hence, his sublime assurance in the spiritual allegory he expounds.

Just how certain the speaker has become may be measured by comparing chapter 16 with chapter 11, quoted above. In the latter, Augustine ponders the interrelations among the Persons of the Trinity through a series of questions. He concludes by wondering at the depth of the mystery: "Who could conceive such things with any ease? Who could state them in any manner? Who could rashly pronounce [*temere pronuntiaverit*] thereon in any way?" (13.11.12).

Just five chapters later, however, Augustine himself pronounces on these issues in the most authoritative fashion: "XVI. For even as you totally are, so do you alone totally know, for you immutably are, and you know immutably, and you will immutably. Your essence knows and wills immutably, and your knowledge is and wills immutably, and your will is and knows immutably." Augustine the speaker simply asserts this as truth. He does not inquire into it, pray over it, or argue for it. In terms of the *inquisitio veritatis* that governs nearly all his *Confessions*, therefore, the speaker does indeed "pronounce rashly" on the mystery of the Trinity. Yet this is of no moment to Augustine the speaker. He seems to feel himself possessed of the truth. The radical change from chapter 11 to chapter 16 suggests that the speaker is possessed *by* the truth, inspired by God.

What could this change possibly mean in terms of a view that only recognizes Augustine the author? Perhaps the questions in chapter 11 are merely rhetorical, and Augustine raises them in order to answer them in chapter 16. Such a response is consistent with the view that books 11–13 constitute a treatise on Genesis 1. Yet why, then, does Augustine imply that no one "could conceive such things with any ease" or "rashly pronounce thereon in any way" in chapter 11 and then proceed, in chapter 16, to conceive such things with ease and pronounce upon them without demonstration? If book 13 is to be seen as a treatise, why separate the questions posed from the answers given by five chapters of allegorical commentary on a different subject? Scholarship on the *Confessions* has an answer to this question: there is no good reason. Augustine is inept at planning a book.

Such ineptitude appears very differently when the *Confessions* is viewed as the progress of a speaker's prayerful encounter with God in an ongoing present. Augustine the author is not inept in planning book 13: he is creating a speaker who undergoes a sudden change, and this profoundly affects the nature of his scriptural exposition. That shift implies, I have suggested, that Augustine the speaker is divinely inspired. Subsequently, the text asserts this explicitly.

The first instance occurs just after the speaker discovers an anomaly in God's commands to "increase and multiply." God so commands the birds and sea creatures, made on the fifth day, and the first human beings, created on the sixth. Yet Genesis does not record this command as having been given to herbs, trees, beasts, and serpents, even though they indeed "by generation increase and preserve their kind" (13.24.35). Augustine insists that this anomaly is significant. Before he offers a figurative interpretation of this crux, he prays: "If I do not understand what you mean by that passage, let my betters, that is, men more intelligent than I am, make better use of it, according as you have given each of them to understand. But let my confession likewise be pleasing in your eyes, for in it I confess to you that I believe, O Lord, that you have not spoken thus to me in vain [*qua tibi confiteror credere me, domine, non incassum te ita locutum*]" (13.24.36). Augustine is not praying, here, to understand the passage, as he so often does in books 11 and 12. The speaker confesses his belief that *God has spoken to him* a true interpretation. He appears to have a certain hesitation about the meaning he will offer, but he does not doubt God's having inspired it.

It may be objected that this does not constitute "inspiration" in an extraordinary way, for God speaks to every Christian. God's responsiveness, as we have seen, constitutes part of the structure of prayer. Nonetheless, the tone of the speaker's prayer here is quite changed from that of the struggling, eager, often anxious searcher in books 11 and 12. Augustine is about to deliver a rather obscure, farfetched figurative interpretation of the crux, and he does so far more confidently than he did earlier, while groping through "the letter" of the first verses of Genesis. His insistence that God has spoken to him explains this change.

This prepares the reader for a more explicit claim to divine inspiration in the following chapter:

> XXV. I also wish to state, O Lord my God, what the following passage in your Scripture brings to my mind. I will speak out, and I will have no fear. I will speak the truth under your inspiration as to what you have willed me to interpret out of those words [*Vera enim dicam te mihi inspirante, quod ex eis verbis voluisti ut dicerem*]. For under the inspira-

tion of none but you do I believe myself to speak the truth [*Neque enim alio praeter te inspirante credo me verum dicere*], for you are the truth, but "every man is a liar." (13.25.38)

Here Augustine emphasizes God's "inspiring" his exposition, twice using the technical term. The syntax of *te mihi inspirante* further underscores, in a striking way, God's possessing the speaker, his embracing and sustaining Augustine's utterance of his truth. The speaker asserts his belief that his allegorical exposition is divinely inspired. This constitutes a different act from praying for God's guidance, as in books 11 and 12, or marveling at how God leads his remembrance of things past (*unde et quo duxisti recordationem meam*, 9.7.16). Augustine is declaring, not petitioning, and "inspiration" names a far more intimate and powerful experience of God than does "guidance."

These two claims to divine inspiration are not relevant simply to the chapters in which they appear. They apply to the entire allegory of God's creating the Church. After reviewing the catalogue of created things in chapter 32, Augustine summarizes his exposition in chapter 34. He introduces it in these words:

> XXXIV. Inspeximus etiam, propter quorum figurationem ista vel tali ordine fieri vel tali ordini scribi voluisti, et vidimus, quia bona sunt singula et omnia bona valde, in verbo tuo, in unico tuo caelum et terram, caput et corpus ecclesiae, in praedestinationem ante omnia tempora sine mane et vespera.

> [We have also examined those things in keeping with that mystical purpose whereby you willed them either to be fashioned in such an order or to be described in such an order. We have seen that things taken one by one are good, and that together they are very good, in your Word, in your Only-begotten, both heaven and earth, the head and body of the Church, in your predestination before all times, without morning and evening.] (13.34.49)

Let us first note that this summary completely ignores the exegeses of books 11 and 12 and of the first eleven chapters in book 13. It focuses solely on the allegory of God's creating the Church, which begins in book 13, chapter 12. Augustine thereby marks that allegory as a coherent and distinct unit within his *Confessions*.

The verbs of the first sentence define the allegorical exposition as inspired. *Inspeximus* implies insight, Augustine's penetrating examination. More strikingly, the object of this insight is not simply the text of Genesis. Its object is God's will (*voluisti*) inspiring the things (*ista*) recorded there. The speaker asserts far more than that his exposition is true. He feels that he has peered into the Truth that lives at the Origin of the text. He feels that he has elucidated the divine purpose inspiring it.

This implies a grace so extraordinary that the speaker accounts it as inspiration. Only God's grace enables a Christian to understand his will, and only unusual grace enables penetrating insight into it. Further, Augustine's analysis of the Trinity envisions the Holy Spirit as God's Will (*velle*, 13.11.12). The speaker's insight into what God has willed in Scripture, therefore, is tantamount to understanding what the Holy Spirit inspired in the text. Only divine inspiration can reveal such truths, especially when they prove so deeply allegorical.

The speaker's claim, it seems to me, goes beyond the kind of divine illumination that scholars have seen in the *Confessions* as a whole. Solignac writes that Augustine "allows himself to be taught by God . . . in the dialogue between the spirit of the man and the Holy Spirit. . . . The *Confessions*, therefore, is a book which, without presenting itself as 'inspired' in the technical sense of the term, is nonetheless *authenticated* (*authentifié*) by a divine light."[7]

Only Scripture, I take it, is "'inspired' in the technical sense of the term," and Augustine's book, to be sure, does not claim to be Scripture. But its speaker, like all Christian men of prayer, seeks the closest possible relationship with God. Throughout the *Confessions*, Augustine seeks divine direction in the search for truth. He hopes for intimate knowledge of God, the grace of certainty in truth. Throughout his *Confessions* Augustine the speaker aspires to be inspired, and the *Confessions*, like every Christian work, strives to be as full of God's truth as Scripture. In book 13 the speaker is convinced that God inspires his reading. He feels that his speaking-writing is "closer to Scripture" than it was in books 11 and 12.

This should not be taken as hubris on Augustine's part. Since there are degrees of grace, there are degrees of illumination and inspiration. Augustine the author has created a speaker who feels an unusual grace of insight into Scripture and he accounts it, in the ardor of his prayer, divine inspiration. Doubtlessly, the author has recreated for his readers an experience, or experiences, he himself has had. At the end of a long and patient *inquisitio*, his speaker bursts forth into a new and strange understanding of Genesis 1. He propounds this new understanding with sublime assurance. He sets it forth in a wholly new mode of commentary.

The new mode of that commentary is characterized by the number, density, and variety of Augustine's quotations from Scripture. The texture of his allegorical exposition proves literally "closer to Scripture" than books 11 and 12 because it is more fully imbued with biblical quotations and allusions. The number of citations tells a large part of the story (see table).

Book 13 clearly contains many more scriptural references than either book 11 or 12. In fact, the thirty-eight chapters of book 13 contain over 70 references more than do the sixty-three chapters of books 11 and 12 together. Within book 13, the number of citations shifts radically from chapter 12 onward. While its first eleven chapters contain 66 references, the following eleven chapters (12–23) contain 210. Augustine's hexameral exposition is largely completed by chapter 27, as the remaining chapters are devoted to summarizing the whole Creation and to reflecting on the sabbath of eternal rest. Chapters 12–27 also contain the vast majority of biblical references in the book, 267.

The sustained frequency, the sheer density of biblical quotation and allusion in these chapters, is unique in the *Confessions*. To be sure, there are other individual chapters, scattered throughout the volume, equally dense with references to the Bible. Michele Pellegrino offers a partial list of some passages that are "an intertwining of Biblical citations": no section of the *Confessions* has more of them, or more closely clustered together, than book 13.[8]

Every such passage, read in terms of an Augustine speaking his prayer in an ongoing present, marks a moment of unusual ardor or

Scriptural references cited in the Skutella-Verheijen edition of the *Confessions*

Confessions	*Number of Biblical References*
Book 11	120
Book 12	169
Book 13	365
Chapters 1–11	66
Chapters 12–27	267
Chapters 12–38	297

illumination, a moment of special grace. Something in his prayerful encounter with God calls forth the inspired words of Scripture with unusual density or force. Indeed, this occurs at many different points throughout the *Confessions*. Nowhere, however, does it occur with such sustained frequency, chapter after chapter, as it does in book 13, after chapter 12.

Number and frequency of citations, however, do not tell the whole story. The style of Augustine's allegory on the Church is difficult, and not simply from density of allusion. The style is somewhat oracular: it contains leaps of thought that juxtapose scriptural allusions with no explicit or apparent connection. This proves rather different from those earlier moments in the volume when Augustine's prayer is densely informed with biblical allusions. Consider this text, which is cited in Pellegrino's list, on Augustine's reading of "certain books of the Platonists":

> Therefore I also read there that "they changed the glory of your incorruption" into idols and various images, "into the likeness of the image of a corruptible man, and of birds, and of fourfooted beasts, and of creeping things," namely, into the Egyptian food by which Esau lost his birthright. For the first-born people worshiped the head of a fourfooted beast instead of you, "and in their hearts turned back into Egypt," and bent your image, their own souls, before the "likeness of a calf that eats hay." These things I found there, but I did not feed upon them. (7.9.15)

The passage contains a series of quotations from the Old and New Testaments, plaited together to form an allegory. Idolatry is the theme throughout. The Israelites' worshiping of the golden calf forms the obvious center for quotations drawn from the Epistle to the Romans, Acts, and the Psalms. Only the allusion to Esau losing his birthright for "Egyptian food" perhaps presents a momentary difficulty. That it refers to idolatry is at least clear. Immediately after this passage Augustine goes on to elaborate the Jacob-Esau allegory to which he alludes.

Consider, in contrast, this passage of equal length, taken from the allegorical exposition in book 13. Here, too, is an interlacing of quotations from the Old and New Testaments to form an allegory. Augustine is commenting on Genesis 1:2–3, the Spirit's brooding over the abyss and the creation of light:

XIII. Yet with us it is still by faith and not yet by sight. "For we are saved by hope. But hope that is seen is not hope." As yet, "deep calls unto deep," but now "in the voice of your floodgates." And as yet he who says, "I could not speak to you as spiritual, but only as to carnal," even he does not think that he has apprehended it, but "forgetting the things that are behind," he reaches out "to those which are before," and he groans, being burdened, and his "soul thirsts after the living God," "even as the hart after fountains of waters" and he says, "When shall I come to it?" (13.13.14)

In the passage quoted from book 7 on idolatry, the Skutella-Verheijen edition cites six biblical references from six different texts.[9] For the passage quoted above, it cites seven references from five different texts (two references each for Ps. 41 and 2 Cor. 5). These numbers would lead one to expect that the latter passage should be slightly easier to follow because somewhat more coherent in its allusions.

Yet the latter passage proves considerably more difficult. How being "saved by hope" relates to "deep calls unto deep" is not immediately clear, to say the least. How both relate to the quotations from Paul immediately following proves even more obscure, and the return to verses from Psalm 41 darker still. Augustine is associating ideas with astonishing and bewildering rapidity. Only by sustained and patient reflection on the text can one possibly hope to fill in the gaps, to reconstruct the allegorical logic that makes this exposition coherent.

Augustine's writing in the *Confessions* changes radically and abruptly in chapter 12 of book 13. Consistently dense with biblical quotations, difficult in its leaps of thought, the writing authoritatively expounds a complex and deeply allegorical interpretation of Genesis 1. As the writing changes, so does the man who is speaking his *Confessions*. His sublime assurance tells us that he feels possessed of certain truth in what he utters. He no longer speaks of himself in the singular, but in the plural.[10] His oracular style, imbued with Scripture, is meant to suggest that he is possessed by certain truth in his interpreting. After pondering the Trinity in chapter 11, Augustine the speaker is infused by a grace that inspires a wholly new understanding of Genesis 1. This enables him to begin his interpretation anew and to complete it swiftly. He completes it in precisely twenty-seven chapters, a perfect trinitarian number $(3 \times 3 \times 3)$ for a divinely inspired allegorical exposition.

How does this exposition, as a whole, bring the *Confessions* to a fitting climax? Some answers to this have already been suggested. The whole volume, like every Christian work, aspires to the condition of Scripture, as it were. Its final twenty-seven chapters are "closer to Scripture" than any other part of the *Confessions*, both in their literal texture and in Augustine's explicit claim to divine inspiration. Similarly, throughout the volume Augustine aspires to the closest possible awareness of God's presence in his life and in his ongoing prayer. In its final twenty-seven chapters, the speaker feels God's inspiring presence with extraordinary force. Finally, the closing meditation on God's eternal *quies*, as many scholars have seen, resolves many themes in the *Confessions* in a deeply satisfying way.

Less obviously, but more importantly, the final twenty-seven chapters fulfill the prayer Augustine makes in book 11, chapter 2, and then revises at the end of book 12. In the former, let us recall, the speaker prays: "Let me confess to you whatsoever I shall find in your books, and let me 'hear the voice of praise,' and drink you in, and consider 'the wonderful things of your law,' from that beginning, wherein you made heaven and earth, even to an everlasting kingdom together with you in your holy city" (11.2.3). This prayer to undertake an impossible task, to examine all of Scripture, may be seen as motivated by Augustine's ardor. Chapter 2 of book 11 contains an astonishingly large number of biblical references, more than forty of them. It would seem that the speaker, quoting so copiously, is quickened with excitement. I suggest that we are meant to understand this prayer as "inspired" (not in the technical sense) by unusual grace.

At the end of book 12, however, the speaker sees that he must revise this prayer. Otherwise, "what tracts of time would suffice to treat all your books in this manner?" Hence, he prays that God may inspire a single focus for his examination of Scripture.

Permit me, then, in these words more briefly to confess to you, and *to choose some single true, certain, and good meaning which you shall inspire* [*et eligere unum aliquid quod tu inspiraveris verum, certum, et bonum*] even though many should occur, where many can occur, in this faith of my confession, that if I should say that which your minister intended, I will say what is right and best. For this I should strive, and if I do not attain it, *I would still say that which your Truth willed by his words to say to me, which also spoke to him what it willed* [*quod mihi per eius verba tua veritas dicere voluerit, quae illi quoque dixit quod voluit].* (12.32.43, my italics)

Clearly, this latter prayer is fulfilled in some respects by the allegorical exposition in book 13. The speaker arrives at a focus for his exposition, the Church, surely a single thing (*unum aliquid*) that is "true, certain, and good" in Augustine's eyes. Probably, this is not quite what the speaker has in mind at the end of book 12, if he has anything very clearly in mind at all. And when he prays that God will inspire (*tu inspiraveris*) some single meaning, he probably does not pray to be possessed by God's truth like some prophet or sibyl. We are meant to understand that God fulfills this prayer beyond the expectation of its speaker, just as he fulfilled Monica's prayers for her son's conversion "far more than she had long begged for" (8.12.30). Similarly, the speaker first prays to understand what God's inspired minister intended in writing Scripture; if that is not possible, he prays to speak "that which your Truth willed by his words to say to me." Again, God fulfills this prayer beyond the speaker's intentions. Augustine later asserts that God's inspiring grace enables him to examine (*inspeximus*) not what his minister meant but *what God himself intended* (*voluisti*) Genesis 1 to mean in a spiritual sense (*propter figurationem*, 13.34.49).

Regarding the earlier, more ambitious prayer, Solignac observes that books 11–13 encompass the sweep of time represented from Genesis to Revelation. These books demonstrate that "time is opened for us out of eternity by the *fiat* of the Creator and it closes in the eternity of the heavenly rest."[11] But Augustine's allegory on the Church in book 13, as we have seen, itself moves from the first verse of Genesis to the sabbath of eternal rest. That exposition thus fulfills the sweep of Augustine's prayer in book 11, chapter 2. In its scope, then, it encompasses the whole of Scripture.

It also contains "all of Scripture" in its style. Its texture, we have seen, is practically a tissue of quotations from the Bible. Augustine quotes from or alludes to over half the books of Scripture, sixteen from the Old Testament and twenty-two from the New. He quotes most abundantly from the Pauline epistles and the Wisdom literature, especially the Psalms. He also quotes frequently from the four Gospels. He uses verses from the major prophets, Acts, the non-Pauline epistles, the Pentateuch, and the historical books of the Old

Testament. Though Augustine does not quote from the book of Revelation, his last four chapters dwell on God's eternal kingdom revealed at the very end of the Bible.

The range of these quotations is perhaps not itself unique in the *Confessions*. But to employ this range with such frequency of quotation, such dense variety of reference, sustained for chapter after chapter, as Augustine does in book 13, is unique in the volume. He fuses quotations and allusions together in such a way that the distinction of the testaments is obliterated. Though that practice is common throughout the *Confessions*, Augustine's allegorical exposition sustains it with unusual intensity and difficulty.

His subject demands it. He treats the biblical text on universal Creation as the creation of the Church. He envisions the Church, the post–New Testament ministry of Christ, in the very first chapter of Scripture. He thereby sees the whole New Testament as "spiritually present" within the first chapter of the Old, just as he foresees the end of all time in the first week of Creation.

Augustine's subject, the Church, can itself be said to encompass the whole of Scripture, and in a number of different ways. As the Spiritual Israel and the Mystical Body of Christ, the Church subsumes the essence of both the Old and New Testaments. More important, the Church is charged with the *magisterium*, to teach and preach the true meaning of Scripture. It thereby functions, like Scripture and like Christ, as a mediator between God and man. As the Mystical Body of Christ, the Church preaches the word of God brought by and revealed in the Word of God. The Church is therefore the guardian of the truth taught in the whole of Scripture. It bears the means of grace whereby mankind is led out of time and back to eternity.

Further, Augustine's allegory implies that creation of the Church subsumes the meaning of the universe and all history. The cosmos was created for man, according to Augustine, and man was created for life with God. The Church offers the means to eternal life, and as Christ's Mystical Body, it is an eternal institution. For Augustine, the Church guides humankind to the goal of rest in God's eternal sabbath, foreseen at the close of Scripture and of the *Confessions*. And in that rest, the Church will be perfected.

In sum, then, the subject of Augustine's allegorical exposition encompasses the whole of Scripture and, hence, the sweep and meaning of all history. It reveals the Church as that "single true, certain, and good meaning" (12.32.43) toward which Genesis 1 and all of Scripture point. The scope of the exposition, from Creation to God's eternal kingdom, itself comprehends the scope of the Bible. And Augustine's style, the densely woven texture of biblical quotations, also draws on all of Scripture. In all of these ways, then, the final twenty-seven chapters of the *Confessions* fulfill Augustine's prayer at book 11, chapter 2, paragraph 3, to "consider the wonderful things of your law, from that beginning, wherein you made heaven and earth, even to an everlasting kingdom together with you in your holy city."

Here again, we are meant to understand that God fulfills this prayer in a marvellous and unforeseen way. In book 11, chapter 2, Augustine the speaker is on fire. He confesses (*confitear*) a desire to consider all the Bible, every verse of every book, it would seem. Such a prayer makes no rational sense in terms of Augustine conceived solely as author, as O'Meara points out. But Augustine the speaker makes it, and he begins a laborious meditation. Seventy-three chapters later, his prayerful meditation catches fire. Within twenty-seven chapters, he completes a meditation on Genesis 1 that encompasses, in its style, themes, and subject, the whole of Scripture. God's grace inspires the speaker's understanding and so fulfills his prayer. His *Confessions* comes to rest.

Augustine the author, one must postulate, plans this entire movement. He plans his speaker to undertake that impossible task near the beginning of book 11 and to revise it at the close of book 12. He composes those prayers in such a way that the allegory on the Church may fulfill their "letter" with its spiritual allegory. Augustine the author plans that exposition to take precisely twenty-seven chapters, a perfect trinitarian number. He plans the "uninspired" exploration, from book 11, chapter 3, to book 13, chapter 11, to take precisely seventy-two chapters, a number with well-known connotations: Jesus chooses seventy-two disciples (Luke 10:1), perhaps to counteract the Babelic dispersal of humankind into seventy-two nations and languages.[12] Augustine plans the entire exposition of Scripture to take precisely ninety-nine chapters: a number both trinitarian (3 × 33) and just one chapter shy of the perfection (one hundred) his final chapters gaze toward. Augustine the author constructs books 11–13 such that the examination of Scripture will be constituted in chapters with significant numbers. He orchestrates digres-

sions, plans a seeming planlessness. He aims all toward the fulfillment of the speaker's prayers in the "inspired allegory" that concludes the *Confessions*.

One can only postulate this Augustine the author. Since the *Confessions* presents itself as a prayer being spoken spontaneously, as it
were, the premise of the writing is that it is *not planned*. Augustine
the speaker prays his often wandering way toward truth. Truth
emerges only through grace in the dynamic of his encounter with
God. According to this premise, whatever structures seem planned in
the volume are not the work of Augustine the speaker but of the God
who guides his *Confessions*.

As I argued in the previous chapter, Augustine the author con-
trives this literary form, in part, to imitate the providential ordering
he has experienced in his own life. God guides the speaker's *Confessions*, just as he has guided, and does guide, Augustine's life. We can
now see that both arrive at fulfillment. God's grace brings the young
Augustine to the "peaceful light" (*luce securitatis*, 8.12.29) of conversion. Divine inspiration fulfills the speaker's desire to consider all of
Scripture. And the *Confessions* ends where Augustine the author aspires to be, the fulfillment of God's eternal *quies*.

In many ways, then, Augustine's "divinely inspired" exposition
of Scripture brings his book to a fitting climax and conclusion. Those
final twenty-seven chapters receive pride of place at the summit of
the volume. Within the *Confessions*, they also function as a kind of
summation of Scripture: a spiritual allegory comprehending, in brief
compass, the "whole Bible." Thus, they articulate a comprehensive
vision of the meaning of the universe and its history. If a coherent
plan is to be found for the volume, some common paradigm must be
found to govern both its first nine or ten books and its treatment of
Genesis. Since Augustine discovers "all of Scripture" in Genesis 1 at
the end of his *Confessions*, we can perhaps discover "all the *Confessions*" in that allegorical exposition.

3 ✤ Book 13 and Books 1–9

In the allegory in book 13, Augustine finds God acting nine times in the week of Creation. God acts eight times in the first six days, and in his ninth act he blesses and sanctifies the sabbath. Augustine discriminates eight distinct hexameral acts on the basis of God's seeing what he makes as "good": "*In seven places I have counted it written down that you saw what you made is good. And this is the eighth*, that you saw all the things that you made, and behold they are not only good, but even very good, as existing all together. For separately, they were only good, but existing all together they are all both good and very good" (13.28.43, my italics). The eighth "good," which is "very good," occurs after God's creation of human beings to his own "image and likeness." In the six days of Creation, God acts twice on the third and sixth days, once on each of the others. Hence, God creates eight separate times in Genesis and then blesses the sabbath, a ninth act.[1]

This pattern must have been important to Augustine. God acts nine times in the week of Creation; Augustine's autobiography comprises nine books. Augustine allegorizes God's ninth act as the "sabbath of eternal life" (13.36.51). Book 9 ends with the death of Monica and a chapter-long prayer for the repose of her soul. Her death is prefigured by the "vision at Ostia," shared with her son: the vision arises from a discussion "as to what the eternal life of the saints would be like" (9.10.23). Book 9, thus, contains certain parallels with the allegory on God's ninth act in book 13. The seven "good" acts of Creation culminate in an eighth, which is "very good"; seven books in the autobiography culminate in an eighth, the young Augustine's conversion, also "very good." God's eighth act, the creation of Adam and Eve, has a moral allegory in book 13: woman is made subject to man, just as the "active appetite is made subject, so as to conceive right and prudent conduct from the rational mind" (13.32.47). In book 8, the young Augustine dedicates himself to continence: he subjects his "womanly" appetite to his reason.

These are but the first, faint traces of a figure. The "inspired" allegory on God's nine acts in Creation provides, I argue, the paradigm, the latent design, for books 1–9 of the *Confessions*. Each of the first nine books corresponds in series to each of God's nine acts, as allegorized in book 13. In each case, the correspondence subsumes certain major themes and images. Here, I shall comment on the most important of these, linking Augustine's "inspired" allegory on each act to its corresponding book in the autobiography.

The premise of the *Confessions*, however, must be kept clearly in mind: these correspondences are not planned by Augustine the speaker, but by God. As the speaker prays his way through books 1–9, he can have no idea what book 13 might hold. As we have seen, he often finds himself surprised at what he has been saying. He is not in complete control of his speaking; he trusts God to guide his *Confessions*. That he should be a divinely inspired interpreter of Scripture is perhaps his hope, but it cannot, obviously, be his plan.

The correspondences we shall trace, therefore, subsume certain major themes and images but not, certainly, every one. The text emerges, according to its premise, through *two* vectors of intentionality. Hence, the volume does not develop according to some tyrannical system that straitjackets every detail. The speaker has a mind of his own and a free will. God guides the *Confessions*; he does not dictate them.

This treatment of correspondence, therefore, attempts to encompass books 1–9 but does not presume to exhaust them. It accounts for certain significant patterns of imagery but not every significant pattern, to be sure. No such exhaustive scheme is possible, given the premise of the *Confessions*: its master plan lies beyond the ken of Augustine the speaker. Equally, many patterns of imagery could be explored in relation to texts other than the allegory in book 13. The water imagery in book 1, for example, certainly echoes the *Aeneid*, and so perhaps does the nautical imagery at the end of book 6 and throughout book 7. Images in books 1–9 can certainly be interpreted in relation to scriptural texts other than Genesis or classical writers other than Virgil. I have not pursued these possibilities, for two reasons. First, such treatment would have prolonged and distracted an already substantial argument. Second, important as other intertextual strands are, the coherence of the *Confessions* turns on internal relations with the allegory in book 13. I have already suggested why this should be the case, pointing to the scope and sweep of Augustine's treatment of Genesis 1. Just as the Bible, for him, is the master text for assessing the truth value of all other literary works, so within the *Confessions* functions the "inspired" allegory containing "all of Scripture." It receives pride of place in the volume at the conclusion of his prayer and the summit of his quest for understanding. The *Confessions'* correspondences with classical literature and even with other biblical texts are meant to be interpreted in its light.

Two scholars have already described master plans for the *Confessions* based on Genesis 1. These differ considerably from each other and from my own. L. F. Pizzolato argues that the *Confessions* is structured according to the six stages of human life.[2] Augustine treats these in the *De Genesi contra Manichaeos*, where he aligns them with the six stages of Creation. Pizzolato appeals to this commentary, which is quite extraneous to the treatment of Genesis in the *Confessions*, to develop a structural scheme for the volume. This scheme has been criticized for being somewhat reductive. Though any such scheme (including the one offered by myself) perforce simplifies Augustine's complex masterpiece, Pizzolato's plan oversimplifies it. Nonetheless, his work deserves attention not only for many fine individual insights but for its commitment to treating the *Confessions* as a comprehensively coherent book.[3]

A more cogent analysis has been developed by Robert M. Durling.[4] He does not appeal to any tradition extraneous to the *Confessions* but, rather, establishes correspondences between the autobiography and Genesis 1. He argues that each of Augustine's first seven books corresponds, in series, with each of the seven days in Genesis. Book 7 embodies "the sabbatical principle"—the young Augustine's experience of "rest" in his intellectual conversion—and books 8 and 9 represent higher realizations of this sabbatical principle, as the young Augustine's intellect and will achieve further integration. Durling's discussion of Genesis in books 1–9 is but part of a more far-reaching treatment of "Platonism and Poetic Form" in the *Confessions*. In the following chapters, I shall return to the principles he articulates. My conception of the volume derives from them.

Nonetheless, the description of Augustine's plan offered here differs considerably from Durling's, as we shall see.

Neither Pizzolato nor Durling conceive of Augustine the speaker as distinct from Augustine the author. Hence, neither offers a convincing rationale for the *latency* of the structure each describes. All Augustine scholars, it would seem, can agree on this one thing, at least: if there is a latent design to the *Confessions*, it is very latent indeed. We are not obtuse readers. Had he wished to, Augustine could surely have clarified some of the work's basic patterns on its "surface," as it were, like Boethius and Dante. But he did not wish to. Boethius and Dante each portray, in retrospect, an "autobiographical" journey with a guide. Augustine's journey, however, is not guided. Or rather, the speaker does have a guide, as he repeatedly insists, but he is not clearly directed.

Hence, the "providential plan" of the *Confessions* is a latent design. The speaker is not aware that a "divinely inspired" understanding of Genesis informs the progress, themes, and metaphors of his autobiographical record. Yet the two prove strikingly aligned. The allegory on God's nine acts in Genesis, the autobiography in nine books: in their progress, central themes, and controlling metaphors, meaningful correspondences abound.

The discussion of metaphor may, perhaps, strike some Augustine scholars strangely. Scholarship on the *Confessions* has been largely historical, philosophical, and theological in its orientations. Therefore, it tends to view rhetorical figures as ornamentation. These *exornationes* are usually seen as external to the real meanings of the text, figures to be penetrated, read *through*.

In literary study of a text, however, scholars tend to *look at* rhetorical figures as forms of meaning in themselves. While acknowledging the historical value of the events and ideas recorded in the work, literary analysts scrutinize the figures of language with which these are expressed, looking for patterns of metaphor and interpreting their meanings. We envision rhetorical figures as essential to the meaning of a work, as woven into its texture, inherent in its structure. Wide reading in scholarship on the *Confessions* would not lead one to expect how richly figurative Augustine's book is. One task of literary study is to examine this somewhat neglected aspect of the work. Perhaps it may inform historical and philosophical studies of the *Confessions* as richly as it has been instructed by them.[5]

With this prolegomenon completed, the treatment of correspondences may begin. It is long. For the reader's convenience, I have numbered each set of correspondences, from I through IX, for easy reference. Each begins with a rather detailed presentation of relevant images and themes from the allegory; each then demonstrates how those figures and ideas inform the corresponding autobiographical book.[6] This arrangement may enable the reader who grants the argued correspondence to leave the things that are behind and hasten on to those that are before.

I

Genesis describes God's first act at the Creation in two parts. Verses 1 and 2 make up the first part. They assert that "In the beginning God created heaven and earth" and describe the earth as "invisible and without form" (*invisibilis et incomposita*).[7] "Darkness" is "upon the deep" (*tenebrae erant super abyssum*), upon the "waters" above which "the spirit of God" is borne. Verses 3–5 constitute the second part of God's first creative act. He creates light (3), sees it as "good," divides it from the darkness (4), and calls "the light Day, and the darkness Night" (5).

Robert M. Durling points to several important correspondences between these verses and book 1 of the *Confessions*.[8] Augustine's autobiography in book 1 falls into two parts: infancy and boyhood (*pueritia*, 1.8.13). Augustine has no personal memories of infancy: that period of life "belongs to the dark regions of forgetfulness" (*ad oblivionis meae tenebras*, 1.7.12). Durling comments: "Darkness is on the face of the deep, and consciousness emerges as the need for language, for the sign which will express his desire. The connection of speech and consciousness is clearly patterned on *Dixitque Deus: fiat lux, et facta est lux*."

Durling goes on to suggest correspondences with God's seeing the light as good. Augustine emphasizes that the elements of reading and writing are good, far better than their use in studying pagan literature (1.13.22) and in learning rhetoric to fulfill vain ambitions (1.17–19). Durling also notes that the book closes by emphasizing the goodness of the boy Augustine, a growing unity derived from God's "most mysterious unity" (*vestigium secretissimae unitatis, ex qua eram*, 1.20.31).

These observations are crucial to understanding the relations between Genesis and book 1. I should like to develop them in the context of Augustine's allegorical exposition on God's first act in Creation, from which new understandings may emerge. In book 13, chapters 12–14, no distinction is drawn between the "two parts" of God's first act. Verses 1–5 are treated as a coherent, allegorical whole. The exposition repeatedly adverts to the imagery of "darkness," "waters," and the "abyss," even after introducing the *Fiat lux*. So, too, does book 1. The "darkness" of Genesis 1:2 does not apply solely to the oblivion that covers Augustine's infancy. The allegory in book 13 envisions it as the "darkness of ignorance" (13.12.13), and these dark and empty waters appear throughout Augustine's critique of his boyhood education, *after* the *Fiat lux* of language.[9]

Augustine's allegory envisions God's creating heaven and earth as the creation of "the spiritual and carnal parts" (*spiritales et carnales*, 13.12.13) of the Church. Before receiving the "form of doctrine," "our earth was invisible and without order" and covered over with the "darkness of ignorance [*ignorantiae tenebris tegebamur*]. . . . But because your Spirit was borne over the water, your mercy did not abandon our misery, and you said, 'Be light made. Do penance. The kingdom of heaven is at hand. Do penance. Be light made'" (13.12.13). The creation of light is linked to the message of the gospel: this is the doctrine that gives form to "our earth." The gospel message insists on conversion, and the text thus links *conversio* to *formatio*, as does chapter 2 of book 13.[10] Both emerge from God's mercy, figured in the Spirit's being "borne above" the formless waters, analogous to "our misery."

The following chapter employs allusions to Psalm 41 and Saint Paul to develop these themes. The "deep" (*abyssus*) of waters below is contrasted with waters coming from above in "the voice of your floodgates" (*in voce cataractarum tuarum*, 13.13.14, and Ps. 41:8). The waters from above are God's "deep," the *abyssus* of his judgments (13.12.13). They are a positive, creative force: the "floodgates of the gifts" of the Spirit, God's pure "fountains of waters" for which Saint Paul thirsts "even as the hart" (13.13.14, Ps. 41:1). "'Desiring to be clothed with his habitation which is from heaven,' he calls to the lower deep, and says, 'Do not be conformed to this world, but be reformed in the newness of your mind.' And again: 'Do not become children in mind, but in malice be children, that you may be perfect in mind'" (13.13.14). The "lower deep" is thus analogous to "this world." If one follows the "form of doctrine" (13.12.13) of "this world," one is conformed to it in a negative conversion. Formation in terms of the "upper deep," the voice of God's floodgates, however, leads to reformation and newness in mind. The darkness of the lower deep is countered by the Spirit's light from above, and both are figured as *abyssi* and "waters."

Paul's injunctions are then said to derive from his friendship for the Bridegroom, Christ, and his zeal for the Bride, the Church. Paul speaks "in the voice of your floodgates and not in his own voice" (13.13.14). He speaks to the faithful lest "their minds be corrupted from chastity, which is in our Spouse, your only Son." Chastity is thereby linked with the Spirit and the "waters above." The waters below, it is implied, are linked with corruption and sin as *fornicatio* away from God. The latter is made explicit in chapter 7:

> How shall I speak of the *weight of lust* [*pondere cupiditatis*], *dragging downward into the steep abyss*, and of charity lifting up through your Spirit, who was borne above the waters? To whom shall I say this? How shall I say it? There are places into which we are plunged and from which we emerge [*quibus mergimur et emergimus*]. What is more like them, and yet what is more unlike them? *They are affections; they are loves: the filthiness of our spirit, flowing away downwards* with a love that brings but care. (13.7.8, my italics)

The waters below, in this allegory, corrupt, deform, destroy: they are the "waters without substance" (13.7.8). The passage implies a storm or a flood, against which one struggles to avoid drowning: one is plunged in passively (*mergimur*) and must struggle actively to emerge (*emergimus*). The dark and formless waters below clearly represent the storm of passions in "this world."

Such imagery occurs at many points in book 1 of the *Confessions*, most prominently *after* the *Fiat lux* of learning how to speak. Augustine concludes his account of language-learning with this statement of its effects: "When my mouth had become accustomed to these signs, I expressed by means of them my own wishes [*meas voluntates*]. Thus to those among whom I was I communicated the signs of my wishes. *I entered more deeply* into the *stormy society of human life* [*vitae humanae procellosam societatem*], although still dependent on my parents' authority and the will of my elders" (1.8.13, my italics). Even in infancy, the text implies, the child has already entered into the "stormy society of human life." Learning language brings the child "more deeply" into the storm. John Freccero elaborates this insight:

> In the *Confessions*, the insatiable hunger of human beings is inseparable from language. In infancy, language and desire are born at the same time when the paralanguage of gesticulation struggles to name the objects it would possess. At the same time, however, *it is clear that the child eventually learns what to desire from a world that adults have named.* One might say that the outward trajectory of language represents a grammar of desire, while the inward trajectory of language represents a rhetoric of suggestion. *Words can express desire, but the words of others, or of Another, can create it.* This explains the polemic against pagan literature and the threat it poses to the adolescent.[11]

Augustine's critique of his education adverts again and again to the imagery of storms, water, darkness, and confusion. Being able to speak and learning to read expose the young Augustine to *formatio* according to the words he heeds, is taught to heed. In the terms of book 13, those words do not come from the voice of God's floodgates, the pure *fontes aquarum* from above. They come from his education in pagan literature, and so they conform him to the "waters below" of "this world," of "our misery." The result, according to Augustine the speaker, is disastrous.

This nexus of images appears prominently in the tears the young Augustine sheds out of sympathy for Dido:

> Who can be more *wretched* than the *wretched* one who takes *no pity* on himself [*Quid enim miserius misero non miserante se ipsum*], who *weeps* over Dido's *death*, which she brought to pass by *love* for Aeneas, and who does not *weep* over his *own death*, brought to pass by not loving you, O God, light of my heart, bread for the inner mouth of my soul, *power wedding* together my mind and the bosom of my thoughts? *I did not love you, and I committed fornication against you* [*fornicabar abs te*], and amid my fornications from all sides there sounded the words, "Well done! Well done!" *Love of this world is fornication against you.* (1.13.21, my italics)

The polyptoton on *miserare* emphasizes the "misery" that the bishop sees in his youthful tears. The text links this misery with the water of weeping, with death, and sinful "love of this world," depicted sexually as *fornicatio* away from God. All these notions, as we have seen, are linked with the "waters below" in the allegory of book 13.

The imagery recurs, more obviously and violently, in chapter 16. Augustine recalls a scene from Terence, in which a young man "arouses himself to lust, as if by heavenly instruction" (1.16.26) when he sees a painting of Danae and Jove's "shower of gold." The "shower" (*imbrem*) suggests both the "waters below" and orgasm, images of dissolution for the chaste Augustine.

What rouses his fiercest polemic, however, are the moral values of pagan society enshrined in a classical education. Study of such works implies a disastrous moral *formatio*, portrayed in images of a dark and torrential flood:

> Woe to you, O torrent of men's ways! Who will stand up against you? How long will it be until you are dried up? How long will you sweep [*volves*] the sons of Eve down into that mighty and hideous ocean [*mare magnum et formidolosum*], over which even they who are borne upon the Tree can scarcely cross? . . .
>
> Nevertheless, O hellish flood [*flumen tartareum*], the sons of men are thrown into you [*iactantur in te*] with fees paid, so that they may learn these fables. A great thing is made of it when some of this is acted out publicly in the forum, supervised by laws decreeing salaries over and above the students' fees. You dash against your rocks, you roar and say: "Here is the learned use of words! Here eloquence is acquired, most necessary for winning cases and expressing thoughts." (1.16.25–26)

Here, and elsewhere, Augustine relentlessly criticizes the worldly values that bring parents to "drown" their sons in such an educational system. Their children are thereby exposed to a moral storm that few can successfully withstand. In the following chapter, the young Augustine's prize-winning version of Juno's first speech in the *Aeneid* also implies this storm imagery. The boy is taught to think through, feel through, and act out the vindictive storm of Juno's emotions. In the *Aeneid*, these lead to the "real storm" unleashed against Aeneas's fleet.

This polemic clearly implies a new, and Christian, educational program, based on the study of Scripture. In the terms of book 13, such study would provide the *formatio* of Christian doctrine through the "voice" of God's "floodgates." It would lead students to be "reformed in newness of mind." It would form their desires to thirst for the pure "fountains of waters" that come from above (13.13.14).

Unlike Augustine's education, it would teach, "Do not become children in mind, but in malice be children, that you may be perfect in mind" (13.13.14). The bishop attacks his teachers for having been adults in malice. Bested by "a fellow teacher in some trifling discussion, he was more tormented by anger and envy than I was when beaten by a playmate in a ball game" (1.9.15). For a full chapter, Augustine criticizes the teachers' concern for purity of pronunciation, their utter lack of regard for purity of heart (1.18). Under their tutelage, the young Augustine is "far from your face in the darkness of my passions" (*in affectu tenebroso*, 1.18.28) and in "a whirlpool of filth" (*voraginem turpitudinis*, 1.19.30). He flounders in the dark chaos of the "waters below."

Thus, the central images in Augustine's allegory on God's first act inform the central themes of book 1, where they occur repeatedly. A few other correspondences may be noted more briefly. God's creating "the spiritual and carnal parts" of the Church is clearly analogous to his forming the soul and body of the child Augustine. This creation, as Durling observes, is good: book 1 closes with the "goods" and "gifts" that make the boy a "trace" (*vestigium*) of God's "most mysterious unity" (1.20.31). The final sentence in the allegory makes a similar point: "What have we that we have not received from you?" (13.14.15).

The paradigmatic figure for this generosity is the Spirit, "the gift of God" (13.9.10). Through the Spirit God pours "the floodgates of his gifts" that make his people joyful (*cataractas donorum suorum, ut fluminis impetus laetificarent civitatem tuam*, 13.13.14). The Spirit thus represents God's mercy coming to meet human misery, because "he was mercifully borne above our dark and fluid inner being" (13.14.15). Augustine's portrayal of his infancy corresponds to this paradigm in several ways.

Augustine portrays the infant as without *mores*. In early infancy, the child is governed wholly by sensations and desires, for he knows "only how to seek the breast, to be satisfied with pleasant things, and to cry at bodily hurts, nothing more" (1.6.7). Above this moral *informitas*, like the Spirit above the waters, are the love and care of his *maiores*:

Your consolations and *mercies have raised me up*, as I have heard from the parents of my flesh, for by one and in the other you fashioned me in time. *I myself do not remember this.* Therefore the comfort [*consolationes*] of human milk nourished me, but neither my mother nor my nurses filled their own breasts. *Rather, through them you gave* me an infant's food in accordance with your law and out of the riches that you have distributed even down to the lowest level of things. *You gave me to want no more than you gave, and you gave to those who nursed me the will to give what you gave to them. By an orderly affection* [*per ordinatum affectum*] they willingly gave me what they possessed so abundantly from you. (1.6.7, my italics)

The text repeatedly insists that *God gives* nourishment to the infant by means of his mother and nurses. He takes rest and joy in this flow of nourishment, "the comfort of *human* milk." This is analogous to the rest and joy (*laetificarent*) that the city of God takes in the flood of his gifts through the Spirit (13.13.14). The child is nursed by an "orderly affection" that conforms to the flood of gifts from above. His desires are natural and good, easily satisfied. His nurses feed him from their God-given abundance. Milk comes to the infant from his *maiores*, adults placed above him in authority, wisdom, and love. Analogously, the Spirit "borne above the waters" brings the "floodgates of His gifts" to make God's people happy (13.13.14). The correspondences between book 1 and the allegory, here, prove thorough and precise.

II

God's second act in the Hexameron again involves the dark and formless waters of "the earth." On the second day God creates the firmament of heaven and divides "the waters that were under the firmament from those that were above the firmament" (Gen. 1:7). The "waters below," it is implied, remain *invisibilis et incomposita* (1:2). God calls the firmament heaven (1:8): His naming it and its firm formation imply a structured order to the "waters above" that does not obtain "below." This distinction is important in Augustine's allegory on Genesis and proves crucial to the structure of imagery-and-theme in book 2.

In book 13, Augustine interprets the firmament of heaven as Scripture. Both heaven and Scripture are works of God and "above" mankind: Augustine repeatedly emphasizes the Bible's "sublime authority" (13.15.16). He draws on Psalm 103:2, where God is said to have "stretched out the sky like a skin," to make an analogy between the "skin" of Scripture and the skins with which God clothes sinful Adam and Eve (Gen. 3:21). Augustine thereby relates the Fall to mankind's need for Scripture, mediating God to man.

The allegory quickly, if implicitly, underscores this connection. Augustine asserts that no other books so effectively "destroy pride," the cause of the Fall and the "beginning of all sin" (Ecclus. 10:15): "For we do not know of any books which so destroy pride, which so destroy "the enemy and the defender," who resists your reconciliation by defending his own sins. I do not know, O Lord, I do not know any such pure words [casta eloquia] which so persuade me to make confession and make my neck meek to your yoke, and invite me to serve you without complaint" (13.15.17). The "sublime authority" of Scripture (13.15.16) destroys pride by persuading submission to God's word and to his will.

Augustine then notes that there are "other waters" placed "above this firmament" of heaven and Scripture. They are, allegorically, the angels, "supercelestial peoples" who are "free from earthly corruption" (a terrena corruptione secretae, 13.15.18). "Earthly corruption," Augustine implies, is figured by the "waters under the firmament." Being placed above the firmament of Scripture, the angels know God's Word directly: "they always behold your face, and without any syllables of time, they read upon it what your eternal will decrees" (13.15.18). The angels gaze directly at God for eternity. Hence, "their book is never closed, nor is their scroll folded up, because you yourself are this to them" (13.15.18).

The mortal and human reading of God's will in the firmament of Scripture, however, is far different. It operates in time, not eternity, through scriptural mediation, not "face to face." Gazing upward to the firmament of heaven-Scripture, as it were, God's Word "now appears to us under the dark figure of the clouds and in the mirror of the heavens," in aenigmate and per speculum, "not as it is" (13.15.18). Here, the verbum Dei means both Scripture and the Son. It modulates toward the latter, for the chapter concludes with the hope of the beatific vision: "when he shall appear, we shall be like him, because we shall see him as he is" (13.15.18).

This leads to a brief declaration of the eternally perfect and interpenetrating esse, nosse, and velle of the Trinity (13.16.19). Augustine contrasts God's immutability, analogous to the solid firmament of heaven, with human mutability and lack of self-sufficiency. He closes his treatment of God's second act by recalling his allegory on the first: "Therefore, 'my soul is like earth without water unto you.' Just as it cannot of itself enlighten itself, so it cannot of itself be sufficient to itself. Thus, 'with you is the fountain of life,' even as 'in your light we shall see light'" (13.16.19). He associates the "waters above" once again with Scripture: God's pure *fontes aquarum* (13.13.14) and with the creative-converting Light-Word that comes through the Spirit, "borne above the waters" below (13.12.13). Once again, Augustine implies that the "waters below" are dark, impure, and "far away" from God. Indeed, they are the waters of "earthly corruption" (13.15.18).

The recurrent use of water imagery in Genesis 1 provides the basis for this allegory. And this allegory provides the latent design for Augustine's recurrent use of water imagery in the early books of his *Confessions*. Hence, the analysis to be offered for book 2 proves similar, in some respects, to that for book 1, because Augustine allegorizes the water imagery in Genesis in consistent ways.

This imagery dominates the first three chapters of book 2. Augustine analyzes his adolescent sexuality as corrupt and dissolute, and thus tending to dissolve him:

> What was there to bring me delight except to love and be loved? But that due measure between soul and soul, wherein lie the *bright boundaries* of friendship [*luminosus limes amicitiae*], was not kept. Clouds arose from the *slimy desires of the flesh* [*de limosa concupiscentia carnis*] and from youth's *seething spring* [*scatebra pubertatis*]. *They clouded over and darkened* my heart, so that *I could not distinguish the calm light of chaste love from the fog of lust* [*serenitas dilectionis a caligine libidinis*]. Both kinds of affection seethed *confusedly* within me and *swept* my feeble youth over the crags of desire and *plunged me into a whirlpool of shameful deeds* [*mersabat gurgite flagitiorum*]. (2.2.2, my italics)

The passage clearly contrasts the "bright boundaries" of true friendship with lust. The former is associated with *serenitas dilectionis*, which implies the bright light of a clear sky (*serenum*). *Concupiscentia carnis* and *libido*, in contrast, "cloud over and darken" that clear light from above with a "fog" that arises from "the flesh." Fleshly desires are formless, muddy and watery, and they cloud the clear light of true friendship. In the final sentence, these desires are portrayed as a torrent that "sweeps" the young Augustine over a waterfall and immerses him in a whirlpool below.

The metaphor controlling this imagery is implied in the allegory of book 13. The "heaven and earth" that God creates, the "spiritual and carnal parts of the Church" (13.12.13), are analogous to the spirit and the flesh of the young Augustine. His fleshly desires, therefore, are "of the earth." On the second day of Creation, the earth is still *invisibilis et incomposita*: the dark, unsteady, formless "waters below." There is a clear light in the firmament of heaven, the *serenitas dilectionis*; the allegory associates it with Christian love which shines forth from Scripture. "The earth" of the young Augustine's "flesh," however, obscures it with watery exhalations.

Augustine goes on to portray himself wandering further and further away from God. His continued use of water imagery creates a powerful portrayal of male adolescent sexuality: "I wandered further away from you, and you let me go. I was tossed about and spilt over in my fornications; I flowed out and boiled over in them [*iactabar et effundebar et diffluebam et ebulliebam per fornicationes meas*] and you were silent" (2.2.2). The imagery of dissolution is associated with orgasm and death. The young Augustine's physical and mental unity was praised, at the end of book 1, as deriving from God's unity. Now the young man is dissipating and destroying himself. Like the prodigal son, he is wasting his substance through his "fornications" (Luke 15:13, 30). The "little death" of orgasm is clearly linked to the danger of spiritual—and even physical—death through these images of dissolution. Immersion in the formlessness of the earthy "waters below" clearly leads to moral deformation. As the chapter continues, Augustine recurrently appeals to water imagery, speaking of "the flood of my youth" (*fluctus aetatis meae*, 2.2.3), "the sweeping tide of my passions" (*impetum fluxus mei*, 2.2.4), and so on. This moral chaos is analogous to the dark watery chaos of the earth *invisibilis et incomposita*.

In the passage quoted above Augustine asserts that God was silent. In the following chapter, however, the speaker realizes his error. His mother, Monica, repeatedly urges the young Augustine "with great solicitude" to "keep from fornication, and most of all from adultery with any man's wife": "Ah, woe to me! Do I dare to say that you, my God, remained silent when I departed still further from you? Did you in truth remain silent to me at that time? *Whose words but yours were those that you sang in my ears by means of my mother, your faithful servant? Yet none of them sank into my heart, so that I would fulfill them"* (2.3.7, my italics).

Again, the allegory of book 13 provides the latent design for this realization. God is not silent about the young Augustine's sins: Monica is the mediator for his words. Monica is here analogous to the firmament of Scripture. She stands properly above her son in familial authority, his *maior*. She stands above him also in moral authority and intelligence. The text describes her Christian heart in terms that echo God's establishing the firmament of heaven: "But you had already begun to build your temple within my mother's breast and to lay there the foundations of your holy dwelling place [*incohaveras templum tuum et exordium sanctae habitationis tuae*]" (2.3.6). Heaven is God's "holy dwelling place." Its sempiternal firmament is created in a moment. God's firmament in Monica, Augustine asserts, is already surely founded when she counsels him against fornication and adultery.

The text asserts that the young Augustine remains obdurately ignorant of his true moral state, for none of Monica's words sink into his heart (2.3.7): "Such words seemed to be only a woman's warnings, which I should be ashamed to bother with. They were your warnings, and I knew it not" (2.3.7). Here, the text implies, is a crucial reason for the young Augustine's dissolute life. God provides a "firmament of heaven-Scripture," and the adolescent refuses to heed it. The young Augustine ought to have "looked up to" his mother and obtained moral firmness from heeding the divine firmament of her counsel. Because he refuses to look up to that firmament, he abandons himself to the fleshly "waters below," with all their formlessness and corruption.

The young Augustine's obduracy, however, does not spring solely from the turmoil of adolescent sexuality. As book 1 makes clear, his classical education provides him a moral formation— Augustine would say, a moral deformation—in the passions treated by pagan literature. As we saw in book 1, the "waters below," the waters "of this world," are full of voices urging conformity to its values. As a boy with extraordinary verbal gifts, the young Augustine is immersed perhaps all the "more deeply in the stormy society of human life" (1.8.13).

In book 2, the voices of "this world" continue to ring in the young Augustine's ears. His father, noticing his first pubic hairs in the bath, crows to Monica about his son's growing manhood (2.3.6). More important, according to the text, are the voices of the boy's friends. Not recognizing that Monica's words are from God, the young Augustine despises both Monica and God (*contemnebaris a me*, 2.3.7) to heed his comrades: "But I did not know this, and I ran headlong with such great blindness that I was ashamed to be remiss in vice in the midst of my comrades. For I heard them boast of their disgraceful acts, and glory in them all the more, the more debased they were. There was pleasure in doing this, not only for the pleasure of the act, but also for the praise it brought" (2.3.7).

Clearly, the young Augustine's motive in joining such a contest in vice is partly social, as much pride as pleasure: his love of "praise," his desire to "glory." He even pretends to have done things he has not actually done, so as not to be outdone (2.3.7). He actively embraces the values of "this world" as though they possess real worth. The bishop excoriates his past error, alluding to the "earthly corruption" of the "waters below" (13.15.18): "See with what companions I ran about the streets of Babylon, and how I was rolled about in its muddy filth [*volutabar in caeno eius*] as though in cinnamon and precious ointments" (2.3.8). Heeding his companions, the young Augustine is conformed to their stormy society and is rolled about in its torrent. Had he obeyed Monica's words, in contrast, he would have been made firm according to the firmament of Scripture. He would have been "reformed in newness of mind" (13.13.14), gazing upward to the light.

In sum, books 1 and 2 associate the "waters below" with "this world" and fleshliness: not simply physical desires but the voices and values that direct them. The allegory of book 13 illuminates this imagery. What Augustine implies by his negative portrayal of pagan education is explicitly clarified in book 13. Just as the "waters below" of pagan texts and worldly values deform moral sensibilities, so do the "floodgates" (13.13.14) of God's gifts in the firmament of Scripture reform them. The recurrent images and concerns of books 1 and 2 are thus illuminated by their latent design in the allegory of book 13.

The centerpiece of book 2, it is often said, is the "theft of the pears," regarded as one of the most dramatic incidents in Augustine's autobiography. I would argue that this view, so formulated, is imprecise. The central drama of book 2 resides not in the theft of the pears but in the bishop's inquiry into the nature of that act. Augustine barely narrates the theft: he devotes but two sentences to the act itself (2.4.9). He mentions the pear tree (*pirus*) but once (2.4.9) and "pears" not at all: his meditation on the act recurs again and again to the more general *fructus*, for its broad moral overtones. In fact, it should be noted that Augustine refuses to dramatize the sinful act itself. Rather, what emerges most powerfully in book 2 is Augustine the speaker's prayerful and anguished inquiry into the motives underlying his past crime. In chapter 1, I outlined the development of that inquiry, how the speaker's prayer leads him to a new understanding of that sin. The motives he considers are all counterpointed in the allegory in book 13. More important, the process unfolds as Augustine the speaker learns to read the "book of his soul" under God's guidance. That metaphor occurs at the climax of his investigation, in the revelation that constitutes Augustine's new understanding of the pear theft. As we have seen, it is a figure richly developed in the corresponding allegory in book 13.

Augustine first recalls the pear theft in chapter 4. His portrayal of the adolescent gang in chapter 3, their internal rivalry for praise and glory through shameful acts, sets the stage. The *superbia* implied in "love of praise" proves central to the speaker's subsequent meditation on the boy's motives. When Augustine examines each of the vices as a "perverse imitation" (2.6.13–14) of God, pride leads the list. He closes the passage by characterizing sin as *fornicatio*, and a rising up in rebellion against God (2.6.14); this implies *superbia*. Pride is "the beginning of all sin" (Ecclus. 10:15) for Augustine; his analysis of man's first sin and Fall adverts to this principle again and again. Similarly, scholars have long recognized that the pear theft in book 2 resonates with allusions to the Fall: Kenneth Burke calls it Augustine's "equivalent of *Adam's* first sin," not temporally but "in the sense of being a *foremost* or *representative* sin."[12]

Each strand in this nexus of themes—pride, *fornicatio*, the Fall— is counterpointed in the allegory in book 13. Augustine there equates Scripture with the skins God makes for Adam and Eve "when by sin they became subject to death" (*cum peccato fierent mortales*, 13.15.16). Scripture, thus, provides protection for naked, fragile man after the Fall. This protection lies in the power of Scripture to "destroy pride": no other book is so full of a "chaste eloquence" (*casta eloquia*) that persuades a reader to make confession and humble himself to God's service (13.15.17).

Clearly, the *casta eloquia* of Scripture works against the *fornicatio* of sin. In book 2 the boy Augustine scorns the *casta eloquia* of God's words in Monica and so runs "headlong" (*praeceps ibam*, 2.3.7) into all kinds of *fornicationes*, including the theft of the pears. Scorning the "Scripture" that would humble him to God's service, he indulges in sinful pride, and even prides himself on his sins. The Fall that brings God to fashion the "skins" of Scripture is recapitulated when the young Augustine repudiates Monica and adheres to the gang that steals the pears.

Augustine's praise of Scripture in the allegory is also relevant to the writer's awareness of his own enterprise in book 2. The words of Scripture destroy the pride of "'the enemy and the defender,' who resists your reconciliation by defending his own sins" (13.15.17). Clearly, Augustine in book 2 heeds this principle and *accuses* his own sins. Further, the book contains Augustine's first explicit statements as to why he is narrating his *Confessions*: "To whom do I tell these things [*cui narro haec*]? Not to you, my God, but before you [*apud te*] I tell them to my own kind, to mankind, or to whatever small part of it may come upon these books of mine. Why do I tell these things? It is that I myself and whoever else reads them may realize from what great depths we cry to you. *And what is closer to your ears than a contrite heart and a life of faith?*" (2.3.5, my italics). The *casta eloquia* of Scripture persuades him to make confession in the first place (13.15.17). Augustine here aligns the aim of his writing with that of Scripture: to lead others to the "contrite heart" of humble confession. Not to refute the heretic, not to teach doctrine, certainly not to construct an *apologia* for himself: the writer defines his aim as instructing his readers in humility. Precisely what he asserts Scripture does so well in book 13, chapter 15.

Furthermore, in book 2 Augustine describes the mode of his writing as analogous to Scripture: He asserts that his writing is guided by God: "'What shall I render to the Lord,' *for he recalls these things to my memory*, but my soul is not made fearful by them?" (2.7.15, my italics). In the spontaneous and dynamic interplay of his ongoing prayer, the speaker-writer is responsive to the promptings of God's grace: "Who is there to teach me, except him who enlightens my heart and uncovers its darkness? What else is it that has aroused my mind to seek out, and to discuss, and to consider these things?" (2.8.16).

These assertions that God guides his text occur as the writer interrogates the motives that underlay his theft of the pears. As we saw in chapter 1 of this book, Augustine's understanding of those motives changes as he continues to inquire prayerfully into them. In chapter 6 of book 2, he cannot discover "What it was that I, a wretch, loved in you, my act of theft" (2.6.12): the act seems to have no rational motive. In chapter 9, however, the writer realizes that he acted out of a love for friendship: "But that deed I would not have done alone; alone I would never have done it. *Behold, the living record of my soul lies before you, my God [Ecce est coram te, deus meus, viva recordatio animae meae]*. By myself I would not have committed that theft in which what pleased me was not what I stole but the fact that I stole" (2.9.17, my italics).

Augustine exclaims ("Behold") at what he feels to be a divine revelation about his past. In so doing, he uses the metaphor of his soul as a book, "a living record," which is always "before God" and understood by him. This image of the writer's soul as a book underlies his whole inquiry into the theft of the pears: Augustine is trying to "read" the "living record of his soul," understood fully only by God. His patient, prayerful inquiry finally arrives at a "revealed truth," recognized by the speaker as such, and Augustine brings book 2 to a close in the following chapter.

Again, these themes are counterpointed in the allegory of book 13. Six times in four sentences the text describes the angels' "reading" God without intermediary, "face to face." God is their codex and their book (*liber*), and he will never be closed (13.15.18). This perfect reading endures eternally, beyond "the syllables of time" (13.15.18). The human reading of Scripture, however, is in time, "under the dark figure of the clouds and in the mirror of the heavens" (13.15.18). So, too, Augustine's reading of his own heart in book 2 is cloudy, *in aenigmate*, until God reveals the truth.

Augustine closes chapter 15 with a Joannine text on the beatific vision: "we shall be like him (Christ), because we shall see him as he is" (13.15.18; 1 John 3:2). This eschatological transformation "into Christ" is counterposed, in book 2, by the young Augustine's deformation, like Adam in the Fall. At the end of time, Augustine believes, nothing will be hidden, everything will be revealed in the vision of God. The "living record" of his soul will be made clear to him in all particulars. For in eternity he shall know God even as, in time, he is known by him (1 Cor. 13:12).

Curiously, book 2 is the only one in the first nine that does not portray the young Augustine pondering a text. In every other book, the writer recalls his having read, or heard, or written, a particular text. This absence is especially striking given the allegory to which book 2 corresponds, God's creating the firmament of Scripture. Nonetheless, the correspondence is fulfilled, subtly but effectively, by the "Scripture" of Monica's counsel, the "Scripture" of Augustine's own writing, and by his attempt to read "the book of his soul."

III

On the third day of the Hexameron, God performs two acts. First, he commands the "waters below" to be gathered into one place that the dry land may appear (Gen. 1:9); he calls the latter "earth" and the former "sea," and sees that his work is good (1:10). Second, he commands the earth to germinate (1:11) and it brings forth grass and trees that bear fruit, "having seed each one according to its kind," all of which God sees as good (1:12).

Clearly, these two acts are closely related in Scripture, and Augustine allegorizes both in a single chapter of book 13. Hence, though the program of correspondences traced here aligns God's third act with book 3 and his fourth with book 4, the same terms in Augustine's allegory encompass both. Certain close similarities of imagery and theme, therefore, occur in this and the following section.

These similarities are not based solely on the allegory in book 13. Books 3 and 4 in Augustine's autobiography encompass the period of his most intense commitment to Manichaeism. Early in book 3, the young Augustine "falls in with" (incidi, 3.6.10) the sect and then later describes his period of adherence to it: "For almost nine years passed, in which I was tossed about 'in the mire of the deep' and in the darkness of error, and although I often strove to rise out of it, I was all the more grievously thrust down again" (3.11.20). Here Augustine draws on the imagery of the third day in Genesis. He describes the "almost nine years" of his Manichaeism as floundering about in a sea, struggling not to drown. Shortly thereafter he opens book 4 by recalling this text: "For the same period of nine years, from the nineteenth year of my age to the twenty-eighth . . ." (4.1.1). These words govern the whole of book 4, for not until book 5, chapter 6, does the work explicitly record the young Augustine's doubting and questioning Manichaean doctrines. By the end of that book the young Augustine resolves "that the Manichaeans must be abandoned" (5.14.25). Hence, books 3 and 4 encompass the period of the young Augustine's firm commitment to Manichaeism and, equally, correspond to the allegory on the third day of Creation, God's third and fourth acts.

That allegory envisions God gathering together the "waters below" into the sea, a "society" of the "embittered" (*amaricantes*, 13.17.20) against God, the heretics. This sea still retains the characteristics of the "waters below" of "this world": "For all of them, there is one same end of temporal and earthly happiness, because of which they do all their deeds, although they waver back and forth amid a countless variety of cares" (*quamvis innumerabili varietate curarum fluctuent*, 13.17.20). This sea is contrasted with the "dry land" of all those who "thirst after" God, the Christian faithful. This land provides a region of order, of moral firmness, that "restrains" the sea of heresies: "You restrain the wicked lusts of souls [*malas cupiditates animarum*], and fix limits for them, as to how far the waters may be permitted to go, so that their waves may break upon one another [*ut in se comminuantur fluctus earum*]" (13.17.20).

Augustine clearly implies a relation between the "dry land" of the Christian faithful and the "firmament of Scripture," created on the second day. Both the "dry land," below, and the firmament of heaven, above, provide restraining, ordering limits to "the waters." Clearly, the "dry land" of the Christian faithful are made firm through their regard for the firmament of Scripture. The "bitter sea" of the heretics, in contrast, chaotically confounds itself with its doctrinal "waves," which gain nothing against the "dry land."

At a deeper level, the binary opposition of land versus sea is structured analogously to that of eternity versus time. The Church is an eternal institution for Augustine, based on the firmament of God's word, "which endures forever" (13.15.18). Heretical doctrines, in contrast, are as restless and mutable as the sea. For all heretics, "there is one same end of temporal and earthly happiness" (*temporalis et terrenae felicitatis*, 13.17.20), while the faithful "dry land" seeks eternal happiness. Hence the latter mirrors, in its form, the stability of eternity. Augustine explicitly links the "sea" of heresy with the chaos and instability of temporal cares, especially the search for happiness in this world. He clearly contrasts to this cluster the "dry land" of Christian faith, which partakes of God's eternally stable truth, will, and joy. His sea-land opposition is founded on the Christian-Neoplatonist contrast between time and eternity.

Augustine's allegory on God's fourth act draws on Genesis 2:6 to explain how the earth brings forth grass and trees. The "dry land" of the faithful is not watered by the "bitter sea." Rather, God himself waters it "by a sweet and hidden spring" (*occulto et dulci fonte inrigas*, 13.17.21) "that the earth too may bring forth her fruit" (*ut et terra det fructum suum*). Augustine's "too" (*et*) implies that the "sea of the embittered" also brings forth an allegorical fruit. By the command of God (*te iubente*), figured as the "sweet fountain" of his word in the gospel, "our soul germinates works of mercy according to its kind" (13.17.21). Augustine implies, therefore, that the bitter sea of the heretics produces works after *its* kind: works of *misery*. Christian charity, which is "sweet," is contrasted with the "wicked lusts" (*malas cupiditates*, 13.17.20) of the "embittered" against God, which can only produce misery.

When Augustine summarizes his allegory in book 13, chapter 34, the "dry land" is analogous to the "zeal of the faithful" (*studia fidelium*) and is contrasted with the "society of unbelievers" (*societatem infidelium*, 13.34.49). The "sea" of the latter is gathered "into one conspiracy" (*in unam conspirationem*). Where the faithful are made zealous by God's Spirit and constitute a firm, well-ordered Church that obeys God's inspired word in the firmament of Scripture, heretics form a con-spiracy, a wicked anti-Church, chaotic, windy with human vanities.

For Augustine, this allegory describes the distinction between the true Church and any and all heresy. In context of the whole *Confessions*, however, the "society of unbelievers" refers primarily to the Manichaeans. They are the object of the bishop's most vigorous and frequent polemics in the volume. In contrast to pagan philosophy and astronomy, Manichaean doctrines are attacked as completely false, utterly fanciful, and pernicious. The sea of these "embittered" heretics is gathered together in God's third act of Creation; the young Augustine joins their sect in book 3 of the *Confessions*.

Augustine's allegory on God's third act further develops the meaning of the water imagery in God's first and second acts. The waters of the sea still represent cupidity, carnality, desire for earthly happiness, and, hence, the fluctuant chaos of the passions. Now, however, they are gathered together "into one conspiracy" (13.34.49) and the brine of the sea symbolizes the "bitterness" of heresy.[13]

When this development is aligned with the water imagery in books 1–3, the young Augustine's "fall" (3.6.10) into Manichaeism is linked to his being educated in the pagan values of "this world" (book 1) and to his youthful sexual desires (book 2). Near the end of book 3, as we have seen, the text portrays Manichaeism as a stormy sea in which the young Augustine almost drowns: "For almost nine years passed, in which I was tossed about in the mire of the deep and in the darkness of error, and although I strove often to rise out of it, I was all the more grievously thrust down again [*ego in illo limo profundi ac tenebris falsitatis, cum saepe surgere conarer et gravius alliderer, volutatus sum*]" (3.11.20). As in all heresy, according to the allegory of book 13, the Manichaean "waves break upon one another" (13.17.20) in a chaos of conflicting doctrines that lack the stability of truth. The passage above portrays a storm at sea that darkens the sky ("the darkness of error") and roils up mud from the ocean floor ("the mire of the deep"). It also recalls the water imagery of books 1 and 2: the "stormy society of human life" (1.8.13), the "torrent of men's ways" (1.16.25) in "this world," "the whirlpool of shameful deeds" (2.2.2) of his adolescence.

Augustine's initial depiction of the Manichaeans clarifies the relations in this strand of imagery: "And so I fell in with certain men, doting in their pride, too carnal-minded and glib of speech [*superbe delirantes, carnales nimis et loquaces*], in whose mouth were the snares of the devil and a very birdlime confected by mixing together [*commixtione*] the syllables of your name, and the name of our Lord Jesus Christ, and the name of the Paraclete, our comforter, the Holy Spirit" (3.6.10). Like the young Augustine of book 2 and his teachers in book 1, the Manichaeans are proud, carnal, and glib of speech. Hence, all are characterized as analogous to the "waters below." The Manichaeans, however, are the worst: they are "deliriously proud," "excessively carnal," and their speech is not simply in error but a "snare of the devil." In the terms of book 13, they are not simply chaotic and fluctuant like the "waters below": the Manichaeans, further, are organized into a "conspiracy" of "bitter men" (*amaricantes*, 13.17.20), combating by deceit the truth of the Holy Spirit.

Augustine goes on in the chapter to attack Manichaeism as a greater evil than paganism. He vilifies the "corporeal fantasies" (*corporalia phantasmata*, 3.6.10) of the heavenly bodies which they served up to him as "truth." Such doctrine is far more pernicious, he asserts, than his boyhood education in the "poetic fables" (*poetica figmenta*, 1.13.22, 1.17.27) of Virgil. The latter are associated with the passions and the chaotic "waters below" in book 1, while Manichaean doctrine is a stormy and bitter sea of folly in book 3. Augustine can at least convert those *poetica figmenta* into "good food" through allegorical interpretation, but not the Manichaean *phantasmata*: "For I can turn verse and song into good food. Again, although I sang of Medea flying aloft, I did not assert that it was a fact; although I heard it sung, I did not believe it. But I did believe in those fantasies. Woe, Woe!" (3.6.11). Classical poetry does not demand religious faith of its readers, as does Manichaean doctrine. Augustine grants that the former may contain allegorical truths, but not the latter. Christian Scripture, the bishop implicitly reminds his readers, is true both literally and allegorically, in multiple ways.

Augustine describes, and thus explains, his having been led into the folly of Manichaean belief: "I met with that bold woman, void of prudence, Solomon's riddle, seated on a stool at her doorway and saying to me, 'Freely eat you of secret bread and drink of stolen waters.' She seduced me [*me seduxit*], for she found me dwelling outside myself in my fleshly eye [*in oculo carnis meae*], and chewing over within myself such things as I had devoured through it" (3.6.11). The woman of Solomon's riddle, of course, is Folly. She offers the young Augustine the "food of truth" and appeals to his pride by suggesting that this truth is "secret," given only to deserving initiates.[14] The text alludes to Proverbs 9:13–18, where Folly is "full of allurements" (9:13) and her seduction has obvious sexual overtones, as in Proverbs 7:4–23. Folly is always a "harlot" in the book of Proverbs, and thus she invites the foolish to *fornicatio* away from God.

Augustine portrays himself here as "carnal" in his vision, like his fellow Manichaeans. The sexual overtones in this passage relate his Manichaeism to his *fornicationes* in book 2, and both, as we have seen, are portrayed through water imagery. The sins of book 2, however pernicious, arise from his adolescent sexual desires and his desire "to love and be loved" (2.2.2), to be admired and applauded by his companions in "this world." Such sins, at least, can be explained rationally. The young Augustine's Manichaeism, in contrast, is an intellectual *fornicatio*. The writer vilifies it with bitter sarcasm as utterly foolish.

The young man's "carnality" and *fornicationes* in book 2 clearly lead him to being seduced by Manichaean folly. Book 3 opens with themes and imagery that recall the early chapters in book 2: "To love and to be loved [*Amare et amari*] was sweet to me, and all the more if I enjoyed my loved one's body. Therefore, I defiled the very source of friendship [*venam amicitiae*] by the filth of concupiscence, and its clear waters I clouded with the lust of hell [*candoremque eius obnubilabam de tartaro libidinis*]" (3.1.1). This passage recalls book 2, chapter 2, which begins "What was there to bring me delight except to love and to be loved [*nisi amare et amari*]?" The text above pictures the young Augustine's concupiscence metaphorically as a perhaps brackish water that befouls a "pure spring" (*venam*) of friendship. The water rises from below the earth (*de tartaro*) to darken a source at or near the surface. The imagery of "clouding" in *obnubilabam* subtly reinforces the water imagery. It also recalls book 2, chapter 2, where the same verb (*obnubilabant*) is used. In book 2, this imagery implies physical (and moral) *fornicationes*. In book 3, the same carnality leads to his intellectual *fornicatio* with Manichaean folly, because the young Augustine is "dwelling outside myself in my fleshly eye" (3.6.11). Just as the "bitter sea" of heresy proves a greater danger than the "waters below," so is intellectual *fornicatio* graver than physical.

In book 4, Augustine provides the rationale that links the latter to the former: "Full of words and folly as I was, I said to them, 'Why, then, does the soul, which God has created, fall into error?' But I did not want them to say to me, 'Why, then, does God err?' *I would rather argue that your unchangeable substance was necessitated to err than confess that my mutable nature had gone astray of its own accord*, and that to err was now its punishment" (4.15.26, my italics). Manichaean doctrine allows the young Augustine to blame his fleshly desires on an alien force within him, distinct from and opposed to his "true nature." Inclined to "fleshliness" by youth and education, he can continue to enjoy his mistress and indulge his sinful attachments to "this world" without acknowledging his own responsibility for his conduct. His adolescent *fornicationes*, in these terms, prepare him for Manichaeism.

In sum, then, water imagery frames and governs book 3. The foul, "underground waters" of sexual desire (*de tartaro libidinis*) in chapter 1 recall the water imagery of book 2 and foreshadow the young Augustine's intellectual *fornicatio* with Manichaean folly in chapter 6. The penultimate chapter describes his nine years in the sect as his being "tossed about in the mire of the deep and the darkness of error" (3.11.20), struggling not to drown in a stormy sea. Since Augustine examines his past Manichaeism from chapters 6 to 12, that period in his book and his past may be said to be governed by this image of the sea. The water imagery at the opening and close of book 3 further develops that imagery from books 1 and 2, and does so in a manner precisely analogous to Augustine's developing allegory of the water imagery in book 13.

Book 3 is also framed by images of weeping, another kind of water. In its final two chapters, Monica weeps prayerfully for her son's conversion away from heresy and to Christianity. In chapter 2, Augustine recalls his pleasure in weeping at the theater. Surely the bishop is asking us to compare the tears of the young heretic and his Christian mother. What emerges from the comparison is counterpointed by the allegory of book 13.

Augustine introduces Monica's prayers for the state of his soul with these words:

> "You put forth your hand from on high," and you drew my soul out of that pit of darkness [*de hac profunda caligine*], when before you my mother, your faithful servant, wept more for me than mothers weep over their children's dead bodies. By that spirit of faith which she had from you, she saw my death, and you graciously heard her [*exaudisti eam*], O Lord. Graciously you heard her, and you did not despise her tears when they flowed down from her eyes and watered the earth beneath [*cum profluentes rigarent terram sub oculis*], in whatsoever place she prayed. (3.11.19)

Here, and elsewhere in chapters 11 and 12, the text dwells on the abundance of Monica's prayerful tears. They are immediately effective. The passage insists that God draws the young Augustine's soul "out of that pit of darkness" at the very time when Monica begins to weep for him, even though he spends almost nine years as a Manichaean. God has mercy on the young Augustine's soul, for he hears and heeds (*exaudisti*) Monica's tears and prayers for mercy. God also consoles`her (*consolatus es*, 3.11.19) with a dream that her son will one day stand on a "rule" with her, the "rule of faith" (8.12.30).[15] At the very end of the book, a bishop prophesies her son's conversion by saying, "As you live, it is impossible that the son of such tears should perish" (3.12.21).

The writer approves and admires these tears, full of Christian charity for the spiritual welfare of another. He portrays his youthful pleasure in weeping at the theater in rather different terms:

The theater enraptured me, for its shows were filled with images of my own miseries [*imaginibus miseriarum mearum*] and with tinder of my fires. Why is it that a man likes to grieve [*vult dolere*] over doleful and tragic events which he would not want to happen to himself? The spectator likes to experience grief [*dolorem*] at such scenes, and this very sorrow is a pleasure to him [*dolor ipse est voluptas eius*]. What is this but a pitiful folly [*mirabilis insania*]? For the more a man is moved by these things, the less free he is from such passions. *However, when he himself experiences it, it is usually called misery; when he experiences it with regard to others, it is called mercy. But what sort of mercy is to be shown to these unreal things* [*in rebus fictis*] *on the stage?* (3.2.2, my italics)

Clearly, the young Augustine's "rapture" with fictive "imaginings" (*imaginibus*) rousing his grief recalls his boyhood fascination with the *Aeneid* in book 1. It also prefigures his embracing the folly of belief in the Manichaean *phantasmata*, an *insania* even more *mirabilis* than his rapture with the stage. Augustine identifies his love of theatrical *dolor* with "misery" here; he distinguishes it sharply from "mercy," a feeling allied to charity. Later in the chapter, the writer calls the young Augustine "wretched" (*miser*, 3.2.4) and finds in that misery the reason that he "loved to feel sorrow."

Monica's tears of mercy, in short, are contrasted with the young Augustine's tears of misery. Monica, a member of the "dry land" of the Christian faithful, is watered "by the sweet and hidden spring" of God's grace (*occulto et dulce fonte inrigas*, 13.17.21). Hence, her tears emerge from his Spirit out of concern for her son's spiritual welfare. Her soul "germinates works of mercy according to its kind" (13.17.21). They are virtuous tears of charity and mercy.

The young Augustine, in contrast, is not a member of the "dry

land" of Christianity and is about to join the "society" of the "embittered" in the "sea" of heresy (13.17.20). His spiritual constitution is
already "watery" from his *fornicationes* and is shortly to become
worse. He, too, brings forth fruits after *his* kind: the writer explicitly
identifies them with "misery." Augustine recalls his pleasure in love
stories when "at the theater I felt joy together with the lovers when
by shameful means they had joy in one another" (3.2.2). He associates
that pleasure with vice and disease (3.2.4). The young Augustine's
"tears of misery" are roused by the fictive imaginings of carnal love
and its pains, with which he identifies himself. His tears are self-
indulgent and vain. Far different are Monica's tears of mercy: they
perform a *work* of mercy and effect her son's salvation.

At a deeper level, the land-sea, eternity-time oppositions inform
Augustine's response to certain Manichaean objections to Christianity. He introduces the three-chapter meditation with these words:
"For I did not know that other Being, that which truly is, and I was as
it were subtly moved to agree with those dull deceivers when they
put their questions to me: 'Whence is evil?' 'Is God confined within a
corporeal form?' 'Does he have hair and nails?' 'Are those to be judged
just men who had many wives, killed other men, and offered sacri-
fices of animals?'" (3.7.12, my italics). The young Augustine's ignorance of God as eternal Being leads to his falling in with the Manichaeans. The bishop's response to the final question, above, turns on
his knowledge of him "who is eternally."

Augustine distinguishes between God's "justice" of "law" (*lex*),
which is eternal, and human "custom" (*mos*), which changes with
changing times. "By this law the customs of various regions and
times were adapted to times and places" (3.7.13). Having established
his principle in chapter 7, he goes on to argue that God's commands
must always be obeyed, even if they should contravene custom
(3.8.15–3.9.17). God's commands to men may change (3.9.17) but his
justice is eternal, never "at variance with itself and changeable"
(3.7.13).

Chapters 7–9 constitute a lengthy, sustained meditation on this
principle. To be sure, the contrast between eternity and time, immutability and change, is central to all the *Confessions*, to all of Augustine's thought. It could be argued that the contrast is implied in
every chapter of the volume. Nevertheless, in Augustine's autobiography it stands explicitly at the center of a sustained meditation

but rarely. It cannot be found in books 1 or 2: their sustained meditations are moral critiques.[16] Nor can such a meditation be found in books 5, 6, 8, or 9. Yet chapters 7–9 of book 3, chapters 8–12 of book 4, and chapters 10–13 of book 7 are wholly and explicitly concerned with the relationship of the temporal to the eternal. Is this merely adventitious? Why should this be the case?

One plausible explanation may be found in the correspondences traced in this chapter. The allegory for God's third, fourth, and seventh acts in Genesis turns on land-sea, eternity-time binary oppositions. The latter pair, to be sure, informs the whole allegory: it is as important for God's second act, creating the firmament between the waters, as it is for the third, fourth, and seventh. Yet the allegory on those latter three acts alone concerns the "dry land" of the Christian faith as distinct from the "sea of heresy" and of "this world." And only books 3, 4 and 7 in Augustine's autobiography contain sustained and explicit treatments of the relationship between the temporal and the eternal. A common, uniquely sustained thematic concern links those books; a common, unique land-sea binary pair links their corresponding allegories.

The rationale governing this pattern, it seems to me, appears in the association of the "dry land" with Christianity. Outside that faith, for Augustine, there is no salvation. Beyond its foundations, mankind is abandoned to the sea of temporality. That faith alone gives the saving knowledge of eternity. Only on the Christian "earth" can the soul participate in God's eternally stable truth or journey to its true country (*patria*, 7.20.26). For Augustine, one can perceive God's eternal law and justice (3.7–9) or "return to the Word" (4.9–12) or adhere to the immutably good Creator (7.9–13) only because God creates the "dry land" of the faith (his third act) and commands it to bring forth seed (his fourth act) and "living soul" (his seventh act). Apart from the Christian "earth," eternity has no meaning in the life of the soul, which drowns in a restless sea of temporal cares.

IV

As in book 3, the tears of the young Augustine are also a "work of misery" in the central event of book 4. Fully half of the book, eight of its sixteen chapters, narrate and meditate upon the young Augustine's desolate grief over the death of an intimate friend. Their friendship, the young man's death, and the young Augustine's wretched sorrow are narrated in chapter 4. Chapters 5–12 critically ponder his misery. The images and themes of Augustine's allegory on God's fourth act in Genesis resonate throughout these chapters.

Augustine introduces the friendship with an image drawn from God's fourth act: the creation and germination of plants, each "having seed according to its likeness" (13.17.21). The two young men are "flowering together in the flower of youth" (*conflorentem flore adolescentiae*, 4.4.7). The text emphasizes their likeness of spirit as well as of age, their common interests and pursuits (*societate studiorum; parilium studiorum*, 4.4.7). They are flowers of the same species, "having seed according to their likeness."

Yet theirs is not, the text asserts, a true friendship. This occurs only when God cements it by "the charity poured forth in our hearts by the Holy Spirit, who is given to us" (4.4.7). The young Augustine has turned his friend "away from the true faith" to Manichaeism. And yet God converts him back to himself "in a marvelous manner" (4.4.7). Baptized while unconscious in his final illness, the young man, on regaining consciousness, fiercely affirms the sacrament against the young Augustine's remonstrations. The young Augustine is confident that, in time, his friend will return to his influence. Instead, the friend is "snatched away from my madness, so that he might be kept with you for my consolation" (4.4.8). While the young Augustine is absent, his friend dies. Chapter 4 concludes with a compelling portrayal of the young Augustine's distraught grief.

Chapters 5–7 elaborate and interrogate the young Augustine's misery, his bitter grief, and the sweetness he finds in weeping. Here is Augustine's real subject. The friend's dying is narrated but briefly, while the young Augustine's response to that death is given much greater attention. Yet the heartfelt depiction of that response is itself colored darkly by the bishop's inquiry into the reasons for his wretched and demented grief. Augustine locates those reasons in the young man's Manichaeism, and his treatment is richly informed by the images and themes of the allegory on God's fourth act in Genesis. Again and again the text adverts to the Manichaean futility of the young Augustine's tears of misery:

> Whence is it, then, that *sweet fruit* is plucked from *life's bitterness*, from mourning and weeping, from sighing and lamenting? *Does sweetness lie*

there because we hope that you will graciously hear us? This rightly
holds for our prayers, since they contain our desire of attaining to you.
But does it hold for that grief and mourning over what was lost, with
which I was overwhelmed? I did not hope that he would come back to
life, nor did I beg for that by my tears; I only sorrowed and wept, for I
was wretched [miser] and had lost my joy. Or is weeping itself a bitter
thing, and does it give us pleasure because of distaste for things in which
we once took joy, but only at such times as we shrink back from them?
(4.5.10, my italics)

This passage raises the possibility of prayer in grief, even as it asserts
that the young Augustine does not pray. We are being reminded of
Monica's tears at the close of book 3 and being asked, again, to compare the young Augustine's tears with hers.

Monica's prayerful tears, let us recall, effect her son's salvation.
A member of the "dry land" of the Christian faithful watered by
God's "sweet and hidden spring" in the gospel, her "soul germinates
works of mercy according to its kind" (13.17.21). The young Augustine, in contrast, is a member of the "sea" of those "embittered" in
heresy (13.17.20). The works he performs according to his kind are
"works of misery." He does not pray for his friend's salvation because
he does not believe in eternal life. He prays for nothing because he
cannot pray. Hence, his tears effect nothing; they are simply the expression of his grief. As a member of the "bitter sea" of heresy, his
spirit is "watery." It finds its sole rest in weeping: salt tears, bitter
sorrow, a restless sea of grieving that effects nothing for anyone else
and little for the young Augustine himself. Only God's mercy working "in a marvelous manner" (4.4.7) prevents him from an even
greater "work of misery": reconverting his baptized friend to Manichaeism. For this reason, the bishop finds consolation precisely in
the death that the young Augustine so bewails. By that death his
friend is "snatched away" from the "madness" of the young Augustine's heresy (*dementiae meae*), "so that he might be kept with
you for my consolation" (4.4.8).

The metaphor of illness underlies much of the treatment of the
young Augustine's grief in the *dementia* of his Manichaeism. Bitter
things taste sweet only to the sick person, and only the demented find
a certain rest in misery itself. But the Manichaean, accustomed to
folly's "sweet stolen waters" (3.6.11), has been drinking from the
salty and bitter sea of heresy as though it were "sweet." His *sapientia*

(reason, soundness of mind, wisdom)—a word whose root is related to words for "taste" (*sapor, sapio*)—is thereby perverted. Drinking the fresh water of Christian truth satisfies thirst; the saltwater of heresy, in contrast, exacerbates thirst and causes illness. It thereby leads to misery, to works of misery, in which a perverted *sapientia* finds the bitter to be sweet:

> Wretched [*miser*] was I, and wretched [*miser*] is every soul that is bound fast by friendship for mortal things, that is torn asunder when it loses them, and then first feels the misery [*miseria*] by which it is wretched [*miser*] even before it loses those things. Such was I at that time, and I wept most bitterly, and I found rest in my bitterness. So wretched [*miser*] was I that I held that life of wretchedness [*vitam ipsam miseram*] to be more dear to me than my friend himself. (4.6.11)

The *dementia* of his Manichaeism also prevents the young Augustine from finding any real consolation for his grief. He does not pray, for he has no true belief upon which to found his prayer. He is a member of the "sea" of heresy, and the objects of his Manichaean faith are as insubstantial as the sea: "To myself I became a great riddle [*magna quaestio*], and I questioned my soul as to why it was sad and why it afflicted me so grievously, and it could answer me nothing. *If I said to it, 'Hope in God,' it did right not to obey me, for the man, that most dear one whom she had lost, was more real and more good to her than the fantasy [phantasma] in which she was bade to hope*" (4.4.9, my italics). The intensity of the young Augustine's grief confounds him. He is swept up in a storm of grief, like the Manichaeism whose "mire of the deep" (3.11.20) nearly drowns him. Just as his vain and bitter tears correspond to the "bitter sea" of heretical folly, so his inner disturbance is paralleled by the chaos of Manichaean doctrine, whose "waves break upon one another" (13.17.20). Had he been a member of the "dry land" of Christianity, the text implies, he could have "hoped in God," grappled with his inner disturbance, and been consoled.

Only a member of the Christian "dry land" has a firm, well-established belief on which to found his hopes and prayers. Only in weeping, however, can a "watery" Manichaean find "a little rest":

> All things grew loathsome, even the very light itself; and whatsoever was not he was base and wearisome to me— all except groans and tears, for in them alone was found a little rest. But when my soul was withdrawn

from these, *a mighty burden of misery* weighed me down. *To you, O Lord, ought it to have been lifted up, to be eased by you. I knew it, but I willed it not, nor was I able to will it, and this the more because for me, when I thought upon you, you were not something solid and firm.* For to me then you were not what you are, but an empty phantom [*vanum phantasma*], and my error was my god. (4.7.12, my italics)

Lacking such a firm, well-founded faith, the young Augustine is "watery" of will and of intellect. He "knows" how to find consolation but does not "will" to, nor is he "able to will it." His adherence to the "sea" of heresy and rejection of the Christian "dry land" cause this incomprehension of himself. It all arises from his failure to have "solid and firm" conceptions of God.

These metaphors, parallel to those used in Augustine's allegory on God's third and fourth acts, recur in book 4. Discussing his having dedicated his first book to a famous orator he had never met, Augustine writes:

See where a man's feeble soul lies stricken when it does not cling to the *solid support of truth. Just as blasts raised by their tongues blow out of the breasts of those who think they know, so also the soul is borne about and turned around, bent this way and that. The light is clouded over from it, and it does not descry the truth.* But look! it is before us! It was to be a great thing for me, if my style and my studies became known to that man. If he should approve of them, I would be all the more on fire. But if he disapproved of them, my heart, *void and empty of your solidity,* would have been deeply wounded. (4.14.23, my italics)

The imagery, here, is of a storm at sea: the sunlight "is clouded over" from the blasts of the winds, and the soul is driven out of control like a ship "borne about and turned around, bent this way and that." The imagery, to be sure, is traditional for *vanitas,* often linked paronomastically with *ventus* (wind). The winds "blow out of the breasts of those who *think* they know." Yet the metaphorics of the allegory in book 13 structure the image. The soul that does not harbor in the "dry land" of Christianity, "the solid support of truth," is blown about and risks destruction. Since the passage concerns the young Augustine's worldly ambitions, it alludes primarily to the "stormy sea" of "this world" of pagan values. And yet we have often seen close correlations between the developing water imagery of the first three books and that imagery in the allegory on the first three days of Cre-

ation. As a part of the "sea" of heresy, the young Augustine is "void
and empty" of God's "solidity," subject to all the vanity and folly of
"this world."

Augustine states this principle again in the final chapter of book
4, and in terms relevant to the fourth act of Creation: "What I have
conceived of you was falsity itself; it was not truth. *It was a figment
of my own misery; it was not the firm reality of your happiness (et
figmenta miseriae meae, non firmamenta beatitudinis tuae). For you
had commanded it,* and so it was done in me, *that the earth should
bring forth thorns and thistles for me* and with labor should I earn my
bread" (4.16.29, my italics). The paronomasia of *figmenta* and *firmamenta* underscores the contrast between the watery, insubstantial
falseness of heresy and the terra firma of Christian faith. The final
sentence of the passage alludes directly to Genesis 3:18, God's curse
on Adam's labor. Nonetheless, at the same time, it resonates against
God's command that the "earth bring forth her fruit" (13.17.21). In
Augustine's allegory, the Christian earth "germinates works of mercy
according to its kind" (13.17.21). The "earth" of the young Augustine,
however, brings forth no fruit, only "thorns and thistles," at God's
command.[17] Similarly, in his furious grief, the young Augustine is
"an unhappy place to myself (*ego mihi remanseram infelix locus*)
where I could not abide and from which I could not depart" (4.7.12).
Infelix here resonates with its primary agricultural meaning, "yield-
ing nothing useful, unproductive."[18] This meaning is clarified in
counterpoint with a sentence earlier in the chapter, which lists all the
diversions that no longer divert the young Augustine: "Not in pleasant groves, not in games and singing, not in sweet-scented spots (*nec
in suave olentibus locis*) . . . "[19]

In sum, then, the young Manichaean's response to his friend's
death and the bishop's critique of that response are deeply structured
by the metaphors that govern Augustine's allegory on the third day of
the Hexameron. In the latter and throughout book 4, Christianity is
the "dry land" of firm truth, nourished by God's "sweet fountain"
(*dulci fonte*, 13.17.21). Distinct from and beating vainly against it is
"the society of the sea" of heresy, a conspiracy of "bitter men," chaotic with conflicting doctrines lacking the substance of truth. Just as
God waters the "dry land" so that it "brings forth fruit," the works of
mercy (13.17.21), so the sea of heresy by itself brings forth empty and
useless "fruit," works of misery.

To be sure, Platonists traditionally depict truth as solid and firm, falsehood as insubstantial and chaotic, and Augustine draws on this imagery at various points throughout the *Confessions*. What is striking is that this structure controls the central themes and images of books 3 and 4 as well as Augustine's allegory on God's third and fourth acts in Genesis. The structure does not, of course, govern every theme and every image in books 3 and 4. It does, however, control the majority of images that depict the young Augustine's Manichaeism.

And it does so in crucial places. At the very beginning of chapter 13, the text asserts that the young Augustine enters more deeply into the "sea" of false beliefs: "I did not know all this at the time, but I loved lower beautiful creatures, and *I was going down into the very depths (ibam in profundum)*" (4.13.20, my italics). "All this" refers to the bishop's Christian critique of "friendship for mortal things" (4.6.11) in chapters 6–12. The metaphor of going deeper into the sea, thus, governs the young Augustine's Manichaeism, which underlies all those chapters.

Further, this sentence from chapter 13 introduces Augustine's meditation on his first book, "De Pulchro et Apto." The meditation concludes, at the end of chapter 15, with another sea and drowning image, framing his recollection of his first book with images from the allegory: "I thought all the time upon the beautiful and the fitting [*de pulchro et apto*]: *I desired to stand fast [cupiens stare]* and hear you, and to "rejoice with joy because of the bridegroom's voice." *I could not*, because I was carried away outside myself [*rapiebar foras*] by the voices of my error, and *under the weight of my pride I sank down into the depths [pondere superbiae meae in ima decidebam]*" (4.15.27, my italics). The young Augustine is unable "to stand fast" because the foundation of his spirit is a "sea" of error. Hence, he sinks "down into its depths." The three chapters that concern Augustine's first book are framed and thus governed, at the beginning and at the end, by imagery drawn from the allegory in book 13.

In a different way, at a deeper level, this imagery has analogues in Augustine's meditation on time, change, and death in chapters 6–12. The sea is, in Platonism, the proverbial image of inconstancy, the instability of all earthly things, which change over time. Book 13 finds the cause of heresy in attachment to the inconstant things of this world: "For all of them, there is one same end of temporal and earthly happiness [*temporalis et terrenae felicitatis*], because of which they do all their deeds, although they waver [*fluctuent*] back and forth amid a countless variety of cares" (13.17.20). The heretics waver (*fluctuent*) on the waves (*fluctus*) of a sea of shifting cares.

Similarly, Augustine finds the cause of the young Manichaean's painful grief in his attachment to "mortal things" (4.6.11). The Christian bishop urges us to direct our love not to changeable things but to their Maker: "In themselves they are but shifting things (*mutabiles*); in him, they stand firm (*fixae stabiliuntur*); else they would pass and perish" (4.12.18). Specifically, Augustine urges return to the Word, for "with him is a place of quiet that can never be disturbed" (4.11.16). Adhering to the truth of God's Word in the firmament of Scripture will make one firm:

> All in you that has rotted away will flourish again [*reflorescent putria tua*]; all your diseases will be healed; *all in you that flows and fades away will be restored, and made new*, and bound around you [*languores tui et fluxa tua reformabuntur et renovabantur et constringentur*]. They will not drag you down to the place where they descend, but *they will stand fast with you* and will abide before the God who stands fast and abides forever. (4.11.16)

The "wateriness" of one's spirit (*fluxa tua*) will no longer flow away. It will be reformed and renewed, made part of the "dry land" of Christian truth, stable and whole before the God who "abides forever." There, the things of the spirit may "flower again" (*reflorescent*) and germinate works of mercy after their kind.

This Christian-Neoplatonist theme recurs throughout the *Confessions*, not least in the allegory that concludes the volume. To argue that the binary pair of the sea versus dry land of book 13 alone governs this passage would be overstating the case. Clearly, both that binary pair and this passage are informed by the Christian-Neoplatonist contrast of time and eternity. The water imagery of book 4, however, is dominated by reference to the young Augustine's Manichaeism. Because of this predominance, other uses of water imagery gravitate, as it were, to that larger mass and orbit around it. In shape, they are analogous. Yet greater in size and importance, the figure of Manichaeism as an inconstant sea exerts its force on all water images in the book.

As the reader moves on into book 5, a certain narrative oddity emerges. In chapter 6, we learn that "for almost nine years" the young

Augustine awaits the coming of Faustus "with intense longing" (5.6.10). He has "questions and objections" (5.6.10) about certain Manichaean doctrines which he hopes Faustus may resolve. "Almost nine years," however, is the entire period of time the young man is a member of the sect (3.11.20). In other words, his "questions and objections" begin to arise very shortly after he "falls in with" (3.6.10) the Manichaeans. Why, then, does the text delay this knowledge until book 5? Otherwise and for the most part, the *Confessions* narrates events in the "natural order" of their historical occurrence.[20]

This narrative oddity can be explained by appealing to the correspondences with book 13. Books 3 and 4 repeatedly advert to the young Augustine's "wateriness" and misery as he flounders in the "sea" of Manichaeism. Should the text observe his "questions and objections" regarding the sect, he would seem rather less immersed in it than he does. He would seem less a vainly foolish and wretched soul. As it stands, books 3 and 4 portray the young Augustine quite floundering in the sea of heresy as befits the correspondences with book 13.

Saving the record of the young man's doubts until book 5 also functions vis-à-vis the allegory. God's fifth act, and Augustine's commentary on it, have nothing explicitly to do with water imagery. This "movement away from water" in the allegory corresponds with the young Augustine's questioning Manichaean doctrine, his movement away from the sect, and definitive break with it. All these are recorded in book 5, though Augustine asserts that they began from the time he joined the sect, recorded in book 3.

V

God's fifth act, creating the lights in the firmament of heaven, stands at the center of the "first week" in Genesis: it is the fifth of nine acts, performed on the fourth of the first seven days. Augustine's treatment of the act in book 13 finds it a crucial transition in the allegory he is developing. His allegory on each of the first four acts dwells on "the waters" of Creation. He finds meanings *in malo* for "the deep" (*abyssus*) of the "waters below" on the first and second days and for the "sea" that is created from them on the third: the chaotic waters of "this world" (books 1 and 2) and the bitter sea of heresy (books 3 and

4). Water imagery does not occur either in the biblical narrative on the fourth day or in Augustine's allegorical reading of it. When, however, God creates the creatures of the sea on the fifth day, Augustine treats them *in bono*.

Just as Augustine's reading of God's fifth act proves transitional in his allegory, so does book 5 prove transitional in his autobiography of his past.[21] It occupies the mathematical center of books 1–9. It marks the young Augustine's movement away from Africa to Italy, away from Faustus to Ambrose, away from Manichaeism toward Christianity. The transition in Augustine's allegory corresponds to that in his autobiography, and the images and themes of the former underlie the central movements of book 5.

God's fifth act is the creation of the *luminaria* (lights) "in the firmament of heaven." These are made "to divide the day and the night" and to be "for signs, and for seasons, and for days and years" (Gen. 1:14). They are "to shine in the firmament of heaven and to give light on the earth" (1:15). God makes "two great lights," the sun and moon, the former "to rule the day" and the latter "to rule the night" (1:16). He sets these and the stars "in the firmament of heaven to shine upon the earth" (1:17) and he sees his work as "good" (1:18).

In his allegory on God's second act, Augustine treats the "firmament of heaven" as Scripture. He maintains that interpretation in his allegory on the fifth act. Augustine also interprets the biblical shift from the fruit-bearing earth below, in God's fourth act, to the "firmament of heaven," in the fifth, as an allegorical movement from action to contemplation: "As we pass from this lower fruit of action into the delights of contemplation, and obtain the word of life on high [*superius*], let us appear like lights in the world, holding fast to the firmament of your Scripture [*appareamus sicut luminaria in mundo cohaerentes firmamento scripturae tuae*]" (13.18.22).

This statement introduces Augustine's treatment of God's fifth act. It emphasizes "holding fast" to Scripture, contemplating its "word of life," and shining forth "like lights to the world." These same themes close his allegory on the act and thus frame its meaning:

> For behold, it is as if God says, "Let there be lights made in the firmament of heaven," and "suddenly, there came a sound from heaven, as of a mighty wind coming, . . . and there appeared parted tongues as it were of fire, and it sat upon each one of them," and there were made lights in the firmament of heaven, holding the word of life [*verbum vitae habentia*].

Run into every place, O you holy fires, you beautiful fires! You are the light of the world, and you are not put under a measure. He to whom you have held fast has been exalted, and he has exalted you. Run forth, and make it known to all nations. (13.19.25)

The passage interprets God's fifth act in terms of Pentecost: the fiery tongues of the Holy Spirit descend upon the apostles and imbue them with the Spirit. In Acts 2, this immediately leads to the first post-Resurrection sermon, when Saint Peter "spiritually" interprets several Old Testament texts as prophesying the passion and resurrection of Jesus. The creation of "lights in the firmament," therefore, is explicitly linked with the spiritual or allegorical reading of Scripture and with preaching its truth. Since, according to Catholic doctrine, the apostles became the first bishops of the Church in the Pentecostal consecration by the Holy Spirit, the passage implies that the spiritual reading and preaching of Scripture belongs especially to bishops. In the Church, they are the "lights" that "rule" the day and the night (Gen. 1:16, 18) and shine upon the earth of the faithful (1:15, 17).

The "gifts of the Holy Spirit" are as important a theme in Augustine's allegory as the spiritual reading and preaching of Scripture. Augustine interprets the distinction between day and night as that between "intelligible and sensible things." Hence, when Augustine interprets the "lights in the firmament" in terms of the "gifts of the Spirit" named in 1 Cor. 12:7–11, he correlates the sun with "wisdom," for "those who are delighted by the manifest light of truth," and the moon with "knowledge," "a lesser light" (13.18.23). The "word of knowledge" contains "all mysteries (omnia sacramenta) which are varied in their seasons, like the moon" (13.18.23). This is knowledge of "sensible things," which vary in their seasons and are analogous to the night (13.18.22). The sun of wisdom, in contrast, concerns eternal truths, intelligible things. Only the "spiritual man" can regard these steadily. The "natural man," in contrast, must "be content with the light of the moon and the stars" (13.18.23).[22]

Where true wisdom and knowledge lie, where the real gifts of the Spirit can be found—in Faustus or in Ambrose, Manichaeism or Christianity—are the crucial issues in book 5. The book is structured around this polarity. The long-awaited Faustus disappoints the young Augustine; the all-unlooked-for Ambrose fascinates and instructs him. Over the course of the book, he is gradually detached from Manichaeism. When the problems he has with certain doctrines (chapters 3–5) are unresolved by Faustus, the young Manichaean gives up his ambition "to advance in that sect." Nevertheless, he resolves "to be content with it for the time being, unless something preferable should chance to appear" (5.7.13). In listening to Ambrose preach, something preferable does appear. At the close of the book the young Augustine resolves "that the Manicheans must be abandoned" and he determines "to continue as a catechumen in the Catholic Church" (5.14.25).

Book 5 counterpoints the young Augustine's reception of Ambrose's teaching with his response to Faustus. "For almost nine years" the young Augustine awaits "with intense longing the coming of this Faustus" (5.6.10). A prominent Manichaean, the latter has a reputation for being "most highly instructed in all genuine studies and especially skilled in the liberal arts" (5.3.3). The young Augustine has "questions and objections" (quaestionibus obiectis) about the sect that other members cannot answer. All promise that Faustus will resolve "these problems and even harder ones" when he arrives (5.6.10).

The stage is thereby set for Faustus's comic entrance. Faustus proves not at all learned, nor even skilled in the liberal arts (5.6.11). He has a gift for "gracious and pleasant conversation" (5.6.10) but nothing more. To the young Augustine, Faustus's ideas do "not seem the better to me because better expressed, nor true because eloquent, nor was his soul wise because he looked that way and had a suitable flow of words" (5.6.10). Faustus is all style and no substance. Not only is he unable to teach the young Augustine what he wants to know but, ironically, the latter begins to instruct Faustus in "such books as he had heard of and desired to read, or such as I thought proper to his abilities" (5.7.13).

The young Augustine at first hopes to find truth in Faustus and finds only a gift for eloquence. He attends Ambrose's sermons at first, only "to try out his eloquence" (quasi explorans eius facundiam, 5.13.23) and finds truth. Ambrose has a reputation for eloquence, as Faustus does for knowledge. The young Augustine finds the former "less lively and entertaining than Faustus" (5.13.23), but ultimately far more effective, for his words unite style to substance:

> Although I was not anxious to learn what he said, but merely to hear how he said it—for such bootless concern remained with me, although I had

no hope that any way lay open for a man to come to you—yet at the same time with the words, which I loved, there also entered into my mind the things themselves, to which I was indifferent. Nor was I able to separate them from one another, and when I opened up my heart to receive the eloquence with which he spoke, there likewise entered, only by degrees, the truths that he spoke. (5.14.24)

The truths heard by the young Augustine come from sermons in which the bishop expounds Old Testament passages allegorically. Such interpretation "in the spirit" revolutionizes the young man's understanding of these texts, liberating him from Manichaean misconceptions: "I now judged that the Catholic faith, for which I had thought nothing could be said against the Manichean objectors, could be maintained without being ashamed of it. This was especially the case after I had heard various passages in the Old Testament explained most frequently by way of allegory, by which same passages I was killed when I had taken them literally" (5.14.24).

Clearly, Ambrose is a true spiritual descendent of the apostles at Pentecost. Like them, he interprets the Old Testament allegorically and discovers there life-giving truths. A bishop of the Christian Church, God has sent his spirit upon him and made him appear as a light "in the world, holding fast to the firmament of Scripture" (13.18.22). Like the apostles, Ambrose is "holding the word of life" (13.19.25) and preaching it "according to the spirit, which gives life." That Word "has exalted" him and he "makes it known to all nations" (13.19.25).

In terms of the allegory in book 13, Ambrose is a genuine spiritual luminary. His light is real and life giving because it is created by God and holds fast to the firmament of his Scripture. His preaching is brilliant with "the gifts of the Holy Spirit," especially "the word of wisdom" and the "word of knowledge," the allegorical sun and moon (13.18.23).

Faustus, in contrast, is a Manichaean luminary in a Manichaean firmament. Not a man of the Holy Spirit but "a great snare of the devil" (5.3.3), he moves among the "false and falsifying holy ones" (5.10.18), a false luminary in a false firmament. Indeed, Faustus sheds as much spiritual light as do the luminaries of Manichaean cosmology. And they shed no light at all, according to Augustine, for they are merely corporeal fantasies (corporalia phantasmata, 3.6.10), empty and vain. Ambrose is a spiritual luminary analogous to the "great lights" (*luminaria magna*, Gen. 1:16) created in God's fifth act and allegorized in book 13. He illuminates the earth of the Christian faithful. Faustus, however, is a phantasmal light, a man not of the Spirit but of wind.

The Ambrose of book 5, thus, illustrates the intellectual and moral virtues urged by Augustine's allegory on God's fifth act in book 13. Faustus, the Manichaean anti-Ambrose, adumbrates the corresponding Manichaean antivirtues.[23] The text portrays Faustus in mildly comic fashion. Part of Augustine's subtle wit is a set of correspondences in which Faustus is revealed to be like the doctrines he preaches, a phantasmal light.

Another correspondence between book 5 and the allegory in book 13 lies in Augustine's discussion of astronomy. He ridicules, in chapter 5, Mani's false teachings about the heavens and the movements of the sun and moon. In chapter 3, he writes at some length on the astronomers' success in predicting eclipses and criticizes their foolish pride in their own knowledge.

The latter passage contains a subtler correspondence. Augustine's critique turns on a polysemy between *defectus*, "eclipse," and its etymon in the verb *deficere*, which means "to fail, to fall away":

> According to these rules, predictions are made in what year, in what month of the year, on what day of the month, on what hour of the day, and in what part of its light the sun or moon is to be eclipsed [*defectura*], and so it comes to pass, as it is predicted. Men who do not understand such matters stand in amazement and wonder at all of this; those who understand them exult and are elated [*exultant et extolluntur qui sciunt*]. *Out of an impious pride they fall back from you and suffer an eclipse of your light*, so early can they foresee a coming eclipse *but their own present eclipse they do not see* [*et deficientes a lumine tuo tanto ante solis defectum futurum praevident et in praesentia suum non vident*]. (5.3.4, my italics).

The polyptoton is so witty and incisive, the point so resoundingly made, that one feels no need to explore the metaphor.

And yet the metaphor is quite precise, though its terms emerge only by reading this text against the allegory in book 13. There, Augustine correlates the sun with "the word of wisdom" (13.18.23), the apprehension of "intelligible things" (13.18.22), which are eternal and divine. The moon is, allegorically, "the word of knowledge"

(13.18.23), concerned with "sensible things" (13.18.22). In these terms, the astronomers suffer an eclipse of God's light because, in their "impious pride," they place the moon of their own knowledge before, in front of, the sun of divine wisdom. Hence, the astronomers also "do not see their own present eclipse," for their eclipse of God's sun also serves to darken the light of their moon of knowledge. The metaphor in book 5 is both precise and morally instructive, but the precision of its terms can be discovered only by comparing it to Augustine's allegory on God's fifth act. The resonance between these two texts argues that Augustine—Augustine the author—planned the correspondence.

The very last words of book 5 also resonate with the terms of book 13. "Therefore, I determined to continue as a catechumen in the Catholic Church, commended to me by my parents, *until something certain would enlighten me, by which I might direct my course [donec aliquid certi eluceret, quo cursum dirigerem]*" (5.14.25, my italics). The book closes with a nautical metaphor. Significantly, this is the only metaphorical use of water imagery in book 5. The only other use of water imagery in the book notes the young Augustine's safe passage from Carthage to Rome: "you preserved me, all full of execrable filth, from the waters of the sea and kept me safe for the waters of your grace" (5.8.15).[24] When one considers how prominent water imagery is in books 1–4 and, as we shall see, in book 6, the near absence of that imagery in book 5 is all the more striking. After all, until its very last chapter, the young Augustine remains a Manichaean, a member of the "sea" of heresy. The relative absence of water imagery further argues the correspondence of book 5 with the allegory on God's fifth act, where water imagery is completely absent.

The passage quoted above occurs just after the young Augustine resolves "that the Manicheans must be abandoned" (5.14.25). Nonetheless, he still has not reached the "dry land" of Christianity. Therefore, he remains "out at sea." He seeks some point by which to navigate. The text defines it as "something certain" that "would enlighten" (*eluceret*) him. What sheds light for a sailor needing direction for his course is a heavenly body, the Polestar, perhaps, or the movements of the sun. In truth, the young Augustine has already found that "light in the firmament of heaven" by which to direct his course: Ambrose. In book 6, Ambrose's preaching further guides his study of Scripture and points the way to safe harbor in the "dry land" of the Christian faith.

VI

In the sixth act of the Hexameron, God commands the waters to "bring forth creeping creatures having life, and the fowls that fly over the earth" (Gen. 1:20; 13.20.26). Augustine's allegory interprets this next stage in the creation of the Church (13.12.13) as "the instruction of heathen nations" (13.34.49). Out of "corporeal matter" (the waters) God brings forth (*produxisti*) "sacraments, and visible miracles" (sea creatures), "and voices in keeping with the firmament of your book" (birds; 13.34.49). These disseminate the Christian faith to the pagans, and "in them the faithful likewise find blessing" (13.34.49). These themes appear recurrently in book 6. It adverts explicitly to the miracle of the spread of Christianity and devotes several chapters to men whose voices are "in keeping with the firmament of Scripture": Ambrose and Alypius. Also, sea imagery reappears in book 6 with renewed frequency, after being nearly absent from book 5.

In his sixth act, God creates from the sea. He commands it to "bring forth" (Gen. 1:20) and thereby creates "the great whales, and every living and moving creature, which the waters brought forth, according to their kinds, and every winged fowl according to its kind." God sees his work to be "good" (1:21). He blesses his new creatures, commanding them to "Increase and multiply" (1:22). Sea creatures are "to fill the waters of the sea," and the birds are to "be multiplied upon the earth" (1:22).

Augustine's allegory dwells on the evangelical mission of Christianity to the pagans (*gentes*, 13.20.26). "Amid the waves of the world's temptations" (*inter medios fluctus temptationum saeculi*) God's creative word enters as his *sacramenta*, spread "by the works of your saints."

Among these deeds, great wonders were wrought, like great whales, and the voices of your messengers, winged creatures above the earth, in the firmament of your book, which was set in authority over them and under which they were to fly, wheresoever they went. For "there are no speeches nor languages where their voices are not heard," since "their sound has gone forth into all the earth, and their words to the end of the world." For by your blessing, O Lord, you multiplied them. (13.20.26)

The allegory draws particular attention to the birds as God's "messengers" for the spread of Christianity. As creatures of the sky, they are closely associated with "the firmament of Scripture" and mediate its "authority" through their preaching to the earth below. At the time of Christ's Resurrection, the Church had very few such messengers. Yet God's blessing increased and "multiplied them," such that "their words have gone forth to the end of the world."

The fundamental problem of the Christian mission, as Augustine sees it, is how to communicate the "truths of the spirit" to those whose minds are "unspiritual" (1 Cor. 2–3). Because of the Fall, all mankind is subject to "the waves of the world's temptations" (13.20.26). The child of Adam, the "natural man," is "fleshly" and corporeal in his conceptions. Hence, the missionary Church must encounter and evangelize the pagans in "the waters" of their corporeality:

> If Adam had not fallen away from you, from his loins [utero] there would not have flowed that salt sea water, the human race, so deeply active, so swelling in storms, and so restlessly flowing [profunde curiosum, procellose tumidum, et instabiliter fluvidum]. Then there would have been no need for your dispensers [dispensatores] to work corporeally and sensibly amid many waters, and thus produce mystical deeds and words [mystica facta et dicta]. (13.20.28)

The Fall makes all mankind subject to "the flesh" and, hence, as stormy and restless as the sea. The passage associates this sea with orgasm: from Adam's loins flows that salt sea water of the human race. Fallen sexuality and alienation from "the spiritual" thus necessitate that Christian truth be communicated "corporeally and sensibly amid many waters."

These reflections correspond precisely, in book 6, to the young Augustine's inability to conceive a "spiritual substance." As is well known, this proves a crucial issue in his development: his sudden enlightenment on this score in book 7 is often called his "intellectual conversion." In book 6, the young Augustine learns that man's creation "to the image of God" (Gen. 1:27) does not imply, for Christians, that God "is limited by the shape of a human body" (6.3.4). This frees him from a Manichaean misconception (6.3.4–6.4.5). Neverthe-less, he cannot "surmise what a spiritual substance would be like even in a weak and obscure manner" (6.3.4). The following chapter explains why. He does not know "how to conceive spiritual things except in a bodily way" (*spiritalia, de quibus cogitare nisi corporaliter nesciebam*, 6.4.6). The young Augustine's conceptions remain corporeal because, in the imagery of book 13, his soul is still "watery," still "at sea." He remains immersed in "fleshly" preoccupations. He gads about canvassing support for his career and has no time for study and meditation (6.11.18). He arranges a politically advantageous marriage (6.13.23). He repudiates his mistress, yet becomes distraught over her absence, remains "a slave to lust," and procures another for the time being (6.15.25).

Water imagery frames book 6 and is used frequently throughout it to characterize, metaphorically, the young Augustine. The final chapter, just after he sends away his mistress, describes his state:

> Praise be to you, glory to you, *O fountain of mercies*! I was becoming more wretched, and you drew closer to me. At that very moment your right hand was ready to help me, *to lift me out of the mire, and to wash me clean*, but this I did not know [*dextera tua raptura me de caeno et ablatura, et ignorabam*]. All that called me back from *a deeper maelstrom of carnal pleasures* [*a profundiore voluptatum carnalium gurgite*] was the fear of death and of your judgment to come, which never left my soul through all my changing opinions. (6.16.26, my italics)

The passage contrasts the purity of God's spiritual waters with the filth of the young Augustine's "fleshly" waters, in whose "mire" he remains immersed. His "carnal pleasures" are described as a watery whirlpool (*gurgite*). Only his fear of God's judgment keeps him from a "deeper" one.

The text again uses sea imagery to link the young man's intellectual to his moral failings:

> I asked, "If we were immortal, and lived in perpetual bodily pleasure [*in perpetua corporis voluptate*] without any fear of loss, why should we not be happy, and what else would we ask for?" *I did not know that this fact belonged to my immense misery, that being drowned and blinded* [*quod ita demersus et caecus*], *I could not conceive the light of a virtue and beauty that must be embraced for their own sake.* For this the body's eye does not see: it is seen only from within. (6.16.26, my italics)

"Drowned" in "the fleshly" the young Augustine cannot conceive a "virtue and beauty" that are spiritual, to "be embraced for their own sake" apart from the pleasure of the body they might give. And yet his greatest happiness in life *is* spiritual, though his attachment to "the flesh" prevents his realizing it: "In my wretchedness *I did not consider from what source it flowed to me [ex qua vena mihi manaret] that I could discuss so sweetly with my friends these very things,* foul as they were. *For without friends I could not be happy,* even in that frame of mind and *with no matter how great a flood of carnal pleasures [etiam secundum sensum, quem tunc habebam in quantalibet affluentia carnalium voluptatum]*" (6.16.26, my italics). Again, pure, spiritual waters—here, from the flowing spring (*vena*) of friendship—are contrasted with the "flood of carnal pleasures." Again, the young Augustine's immersion in "the waters" of "the flesh" prevents his understanding of the truth.

Sea imagery is also central to the first chapter of book 6. After noting that God created the young Augustine "wiser than the birds of the air," the text describes his state metaphorically: "But I walked in darkness, and upon a slippery way [*ambulabam per tenebras et lubricum*], and I sought for you outside myself, but I did not find you, the God of my heart. *I went down into the depth of the sea [et veneram in profundum maris],* and I lost confidence, and I despaired of finding the truth" (6.1.1, my italics). The dark and slippery way, as though the young Augustine walks in a dark wood after a storm, becomes, by a shift in metaphor, the surface of the sea in a storm. He sinks down "into the depth of the sea," drowning and in despair. Because he seeks God outside himself, he attempts to find the immutable in the changeable, "watery" realm of bodies. The attempt is doomed to failure. Hence, the young Augustine is drowning in his own "corporeal" conceptions and despairs of finding spiritual truth.

Chapter 1 goes on to describe Monica's sea passage to Italy to rejoin her son: "But now my mother, strong in her love, had come to me, for she had followed me over land and sea, kept safe by you in all her perils. *In the midst of storms at sea [nam et per marina discrimina], she reassured the sailors themselves, by whom inexperienced travelers upon the deep are accustomed to be comforted, and promised them that they would reach port in safety, for you had revealed this to her in a vision [per visum]*" (6.1.1, my italics). While there is no reason to doubt the historical truth of this story, its placement immediately after the young Augustine's metaphorical descent "into the depth of the sea" demands a literary interpretation. Augustine did not need to recount the episode, in the first place, and if he did feel compelled to, he did not have to place it here. The proximity of these texts implies that the *historia* of Monica's journey can and should be read allegorically.

The young Augustine is drowning in the metaphorical sea of his "fleshliness." Monica, in contrast, untraveled as she is, remains a rock of confidence in a real sea storm. She even consoles the sailors, themselves accustomed to storms, and assures them they will not perish. True Christian that she is, Monica is part of the "dry land." She has complete faith in God's revelation, in Scripture, and in her vision that the ship shall "reach port." She is no more threatened by storms in the real sea between Africa and Italy than she is by those in the metaphorical sea of "this world," of *cupiditas* and "fleshliness."

This episode also resonates against Monica's first divinely given "vision" in the *Confessions*. She dreams that her heretical son joins her on "a certain rule" (3.11.19), the rule of the faith. She recounts "this vision" (*ipsum visum*, 3.11.20) to the young Augustine at that time; the text uses the same word, *visum*, for what Monica recounts to the sailors. Monica has firm faith in that "vision" of her son's future conversion, so much so that she is not surprised, in Italy, to learn that he is no longer a Manichaean: "Yet when I told her that I was no longer a Manichean, although not a Catholic Christian, she did not leap with joy, as if she had heard something unexpected. The reason was that she had already been assured to that aspect of my wretched state, in which she bewailed me as one dead, but yet destined to be brought back to life by you" (6.1.1). Her bewailing the young Augustine "as one dead" refers to book 3, chapter 11, and underscores the relation between these two passages.

That relation implies the young Augustine's salvation. Like the sailors, he will not perish in the sea. Monica's visions are God's assurance that the young Augustine will, like the sailors, "reach port" (6.1.1), come to the "dry land" of Christianity. This nexus of images, at the very beginning of book 6, alludes to the nautical image that closes book 5.

Such imagery describes the young Augustine at many places in book 6. His doubtful state regarding the Catholic faith is called a "wavering," *fluctuationem* (6.1.1), being tossed on the waves (*fluctus*) of the sea. When such doubts reach greater intensity, they are called *aestus* (6.3.4), the seething waters of a stormy sea. The nautical image subsequently becomes more explicit. After the young Augustine considers the "surpassing authority" that God has given to Scripture "throughout the whole world," the text describes his state: "I thought over these things, and you were present to me. I uttered sighs, and you gave ear to me. *I wavered back and forth, and you guided me* [*fluctuabam et gubernabas me*]" (6.5.8, my italics). Here God is the steersman, the *gubernator*, of the young Augustine's bark, wavering on the waves of "this world" and his carnal attachments to it.

Later, the young Augustine argues to himself that even married men can pursue wisdom: "While I was saying all this to myself and *the winds were shifting and driving my heart now this way and now that* [*et alternabant hi venti et impellebant huc atque illuc cor meum*], time passed, and still I delayed to be converted to you" (6.11.20, my italics). Here, the young man's "heart" is a ship, driven "now this way and now that" by the conflicting "winds" of his own opinions, which constantly shift direction.

In sum, a significant strand of sea imagery runs throughout book 6 to describe, metaphorically, the young Augustine's spiritual state.[25] The imagery is not perfectly self-consistent. Chapters 1 and 16 describe him as "drowning." The images in chapters 3, 5, and 11 suggest that he is aboard a ship, though in a dangerous sea. All these images, however, resonate against the allegory on God's sixth act in creation, where the ocean symbolizes "the waves of the world's temptations" (13.20.26) and the "carnality" of the stormy human race after the Fall (13.20.28).

Yet this is but one strand of theme and imagery in the allegory. Its central concern is the missionary spread of the Christian faith through "great wonders, like great whales" and the preaching of "your messengers, winged creatures above the earth, in the firmament of your book, which was set in authority over them and under which they were to fly" (13.20.26). These themes prove central, also, to book 6.

The text first points to the authority of Scripture and the miracle of its spread "into all the earth" (13.20.26) in chapter 5. God persuades the young Augustine that "not those who believe in your books, which you have established with such mighty authority among almost all nations, but those who do not believe in them are the ones to be blamed" (6.5.7). Shortly thereafter, the spread of Christianity becomes an argument for the truth of the faith. "Therefore, since we were too weak to find the truth by pure reason, and for that cause we needed the authority of Holy Writ, I now began to believe that in no wise would you have given such surpassing authority throughout the whole world to that Scripture, unless you wished that both through it you be believed in and through it you be sought" (6.5.8). According to the allegory in book 13, this is the greatest of "great wonders, like great whales" (13.20.26) wrought in the sixth act of God's creating the Church.

To be sure, this is a common theme in the church fathers. One might well argue that it is implied throughout the *Confessions*. What is striking, however, is that this theme is explicitly treated, in Augustine's autobiography, for the first time in book 6, and in his allegory on the Hexameron, for the first time in God's sixth act. That a theme so common should be introduced at such corresponding points argues a planned correspondence.

The theme receives a third and more definitive articulation as the young Augustine criticizes himself in chapter 11: "It is no vain, no empty thing that the lofty dignity and the authority of the Christian faith are spread throughout the whole world. Never would such mighty things be wrought by God in our behalf if the soul's life ceased after the body's death. Why then do we delay to abandon worldly hopes and devote ourselves to seeking God and a life of happiness [*vitam beatam*]?" (6.11.19). What the young Augustine begins to believe in chapter 5 becomes, in this passage, a firm argument for complete conversion.

The spread of the Christian faith in the allegory on God's sixth act also underlies the chapters on Ambrose and Alypius in book 6. That book devotes more space to figures other than the young Augustine than any other in the autobiography. Chapter 2 treats Ambrose's influence on Monica. Chapter 3 examines the cares of his episcopal life and includes the famous passage on his silent reading. Chapters 3 and 4 trace the influence of Ambrose's preaching and exegesis of Scripture on the young Augustine. Clearly, Ambrose is one of God's "messengers, winged creatures above the earth" (13.20.26) whose teaching is "in keeping with the firmament" (13.34.49) of Scripture.

So, too, was Alypius such a bishop at the time when Augustine wrote the *Confessions*. Four chapters of book 6 are devoted to him. In each, the future bishop learns some lesson, taught providentially, according to the text, that increases his store of wisdom: "But you, O Lord, who rule the course of all things [*qui praesides gubernaculis omnium*], which you have created, had not forgotten that he was to be numbered among your sons as a bishop of your Church."[26] In each chapter on Alypius, the future "dispenser of your Word" becomes "a more experienced and instructed man" (6.9.15). In chapter 7, he learns the effectiveness of even casual words from a respected person. In chapter 8, he learns not to trust in himself what he owes to God.[27] In chapter 9, God allows him to be arrested for a crime he does not commit so that he would "begin to learn this: in cases up for judgment, no man is readily to be condemned with rash credulity by another man" (6.9.14). Chapter 10 illustrates his courageous love of truth and justice.

These chapters on Alypius do not seem necessary to the autobiography of Augustine's past. Neither do the details about Ambrose's life and reading. To be sure, these persons are important in Augustine's life. Perhaps Augustine wanted not simply to acknowledge their influence on his life but, from respect and love, to give each a "place of his own," a part of his autobiography yet apart from it. Such reasons are plausible, though not clear. What is clear, however, is that Augustine grants considerable space to Ambrose and Alypius in book 6. He might have done so in book 5, especially for Ambrose, or in books 7 or 8, especially for Alypius. But he does not. He chooses book 6 to write about Ambrose's life as a bishop and Alypius's moral education to be a "dispenser" (6.9.15, 13.20.28) of God's word. And book 6 corresponds, in the allegory of book 13, to the missionary spread of Christianity through God's "messengers" (13.20.26).

That correspondence also governs, I should like to suggest, the treatment of marriage in chapters 12–15. The theme is introduced, and thus framed, negatively: marriage is a hindrance to the pursuit of wisdom. "Alypius in fact kept me from marrying, since he repeated over and over that if I did so, we would in no wise live together in unbroken leisure in love of wisdom [*securo otio simul in amore sapientiae*], as we had long desired" (6.12.21). Love for women, Alypius argues, is incompatible with the love of wisdom.

The implied argument of these chapters is that celibacy is essential to those who would pursue the Christian mission. The future bishops must remain without wives to perform their vocations truly. Complete dedication to wisdom or to God is impossible for married men. The point is underscored in chapter 14. The young men and several friends make plans for a community, "to live a life of quiet apart from the crowd" (remoti a turbis otiose vivere, 6.14.24). Here would be the leisured retirement, the otium "in love of wisdom," that the young Augustine and Alypius have "long desired" (6.12.21). Plans seem to be maturing rapidly until they all discuss "whether their little wives would permit this" (utrum hoc mulierculae sinerent). Immediately, the project collapses (dissiluit 6.14.24). Clearly, marriage proves incompatible with being a dispenser of God's word, one of his "winged messengers" (13.20.26).

At a deeper level, Augustine's meditation on sexual desire in these chapters (6.11.20–6.15.25) corresponds to his vision of the Fall in the allegory. There, the waters are called a "bitter disease" (amarus languor, 13.20.27), and the disease is spread by orgasm and procreation: from Adam's loins (utero) there flows (diffunderetur) "that salt sea water, the human race" (13.20.28). This imagery appeals loosely to the theory that Adam's sin is communicated to his children physically, through the "passing down" of semen. Augustine's allegory implies that the Fall spreads through procreation "according to the flesh." It is countered only by Christianity, disseminated "according to the spirit."

This principle is implied in book 6 as well. The text gestures but vaguely to "whatever conjugal dignity there is" (si quod est coniugale decus, 6.12.22) in marriage. The real issue is the young Augustine's "insatiable sexual desire" (6.12.21), his being "a slave to lust" (6.15.25):

> I did not believe that the cure for this disease [infirmitatem] lay in your mercy, for I had no experience of that cure. I believed that continence [continentiam] lay within a man's own powers, and such powers I was not conscious of within myself. I was so foolish that I did not know that, as it is written, no man can be continent [continentem] unless you grant it to him. This you would surely have given, if with inward groanings I had knocked at your ears and with a firm faith [fide solida] had cast all my cares upon you. (6.11.20, my italics)

The crux of the young Augustine's conversion in book 8 is clearly set forth here. "Firm faith" is associated with "continence," commitment to the Christian "dry land" (13.17.21) with the "moral solidity" of chastity. Sexual desire, in contrast, is a "disease," an in-firmity. Orgasm represents moral as well as physical dissolution, dispersion of the self into "wateriness." It is of the Fall, whose waters are "a bitter disease" (13.20.27), against which stands the solid earth of Christianity and continence. Before the young Augustine becomes a messenger of the faith, like Ambrose, and begins to labor in the world against the Fall, he must dedicate himself to God in "firm faith." And that, for him, implies continence.

VII

Though *continentia*, in the *Confessions*, refers primarily to sexual continence, it retains its wider meaning of "restraint, self-control, re-pression of one's appetites and passions." All the passions, of course, lead to moral dissolution. Augustine regards sexual desire as the strongest of the passions, and the orgasm to which it tends proves a graphic image of dispersion, dissipation.[28] Sexual passion thus be-comes a synecdoche for all the passions, and "continence" comes to refer primarily to "chastity," though it restrains, by definition, all dis-solute "motions of spirit."

This moral function gives to "continence" a role in the intellec-tual life. The principle is neatly expressed in the polysemy of a single sentence:

> per continentiam quippe colligimur et redigimur *in unum*, a quo in multa defluximus.

> [By continence, we are gathered together and brought *to the One, from whom* we have dissipated our being into many things.] (Ryan's translation)

> [By continence, we are gathered together and brought *into a unity, from which* we have dissipated our being into many things.] (my translation; 10.29.40, my italics)

As continence restrains the "flowing away" (*defluximus*) of desires, it restores "unity," integrity, and health, to the self. In so doing, it en-ables the soul to make the Christian-Neoplatonist "return to the One." The passive voice in the verbs implies that both continence and the "return to God" are gifts of grace.

The development of the young Augustine, from book 6 to 8 in the *Confessions*, can be described as a movement toward *continentia*, intellectual and moral. "Continence" is not raised as an explicit issue in the volume until the passage in book 6 examined at the end of the previous section. In book 2, for example, Monica advises her son to avoid *fornicatio* (2.3.7), but *continentia*, a positive virtue, is not mentioned. Its emergence as an explicit issue in the autobiography is closely related to the development of Augustine's allegory in book 13.

"Continence" is the explicit focus of his allegory on God's seventh act. In Genesis, God turns from creating in the waters, on the fifth day, to creating from the earth, on the sixth. Augustine interprets this movement in moral terms: from the waters of "this world" to continence, in its widest sense. God, however, creates twice on the sixth day. He commands the earth to "bring forth living soul" (Gen. 1:24), cattle and reptiles and beasts "according to their kinds." Then God himself creates man to his own "image and likeness" (Gen. 1:26–27). Augustine's allegory envisions God's creating the "living soul" of continence as the crucial transition from "the waters" of "this world" to the renewal of the soul, through grace, to the image of God. This movement in the allegory parallels, in several important ways, the movement in its corresponding books, 6–8.

Though the biblical text on God's seventh act makes no mention of water, water imagery recurs throughout Augustine's allegory on it. The "faithful earth" is "separated from" (*distincta*) and contrasted with the "waters of the sea, bitter with infidelity" (13.21.29). Here is the same opposition developed in the allegory on God's third act: the "dry land" of the Christian faithful separated from the "bitter sea" of heretics (13.17.20–21). This earth is "established" by God "above the waters" (*quam fundasti super aquas*, 13.21.29): its stability is linked to its superiority, moral as well as physical. Because unfaithful, fallen man has need of God's word, he creates from and for their "bitter waters" his "winged messengers" in his sixth creative act. But the "living soul" of his seventh act arises differently:

> Man's infidelity shows itself to be the reason for the first words of the evangelists, but the faithful also are exhorted and blessed by them many times, day after day. *But the living soul takes its beginning from the earth [at vero anima viva de terra sumit exordium], for it profits no one except the faithful to keep continent from the love of this world [continere se ab amore huius saeculi], so that their soul may live to you, for it*

was dead while it lived in pleasures [*deliciis*], in pleasures that bring death [*deliciis motiferis*], O Lord. For it is you who are the life-bringing pleasures [*vitales deliciae*] of the pure of heart. (13.21.29, my italics)

This text clearly associates the "earth" with "continence" and its "living soul" with love for God, who is its "life-bringing pleasure." The waters of the sea are correspondingly linked with "the love of this world" and with "pleasures" as "the world" conceives them, which prove "pleasures that bring death."

The message of continence is underscored in Augustine's exegesis of "according to its kind" (*secundum genus*, 13.21.31). God's "ministers" must work differently on the faithful "dry land" from the way they do on the "waters of infidelity": "Let them be a pattern [*forma*] to the faithful by living before them and arousing them to imitation. For thus do men truly hear, not merely to hear but also to do. 'Seek God, and your soul shall live,' so that 'the earth may bring forth a living soul.' 'Do not be conformed to this world' [*nolite conformari huic saeculo*]. Keep yourselves from it [*continete vos ab eo*]. The soul lives by avoiding what it dies by desiring" (13.21.30). The passage contrasts the *forma* ("pattern") of God's ministers to the "formless waters" of "this world." Imitation of that *forma* means the refusal to "be conformed to this world." That refusal is summed up as the "continence" of the faithful, the "earth" that "brings forth a living soul." Imitation of that *forma* makes one firm, for in that way "our earth" receives "the form of doctrine" (13.12.13).[29]

The chapter restates these themes by appealing, as so often in the allegory, to a contrast between God's "waters" and those of the *saeculum*:

For the soul does not die in such wise as to lose all action, since it dies by forsaking [*discedendo*] the fountain of life, and so is taken up by this passing world and is conformed to it [*ita suscipitur a praetereunte saeculo et conformatur*].

But your Word, O God, is the fountain of eternal life, and it does not pass away [*non praeterit*]. Therefore, this departure of the soul is *restrained by your Word* [*ideoque in verbo tuo cohibetur ille discessus*], when it is said to us, "Do not be conformed to this world," so that the earth may bring forth in the fountain of life a living soul, a soul *continent in your Word* through the evangelists, by imitating the imitators of your Christ. (13.21.30–31, my italics)

The sea of "this world" is associated with the "passing away" of time. God's fountain, in contrast, is eternal. A fountain, by definition, is associated with "dry land": waters distant from the sea and, hence, sweet and pure, not bitter and foul. God's fountain is thus linked to the "earth" of the Christian faith. The "living soul" adheres to this "fountain of life," restrained in its own continence by obedience to God's Word: "Do not be conformed to this world."

Yet this proves but a step, albeit crucial, to a higher, more perfect life for the soul. Augustine interprets the progress of the Hexameron from God's seventh to his eighth act in terms of the progress of Romans 12:2: "And be not conformed to this world; but be reformed in the newness of your mind, that you may prove what is the good, and the acceptable, and the perfect will of God." Augustine allegorizes the creation of man to God's "image and likeness" as reformation "in newness of mind." The Christian, already continent, becomes perfect. Thus renewed, he "may prove the good, and the acceptable, and the perfect will of God" (13.22.32).

Similarly, book 7 marks a crucial stage in the young Augustine's progress, as is well known. Book 8 records the conversion of his will to continence. In the terms of the allegory, the young Augustine is reformed in newness of mind and accepts, at last, "the perfect will of God." Book 7 prepares him for that grace. His apprehension of God as immutable being brings him, as it were, to continence of the intellect. The images and themes that govern the allegory of continence for God's seventh act also govern book 7.

The book itself traces a movement from "sea" to "land," and its crossing point comes in the young Augustine's intellectual conversion. Its early chapters twice portray his thinking about God in terms of water, and similar metaphors describe, in part, his wavering spiritual state. After the vision of Being in its central chapters, however, such images disappear completely from the book. The sea journey of book 6 becomes a land journey in the second half of book 7. Images of intellectual wavering are replaced by those of moral weakness, of infirmity to be made firm by the "solid foundation of religion" (7.20.26). This movement from sea to land imagery in book 7 corresponds to that same movement in Augustine's allegory on God's seventh act in book 13.

At the beginning of book 7, fleshly of intellect as of will, the young Augustine is unable to conceive of God except in corporeal terms. Robert M. Durling observes that water imagery underlies the following description of his thinking:[30]

> Hence, although I did not think of you as being in the shape of a human body, *I was forced to think of you as something corporeal, existent in space and time, either infused into the world or even diffused outside the world through infinite space [sive infusum mundo sive etiam extra mundum per infinita diffusum].* Even thus did I think of that very incorruptible and inviolable and immutable being which I set above the corruptible, the violable, and the mutable. (7.1.1, my italics)

"Infused" and "diffused" mean, etymologically and literally, "poured into" and "poured through." The controlling metaphor here is water.

That metaphor is made explicit in chapter 5:

> I placed before my spirit's gaze the whole creation, whatever we can see in it, *such as earth, and sea, and air, and stars, and trees, and mortal animals, and likewise whatever we do not see therein, such as the firmament of heaven above, and all the angels, and all its spiritual beings, but I set out even such beings as if they were bodies,* arranged in such and such places, as my imagination dictated. I made your creation into a single great mass. . . . I imagined, Lord, that you encircled in on every side and penetrated it, but you remained everywhere infinite. *It was as if there were a sea, one single sea, that was everywhere and on all sides infinite over boundless reaches. It held within itself a sort of sponge, huge indeed but yet finite, and this sponge was filled in every part by that boundless sea.* (7.5.7, my italics)

Durling notes the significant lack of order in the catalogue of created things at the beginning of this passage. They float, as it were, in a mental confusion. Durling argues that the catalogue "anticipates the procedure that emerges at the center of Book VII . . . "the idea of ascent to God via the interrogation of creatures." Here, there can be no ascent because there is no conception of hierarchical order. Nor is it "yet an interrogation." Durling trenchantly sums up the inadequacies of the young Augustine's thinking: "In terms of the understanding [the young] Augustine will later reach, it provides no place to stand, no principle of fixity. *He is involved in the fundamental absurdity of trying to conceive the transcendentally unchanging with the image of the sea, the very matter of mutability. This will have to be reversed.*"[31]

The young Augustine's inability to conceive a "spiritual sub-stance" (6.3.4) first arises in book 6. Yet despite his intellectual diffi-culties, he has been making spiritual progress. In the first half of book 7, he is less "watery" than in book 6:

> Such things I turned over within my unhappy breast, overladen with gnawing cares that came from the fear of death and from not finding the truth. Yet the faith of your Christ, our Lord and Savior, *the faith that is in the Catholic Church, was firmly fixed within my heart* [*stabiliter haerebat in corde meo*]. In many ways I was as yet *unformed* [*informis*] and I *wavered* from the rule of doctrine [*praeter doctrinae normam fluitans*]. But my mind did not depart from it, nay, rather, from day to day it drank in more and more of it. (7.5.7, my italics)

The passage combines images of watery instability with those of firmness. Like water, the young Augustine is *informis*, lacks a stable form. His "wavering" (*fluitans*) portrays him as floating or drifting on a wave or stream. At the same time, the Christian faith is "firmly fixed" within him. This imagery implies that the young Augustine is a ship anchored near land: still wavering yet firmly fixed as well.

In the final words of book 5 and throughout book 6, as we have seen, the young Augustine is "at sea." God is his *gubernator* (steers-man: *gubernabas me*, 6.5.8); the conflicting winds of his opinions blow the ship of his heart this way and that (6.11.20). In the first half of book 7, however, this ship is moored in the harbor of Christianity. To some extent, the young Augustine drifts about and yet he is "firmly fixed" to the "earth" of the Christian faith.

The text returns to these images and themes shortly before the young Augustine begins to study "certain books of the Platonists" (7.9.13):

> But now, O my helper, you had freed me from my chains, and still I asked, "Whence is evil?" [*unde malum*] but there was no way out. Yet *in none of those wavering thoughts* [*fluctibus cogitationibus*] *did you let me be carried away from that faith* [*auferri ab ea fide*] in which I be-lieved both that you exist, and that your substance is unchangeable, and that you have care over men and pass judgment on them, and that in Christ, your Son, and in the Holy Scriptures, which the authority of your Catholic Church approves, you have placed the way of man's salvation [*viam salutis humanae*] unto that life which is to be after his death. These truths being made safe and fixed immovably in my mind, I asked uncertainly [*aestuans*] "Whence is evil?" (7.7.11)

In his "wavering thoughts," in the swelling surges (*aestus*) of his uncertainty ("*aestuans*"), the young Augustine still remains firmly anchored. God does not allow him "to be carried away" from the "dry land" of Christian faith by waves of doubt.

This is the last water image in book 7. The revelation of God as immutable Being, in chapter 10, resolves the young Augustine's intellectual difficulties. At last, he can answer the troubling *unde malum* and conceive of a spiritual substance. His mental universe becomes well-ordered beneath the divine light of that vision. As Durling shows, creation is no longer a sea (7.5.7) for the young Augustine, but a hierarchy to be ascended by the soul (7.17.23).[32]

Never again does book 7 portray him wavering, as though on water, even when it portrays his unsteadiness. After his intellectual vision of God in chapter 10, the young Augustine moves from "water" to "land," just as God's seventh act, in the allegory, is represented as a movement from "water" to "land." Consider the following passage, which might have used water imagery but does not:

> I marveled that now I loved you, and not a phantom in your stead. Yet *I was not steadfast* in enjoyment of my God [*non stabam frui deo meo*]: I was borne up [*rapiebar*] to you by your beauty [*decore tuo*], but soon I was borne down from you by my own weight, and with groaning *I toppled* [*ruebam*] into the midst of those lower things. This weight was carnal custom [*consuetudo carnalis*]. Still there remained within me remembrance of you: I did not doubt in any way that there was one to cleave to, nor did I doubt that I was not yet one who could cleave. (7.17.23, my italics)

The young Augustine is unable to stand firm (*non stabam*) in his apprehension of the divine light. The "weight" of "carnal custom" carries him back down to "lower things." Those lower things, however "carnal" they may be, are no longer portrayed as watery, for the young Augustine now perceives their relation to immutable Being. The young man doesn't "sink" into these lower things. The verb describing his downward movement, *ruebam*, is an instance not of water but of land imagery: it describes toppling down a slope. The young Augustine remains on the "dry land" of his newly found certainty. To regain his vision of the divine light, he must reascend the levels of being, as the chapter goes on to describe.

The journey of the soul to the One, however, proves easier to describe than to make. Augustine criticizes Neoplatonism for lacking clear directions and practicable means to reach the "land of peace" it envisions:

> It is one thing to behold from a wooded mountain peak the land of peace [*patriam pacis*], but to find no way [*iter*] to it, and to strive in vain towards it by unpassable ways [*per invia*], ambushed and beset by fugitives and deserters, under their leader, the lion and the dragon. It is a different thing *to keep to the way* [*tenere viam*] that leads to that land, guarded by the protection of the heavenly commander, where no deserters from the heavenly army lie in wait like bandits. (7.21.27)

The journey figured in this striking passage is a journey by land. Neoplatonists have no clear path to effect their return to the soul's *patria*, but Christians do have a "way" (*via*) to hold to (*tenere*), one divinely protected. That "way," of course, is Christ, "the way and the truth and the life" (7.18.24; John 14.6).

This figure, from the final sentences of book 7, makes quite explicit a metaphor that begins to emerge three chapters earlier. The young Augustine's journey to truth no longer takes place on the sea, as in book 6, but on land. And this shift from sea to land metaphors for describing the young man's spiritual development is precisely analogous to the shift, in the allegory on Genesis, from sea imagery in God's sixth act to land imagery in his seventh. Having reached harbor on the Christian "earth," the young Augustine sets out to reach the "land of peace" (7.21.27). He is unable to do so, however, because he does not fully recognize that "The Word was made flesh" (7.18–19). He does not hold Jesus (*non tenebam*, 7.18.24) as "the way and the truth and the life" and so he does not "hold to the way" (*tenere viam*, 7.21.24) that leads to "the land of peace." The figure of a land journey is clear in chapter 20. The difference between Neoplatonists and Christians is analogous to that "between those who see where they must travel, but do not see how [*nec videntes, qua*] and those who see the way that leads [*viam ducentem*] not only to beholding our blessed fatherland [*beatificam patriam*] but also to dwelling therein" (7.20.26). A Christian may even reach that heavenly *patria* without first beholding it from afar. Thanks to Scripture, "he who cannot see from afar off may yet walk upon that way [*ambulet viam*] whereby we may come to you, and see you, and hold fast [*teneat*] to you" (7.21.27).

Land imagery also functions in the late chapters of book 7 in

metaphors of building, of establishing a firm foundation. As we have
seen, the earlier chapters, like book 6, use water images to describe
the young Augustine's wavering, his intellectual uncertainty. After
his vision of Being in chapter 10, he is intellectually certain but morally weak. Chapter 18 uses a building metaphor to show how Christ
repairs infirm humankind:

> I did not hold fast to Jesus my God, a humble man clinging to him who
> was *humble* [*humilem*], nor did I know in what thing his weakness [*infir-
> mitas*] would be my teacher. Your Word, eternal truth, surpassingly
> above [*supereminens*] the highest parts of your universe *raises up* [*erigit*]
> there to himself those who have been brought low [*subditos*]. *Amid the
> lower parts he has built himself out of our clay a lowly dwelling* [*in
> inferioribus autem aedificavit sibi humilem domum de limo nostro*], in
> which he would protect from themselves those ready to become submis-
> sive to him [*subdendos*], and bring them to himself. (7.18.24, my italics)

This text links the Incarnation to the founding of the Church.
The eternal Word humbles himself to take on human form and so
raise up "those who have been brought low." As God creates Adam
"from the clay of the earth" (*de limo terrae*, Gen. 2:27), so does the
New Adam build for himself "a lowly dwelling out of our clay." That
physical body modulates, in the image, into the Church, Christ's
Mystical Body, in which he protects those faithful to him. He "raises
up" (*erigit*)—a verb that implies construction—those who acknowledge their humility and weakness.

This the prideful young Augustine cannot do. He is "puffed up
with knowledge" (*inflabar scientia*, 7.20.26). He lacks "the charity
that builds upon the foundation of humility, which is Christ Jesus"
(7.20.26). "Humility," of course, derives etymologically from the
Latin word for "earth, dry ground," *humus*. Hence, it provides a firm
foundation for charity and for the Church, the "humble dwelling
place," that Christ builds "out of our clay" (7.18.24). Augustine goes
on to contrast the humble contrition of Christianity with the pre-
sumption of Neoplatonism. The bishop rejoices that he moved from
the latter to the former: "If I had first been formed [*informatus*] by
your Sacred Scriptures and if you had grown sweet to me by my familiar use of them, and I had afterwards happened on those other vol-
umes [of the Neoplatonists], they might have drawn me away from
the solid foundation of religion [*solidamento pietatis*]" (7.20.26, my
italics). Only such a foundation on the solid earth of the Christian

faith, Augustine believes, can inform and thus make strong the infirm human soul.

In sum, then, book 7 traces a movement from sea metaphors, in its earlier chapters, to land imagery in its later ones. This movement corresponds to that in Augustine's allegory on God's seventh act. The allegory traces a movement from the sea of "love of this world" (13.21.29) to continence in God's Word, associated with the "dry land" of Christianity (13.21.30–31). The young Augustine's "coming to land" implies his reaching a continence of the intellect, one attained through a Neoplatonist vision of the Word (7.9–10). This is perfected in his higher conversion to continence of the will and Christianity in book 8.

The absence of sea imagery in the later chapters of book 7 is rather striking because, in some sense, inappropriate. The young Augustine is not yet, as the book insists, fully on the earth of Christianity. He does not believe in the Incarnation (7.18–19); he does not recognize the "foundation of humility" (7.20.26); he has not yet entered the "lowly dwelling" of the Church that Christ "built for himself out of our clay" (7.18.24). The sea imagery in the earlier chapters describes the young Augustine positively, his current spiritual state. The land imagery in the later ones describes him, for the most part, negatively: what he is not, or not yet. The young Augustine remains prideful. As books 8 and 9 attest, at this time he is still deeply involved in his political and marital ambitions in "this world." Throughout the *Confessions* these themes are associated with water imagery. Only by tacitly ignoring these issues does Augustine achieve in book 7 an internal coherence and, thereby, a correspondence with the allegory in book 13. Such careful evasion suggests an author's conscious plan.

And yet, for Augustine, Neoplatonism does arrive at the dry land of some truths. He presents it, in chapter 9, as a Christianity manqué: partially in agreement with certain New Testament teachings, it lacks the saving truth of the Incarnation. The metaphors of the later chapters accord with this presentation. The young Augustine reaches the land of solid truth but can journey no further. Lacking faith in Christ the way (*via*) he has no clear journey (*iter*) to the *patriam pacis* (7.21.27).

The land-sea opposition in the allegory also underlies the chapters that follow immediately upon the young Augustine's intellectual conversion. Chapters 11–13 and 15 treat the relationship of eternal Being to temporally existent beings. As I suggested in section III of this chapter, the relationship between the eternal and the temporal proves a theme of sustained meditation in the autobiography only in books 3, 4, and 7. And these books correspond uniquely to allegories that feature the land-sea opposition in book 13. As primarily a "land book," book 7 adverts again and again to God's eternal immutability and incorruptibility. Both the book and its corresponding allegory trace a metaphorical movement from sea to land. Reflection on how the temporal is related to the eternal thus proves, analogously, fitting.

Perhaps this seems merely adventitious. God's immutability is, after all, a recurrent theme in the *Confessions*. Since the young Augustine is struggling to conceive of God as a "spiritual substance" in book 7, eternity and immutability prove central. The narrative of his development provides the rationale, not a scheme of correspondences with book 13. Certainly, this proves the case for the writer-speaker of the *Confessions*. Since the dynamic of his prayer has not yet led him to his allegory on Genesis in book 13, Augustine the speaker has no correspondences in mind.

And yet a narrative oddity, a deviation from the "natural order" of the autobiography, suggests that the author has planned such a scheme. The young Augustine begins to meditate on God's "spiritual substance" early in book 6, and yet God's immutability is never mentioned. The text presents his thinking negatively: he learns from Ambrose's sermons that Christians do not conceive of God as "limited by the shape of a human body" (6.3.4). What positive doctrine he learns about God is never treated.

The very first chapter of book 7, however, asserts that even then the young Augustine had some definite ideas: "I, a man—and such a man!—tried to think upon you, the supreme, sole, and true God, and I believed with all my soul that you are incorruptible, and inviolable, and immutable" (7.1.1). At a time corresponding to book 6, chapter 3, therefore, the young Augustine believes fervently in God's immutability. Nowhere in book 6 is this mentioned. Nowhere in book 6 is God's immutability or incorruptibility or inviolability referred to in any context, even briefly. Mention of the young Augustine's belief is delayed until book 7, where it becomes a recurrent theme. Why should an author violate the "natural order" of his narrative in this way?

Certainly, this violation lends book 7 some of its uniqueness. More than any other book in the first nine, it dwells upon the immutability of God's eternal Being. The complete absence of that theme in book 6 makes it stand out all the more sharply in book 7.[33] Yet the scheme of correspondences we are tracing also provides a plausible explanation. In his sixth act, God creates from the waters, and book 6 is a "water book." It dwells on the young Augustine's involvement in the waters of "this world," or treats those "messengers of God," Ambrose and Alypius, whom God creates from the waters in the allegory of book 13. Though God's immutability fits naturally with the narrative in book 6, it proves a theme inappropriate to its correspondence with "the waters." Book 7, in contrast, is a "land book." In the allegory, the "dry land" is always associated with the Christian faith, with the relationship between temporal man and the eternal God. God's immutability thus proves an appropriate theme for book 7, and the violation of "natural narrative order" suggests an author's conscious plan.

A final correspondence between book 7 and the allegory may be more briefly noted, one *not* based on the land-sea opposition. Augustine's allegory explicitly alludes to the Incarnation and the Eucharist: "Of these [creatures from the sea] the earth now has no need, although it feeds upon the Fish, raised out of the deep and put upon that table which you have prepared in the sight of believers. He was taken out of the deep to the end that he might nourish the dry land" (13.21.29). This is Augustine's sole reference to the Eucharist in book 13. Though other texts use the metaphor of "feeding on truth," no other allegory refers to the food of God himself.

Book 7 contains a similar transformation in food metaphors in the *Confessions*. The imagery first becomes prominent in book 3: the Manichaeans feed the false food of vain "truth" to the young Augustine (3.6.10–11). Imagery of the "food of truth" recurs throughout books 3–5 and, indeed, throughout the *Confessions*.[34] In the young Augustine's vision of Being in book 7, however, the "food of truth" becomes the food of God himself: "I found myself to be far from you in a region of unlikeness, as though I heard your voice from on high: 'I am the food of grown men. Grow and you shall feed upon me. You will not change me into yourself, as you change food into your flesh, but you will be changed into me'" (7.10.16).

This passage is echoed in the closing words of chapter 17: "I took with me only a memory, loving and longing for what I had, as it were, caught the odor of, but was not yet able to feed upon." The following chapter relates this imagery to the recurrent concern of book 7 with the Incarnation: "He called to me, and said, 'I am the way and the truth and the life.' He mingled that food, which I was unable to receive, with our flesh, for 'the Word was made flesh,' so that your Wisdom, by which you created all things, might provide milk for our infant condition" (7.18.24). The Eucharist as the food of Christ is mentioned in book 13 only in the allegory on God's seventh act; Augustine's autobiography refers to the sacrament in the same fashion only in book 7. Such a correspondence suggests an author's conscious plan.

Faith in the Incarnation and the sacrament of the Eucharist, these are precisely what Neoplatonism lacks, according to book 7: a "way" that leads the soul to eternity. The young Augustine comes to realize this and, in the last chapter, he turns to the study of Saint Paul. Book 5 and especially book 6 present him thinking and feeling about Scripture, largely through hearing it expounded by Ambrose. Such thinking and feeling are conspicuously absent from book 7, until the final chapter. And then the young Augustine "seizes upon" (arripui, 7.21.27) the text of Scripture for himself, for his own study. In order to accept God's word for his life, he must accept God's Word in history. In order to be "reformed in newness of mind," he must accept God's recreation of humanity.

VIII

God's eighth act in the Hexameron is the creation of humankind. After commanding the earth to bring forth "living soul," he says, "Let us make man to our image and likeness" (Gen. 1:26). He then creates "man to the image of God" (1:27; 13.22.32), commands the male and female to "increase and multiply," and gives them "rule" over the creatures of the fifth and sixth days (1:28).

Augustine begins his allegory on this act by showing how it is related to his treatment of the previous one:

> For behold, O Lord our God, our creator, when our affections have been restrained from love of this world, in which affections we were dying by living evilly, and when by living well a living soul has begun to exist, and

your Word, by which you spoke to us through your apostle, has been fulfilled in us, namely, "Do not be conformed to this world," there follows what you immediately adjoined, and said, "But be reformed in the newness of your mind." (13.22.32)

The soul moves, in this allegory, from moral continence to spiritual conversion, from restraint of the affections to their perfection in service of God's will. Augustine goes on to complete the quotation from Romans 12:2. Paul urges his "children through the Gospel" to "'Be reformed in the newness of your mind, that you may prove,' for yourselves, 'what is the good and the acceptable and the perfect thing'" (13.22.32).

The allegory appeals to a traditional figure: the creation of Adam is a type of man's recreation in grace. Augustine draws explicit attention to God's direct creation of man and, hence, man's direct relation to God: "Therefore, you do not say, 'Let man be made,' but, 'Let us make man,' and you do not say, 'according to his kind,' but 'to our image and likeness.' For since he is renewed in mind and perceives your truth that he has understood, he himself establishes what is your will, what is the good, and the acceptable, and the perfect thing" (13.22.32). Such a creation and renewal in grace make a man "spiritual," for thereby he is "'renewed unto knowledge of God, according to the image of him who created him'" (13.22.32; Col. 3:10). Just as Adam is granted dominion over the creatures, so the "spiritual man" is able to "judge all things," "but he himself is judged by no man" (13.22.32; 1 Cor. 2:15).

The moral dimensions of this allegory are clarified in a later chapter. Augustine summarizes all that "we see" of created things, adhering closely to the literal meaning of Genesis 1. When he reaches the sixth day, however, he turns to moralizing allegory:

> We see the face of the earth, adorned with earthly creatures, and man [hominem], made to your image and likeness, that is, by the power of reason and intelligence, set over all non-rational animals. *And even as in his soul there is one power which is master by virtue of counsel [quod consulendo dominatur] and another made its subject so as to obey, so also for man [viro] in the corporeal order there was made woman.* Because of her reasonable and intelligent mind she would have equality of nature, but *as to bodily sex she would be subject to the male sex, just as the active appetite [appetitus actionis] is made subject, so as to conceive right and prudent conduct from the rational mind.* (13.32.47, my italics)

This familiar allegory alludes to the Creation account in Genesis 2. Woman is associated with appetite and man with reason: the former is "rightly subordinate" to the latter. The allegory of conversion "in the newness of your mind" is thus linked with the rule of reason over appetite, of the masculine over the feminine.

The relevance of this allegory of conversion to book 8 of the *Confessions* is obvious. The book narrates at some length three conversion stories. In chapter 2, Simplicianus tells the young Augustine of Victorinus's conversion, to "exhort" him to "accept Christ's humility" (8.2.3). In chapter 6, Ponticianus tells him about the conversion of two *agentes in rebus*. This tale goads the young Augustine to his own conversion, detailed in chapters 7, 8, 11, and 12, which Alypius imitates. Five conversion stories are thus narrated at some length over twelve chapters. A sixth, the conversion of Saint Anthony (8.6.14 and 8.12.29), is reported but not elaborated.

Furthermore, five of these conversions involve a commitment to sexual continence by these men: to the rule of "masculine" reason over "feminine" appetite. The two *agentes* enter the monastic life, giving up their "affianced brides" (8.6.15), who themselves dedicate their virginity to God. Saint Anthony founded a monastic tradition. Chastity, of course, proves the crucial issue in the young Augustine's conversion, and Alypius also chooses continence at the same time. Rejecting sexual intercourse with women, the young Augustine repudiates the "woman in him," his appetite, and identifies his true self with the "masculine" reason, made "in the image of God." Conversion and the rule of reason over appetite, thus, prove the central themes both of book 8 and of Augustine's allegory on God's eighth act.

The young Augustine's conversion is associated, by this correspondence, with the creation of Adam. So is it also in the very first chapter of the *Confessions*. At the close of book 8, the young man finally arrives at the "rule of faith" (*regula fidei*). God converts him (*convertisti enim me*, 8.12.30) to complete faith in the "Word made flesh." The first use of "faith" (*fides*) in the volume recalls Augustine's conversion: "Lord, my faith calls upon you, that faith which you have given me, which *you have breathed into me* by the incarnation of your Son [*quam inspirasti mihi per humanitatem filii tui*] and through the ministry of your preacher" (1.1.1, my italics). God's "breathing into" (*inspirasti*) the young Augustine faith in the Incarnate Word recalls the creation of Adam, when "the Lord breathed into (*inspiravit*) his face the breath of life" (Gen. 2:7). Again, the typology is traditional. Recreation in grace through the New Adam is analogous to God's creating, in the flesh, the first Adam. Augustine not only appeals to this figure but does so, appropriately, via the account in Genesis 2. There, Adam is created by God and placed in a garden, without a woman. In book 8, the young Augustine is recreated by God in a garden, from that moment on sexually continent—without a woman.

The young Augustine's conversion is closely associated with the Incarnation in another, more subtle way. It can best be approached by asking at what point in the narrative the young Augustine comes to believe in the Incarnation. As a reader completes book 7, this appears to be the next step in the young man's development. He believes firmly in the Catholic faith (7.5.7, 7.7.11). He can conceive of God as a spiritual substance and at last understands *unde malum* (7.10–16). The final chapters of the book turn on the young Neoplatonist's need to accept the "humility" of "the Word made flesh" (7.18–20). For this reason, he turns to the study of Saint Paul (7.21).

And yet, in book 8, the issue seems almost to disappear. In chapter 2, the young Augustine does not yet believe in the Incarnation: Simplicianus tells him of Victorinus's conversion "in order to exhort" him "to accept Christ's humility" (*ut me exhortaretur ad humilitatem Christi*, 8.2.3). Victorinus is portrayed as very like the young Augustine: skilled in the liberal arts, a well-known public figure, a Neoplatonist, a Christian manqué. The final step to his becoming a true "child of Christ" requires him "to bend his neck under the yoke of humility, and to lower his brow before the reproach of the cross" (8.2.3). Victorinus needs to accept not simply that God's Word is eternal but that he humbled himself to human life and a redeeming death. So, too, does the young Augustine.

But belief in the Incarnation disappears as an explicit theme from the rest of book 8, despite its being featured so clearly in the later chapters of book 7. In the first chapter of book 9, however, Augustine describes his conversion to continence in these terms:

> But throughout these long years where was my free will? Out of what deep and hidden pit was it called forth in a single moment, *wherein to bend my neck to your mild yoke and my shoulders to your light burden, O Christ Jesus, "my helper and redeemer!"* How sweet did it suddenly

become to me to be free of the sweets of folly: things that I once feared to lose it was now joy to put away. *You cast them forth from me*, you the true and highest sweetness, *you cast them forth, and in their stead you entered in*, sweeter than every pleasure. (9.1.1, my italics)

This passage suggests that the young Augustine's conversion to continence is marked, simultaneously, by his complete acceptance of the Incarnation. "Christ Jesus," his "helper and redeemer," casts forth from him the "sweets of folly" and *enters the young Augustine* "in their stead." When the young man accepts the Pauline injunction to "put on the Lord Jesus Christ" (8.12.29), God's word enters and redeems him, just as God's Word entered the world to redeem it. In being converted to sexual continence by Scripture, the young Augustine is accepting God's word into his flesh. At the same time, this passage implies, he accepts "the Word made flesh."[35]

Book 8, thus, implies a link between the young Augustine's conversion and the Incarnation: the New Man is created in him even as he accepts the eternal Word as the New Adam. God's "Word made flesh" proves a principle not only of redemption in the past but of hermeneutics and Christian practice, salvation in the present: making God's word "flesh," in the world. And this incarnation of the New Adam in the young Augustine corresponds, in book 13, to God's creation of the first Adam, whole and unfallen. The New Adam, the true "Image of God," begins to renew him "to the image of God" (Gen. 1:27) created in the first Adam. The young Augustine can now "prove what is the good and the acceptable and the perfect thing" (Rom. 12:2, 13:22.32).

A more subtle act of correspondence between book 8 and the allegory turns on Augustine's interpretation of "increase and multiply" (13.24). God gives this command to human beings, in his eighth act, and to the creatures brought forth from the sea, in his sixth. Augustine observes that the beasts of the earth, created in God's seventh act, do not receive this command, though they do indeed "increase and multiply" when one considers "the actual natures of things" (13.24.37). Augustine resolves this anomaly through allegory. His treatment resonates against books 6, 7, and 8, and especially his presentation of Neoplatonism.

Augustine interprets this anomaly allegorically. His interpretation, in fact, concerns the very principles of polysemous allegory:

But as to what may in such wise increase and multiply that a single thing may be stated in many ways and a single statement may be understood in many ways, this we find only in signs corporeally expressed and in things intelligibly conceived [*in signis corporaliter editis et rebus intelligibiliter excogitatis*]. *By signs corporeally expressed* we understand the *generations of the waters,* on account of causes necessitated by fleshly depth; *by things mentally conceived, human generations,* on account of the fecundity of reason. (13.24.37, my italics)

God's sixth act, the creation of sea creatures, is associated with a single meaning expressed through a multitude of different signs. Augustine's example: all the "corporeal rites" and "mystic deeds and words" of the missionary Church signify "God's Word" (13.20.27–28). God's eighth act, the creation of humans, is associated with the multitude of meanings derived from a scriptural text "obscurely uttered in but one way" (13.24.37). Both principles are clearly related. Both, for Augustine, are central to the understanding of Scripture. Both are "spiritually fertile."

It seems to me no accident, therefore, that books 6 and 8 are centrally concerned with the reading of Scripture and with "spiritual fertility." Book 7, in contrast, stands apart from books 6 and 8 on this score. The young Augustine is engaged with the "books of the Platonists," not with the Bible. Just as God does not command the creatures of his seventh act to "increase and multiply," so, these correspondences suggest, do the Platonist books of book 7 lack the "spiritual fertility" of biblical allegory.

The theme of "spiritual fertility" is rather obvious in book 8. The young Augustine is converted to continence. This virtue is personified as *Continentia,* "in no wise barren [*sterilis*] but a fruitful mother [*fecunda mater*] of children, of joys born of you, O Lord, her spouse" (8.11.27). *Continentia* is herself surrounded by her children, "many boys there and girls, there too a host of youths, men and women of every age, grave widows and aged virgins." After the young Augustine joins them, as it were, the book closes with Monica's joy: "You turned her mourning into joy far richer than that she had desired, far dearer and purer [*castius*] than she had sought in grandchildren born of my flesh" (8.12.30). The text implies that Monica shall have "grandchildren in the spirit," born through her son's propagation of the Christian faith. Indeed, book 8 locates the young Augustine's conversion on a family tree of spiritual propagations: Victorinus, Saint

Anthony, the *agentes in rebus*, all stand in a genealogy of conversions that help generate his own.

In book 6, the young Augustine hears, for the first time, the fundamental axiom of biblical allegory: "the letter kills, but the spirit gives life" (6.4.6). This is the generating principle of the "spiritual fertility" of Scripture. The propagation of the faith is a central theme in book 6 and in the allegory on God's sixth act, as we have seen. The book lavishes attention on Ambrose the bishop (6.3.3) and on Alypius, the future bishop (6.7–10). It repeatedly adverts to the spread of the Christian faith (6.5, 6.11). All this propagation "in the spirit" is set against a negative portrayal of marriage and procreation "after the flesh" (6.11–15). Augustine's allegory on "increase and multiply" thus resonates against the young Augustine's experiences in books 6 and 8 in several ways.

In book 7, however, the young Augustine does not read Scripture until the last chapter. Furthermore, his study of Neoplatonism is presented negatively. For Augustine, the New Testament comprehends Neoplatonist doctrine and exceeds it with the revealed truth of "the Word made flesh." Lacking belief in the Incarnation, Neoplatonism fails to see how eternity has united itself to time. It therefore lacks "Christ, the way" to the "fatherland of peace" (7.21.27).

Belief in Christ, of course, is precisely what enables allegorical interpretation in the first place. The dialectic of Old Testament and New, of the "dead letter" and the "quickening spirit," is created by the Word's having become flesh. The "books of the Platonists," therefore, are ultimately sterile in themselves: they are creatures of God's seventh act, as it were, and do not "increase and multiply." They have not "spread their dignity and authority throughout the whole world" (6.11.19), as has Scripture. They have no faith in the union of eternity with time in Christ. Hence, they do not possess that union of spirit and letter that makes Scripture so fertile with meaning and truth, for Augustine.

IX

God's ninth act in Genesis is his blessing and sanctifying the seventh day (Gen. 2:3), because he rests "on the seventh day from all his work which he had done" (2:2). Each of the first six days has an "evening

and morning," but not the seventh. For this reason, Augustine allegorizes the movement from Hexameron to sabbath as that from the
world of history to eternal rest in God:

> This entire most beautiful order of things that are very good, when their
> measures have been accomplished, is to pass away. For truly in them a
> morning has been made, and an evening also.
>
> XXXVI. But the seventh day is without an evening, and it does not
> have a setting [occasum], because you sanctified it to endure for all eter-
> nity, so that by the fact that you rested on the seventh day, having
> fulfilled all your works, which are very good, although you wrought
> them while still at rest, *the voice of your book may proclaim to us be-
> forehand that we also, after our works, which are very good because you
> have given them to us, may rest in you on the sabbath of eternal life.*
> (13.35.50–13.36.51, my italics)

Augustine's language here applies both to the faithful soul and to the
souls of all the faithful, to life with God after death and to eternal life
after the Last Day.

The "peace of rest [quietis], the peace of the sabbath, peace without an evening" (13.35.50) is a recurrent theme in book 9. The first
eight books of the *Confessions* record but two deaths: those of Augustine's father (3.4.7), mentioned in passing, and his friend in book 4.
In book 9 alone, however, Augustine records five: those of his father
(now named Patricius); his son, Adeodatus; his friends, Verecundus
and Nebridius; and, most important, Monica. Monica's "vision at Ostia," death, and burial form the climax of book 9; a prayer that "she
may rest in peace" (9.13.37) concludes it, and so concludes Augustine's autobiography. In all these passages, the theme of "eternal
rest" rings clearly, and, more quietly, it resonates elsewhere, as well.

The first deaths recorded in book 9 are Verecundus's and
Nebridius's. That record is proleptic: it occurs in the aftermath of the
young Augustine's conversion and just before he retires to
Cassiciacum. The bishop remembers his two friends: how both were
converted and subsequently died at a time *long after* that being narrated. This violation of the "natural order" of the narrative serves a
program of correspondences between book 9 and the allegory.

For Augustine dwells on the eternal rest that each of his friends
now enjoys in God. He recalls that Verecundus was baptized just before he died:

Lord, you will reward him with the reward of the just, for *you have already rewarded him with their lot.* Although we were absent, for by then we were in Rome, he was seized by bodily illness and during it he became a Christian and one of the faithful, and he departed from this life. . . . Faithful to your promises, in return for that country place of his at Cassiciacum, where far from the madding world we found rest in you, *you gave to Verecundus delights in your paradise that are eternally fresh, for you forgave him his sins upon earth, in that mountain flowing with milk, your mountain, that richest mountain.* (9.3.5, my italics)

Augustine proves just as lyrical in his belief that Nebridius is enjoying God's eternal sabbath:

This man, not long after our conversion and regeneration by your baptism, also became a faithful Catholic and served you in perfect chastity and continence among his own people in Africa, for his whole household through him became Christian, and you freed him from the flesh. *Now he lives in Abraham's bosom.* . . . There he lives. What other place is there for such a soul? *There he lives,* in that place of which he asked so many questions of me, a poor, ignorant man. No longer does he put his ear to my mouth, but *he puts his spiritual mouth to your fountain, and in accordance with his desire he drinks in wisdom, as much as he can, endlessly happy.* (9.3.6, my italics)

The correspondence with Augustine's allegory on God's ninth act is obvious.

A similar prolepsis governs Augustine's mention of the death of Adeodatus. He recalls his son's extraordinary abilities as he records their baptism together. The bishop is confident that Adeodatus, too, now dwells with God: "Quickly you took his life away from the earth, and now I remember him with a more peaceful mind [*securior*], for I have no fear for anything in his childhood or youth, and none at all for him as a man. We joined him to us, of equal age in your grace, to be instructed in your discipline. We were baptized, and anxiety over our past life fled away from us" (9.6.14). Though Adeodatus, in fact, died some time after Monica, his death is recorded before it. The prolepsis enables the author to create correspondences with the allegory on God's "eternal sabbath" in book 13, while placing Monica's death at the climax of book 9.

That climax is heightened by the famous "vision at Ostia" in the preceding chapter. Monica and her son share a spiritual *ascensus.* It arises from their discussing together the nature of eternal life: "We inquired of one another 'in the present truth,' which truth you are, as to what the eternal life of the saints would be like, 'which eye has not seen, nor ear heard, nor has it entered into the heart of a man'" (9.10.23). After a beautiful description of "passing beyond" all things to hear God's Word in beatifying silence, Augustine returns to this theme:

> if this could be prolonged, and other visions of a far inferior kind could be withdrawn, and this one alone ravish, and absorb, and hide away its beholder within its deepest joys, so that sempiternal life might be such as was that moment of understanding for which we sighed, would it not be this: "Enter into the joy of your Lord?" When shall this be? When "we shall all rise again, but we shall not all be changed." (9.10.25)

The "vision at Ostia" closes with this text on the Last Day. The whole vision arises from, concludes in, and thus is richly informed by, the theme of rest in God "on the sabbath of eternal life" (13.36.51).

The theme is echoed again in Monica's last recorded words in book 9. Shortly after the vision, she speaks confidently of "the advantages of death" to some of her son's friends: "They were amazed at the woman's strength, which you had given to her, and asked if she did not fear leaving her body so far from her own city. She replied, 'Nothing is far from God. I need not fear that he will not know where to raise me up at the end of the world'" (9.11.28). The very next sentence records her death. Monica's last words in the book are not, one should note, the last words in her life. They are spoken while her son is absent, and the young Augustine is at her deathbed to close her eyes (9.12.29). These words function in book 9 as the dramatic climax to a life of courage in the Christian faith. And this climax underscores the correspondence between the book and the allegory on Genesis.

The long last chapter of book 9 is an extended prayer for the repose of Monica's soul. Mindful of human weakness in the best of Christians, the bishop prays ardently that God "enter not into judgment with her" (9.13.35). He concludes by remembering briefly his father and prays that all his readers may pray for his parents. His final words reveal Monica's last request of him: his prayers for her soul. These, Augustine hopes, may be multiplied by the readers of his *Confessions.*

The theme of death and eternal rest in God, thus, is explicit in at least five of the thirteen chapters in book 9. In all the other books of the autobiography, the theme is mentioned but once, and that mention is brief: the young Augustine's friend is "snatched away from my madness so that he might be kept with you for my consolation" (4.4.8). In Augustine's autobiography, book 9 alone dwells on this theme; in book 13, it proves central only to the allegory on God's ninth act.

The allegory also resonates, though more quietly, in other events of book 9. Chapter 7 narrates the confrontation between Ambrose and Justina, mother of the emperor and an Arian. At the very center of the chapter, Augustine recalls the turning point of the struggle: God "revealed" to Ambrose "the place in which the bodies of the martyrs Protase and Gervase lay hidden, uncorrupted in the treasure-house" of God's "secret place" (9.7.16). This discovery serves to "check the mad rage" of Justina, as Augustine goes on to narrate.

This discovery is recorded in lines at the very center of the central chapter of book 9. Such placement at the center gives these "uncorrupted saints" a meaning greater than their narrative role in the book would warrant. Their physical centrality, I would argue, reflects the central theme of book 9 and its corresponding allegory. Clearly, the bodies of Saints Gervase and Protase remain uncorrupted because their souls are uncorrupted, dwelling in "the treasure-house of God's secret place" in heaven. And their placement at the physical center of the book is no accident, though it is not the conscious plan of Augustine the speaker. Immediately upon finishing the story, he wonders: "Whence and whither have you led my recollection so that *I confess also these things to you* [*ut haec etiam confiterer tibi*], mighty deeds that I had almost passed over in forgetfulness?" (9.7.16, my italics). Without God's leading him, the speaker would not "also" (*etiam*) "confess these things." They are not part of Augustine's intention for his autobiography, this text asserts, but they do prove part of God's plan. And God's plan involves correspondences with an allegory on Genesis that he foresees, though the speaker does not. Hence, the mention of "uncorrupted saints" at the very center of book 9 is God's work, according to the premise of the *Confessions*. It resonates against "the sabbath of eternal life" in book 13.

The theme also can be seen in the young Augustine's retirement to Cassiciacum, recorded in chapter 4. This, too, proves a time of rest, though not of *pax* and *quies*, as in the "eternal sabbath." The text describes it as a "respite" (*in pausatione*, 9.4.7), a time of "leisure" (*in illo tunc otio*, 9.4.8) and of "vacation" (*dierum illorum feriatorum*, 9.4.12). Over half the chapter is taken up with a meditation on Psalm 4. Augustine concludes this with sustained allusion to death and the Last Judgment.

> At the next verse I cried out with a deep cry from my heart, "*Oh, in peace, oh, in the Selfsame!*" *Oh, why did he say: "I will fall asleep and I will take my sleep!" For who will hinder us when there "shall come to pass the saying that is written, 'Death is swallowed up in victory.'" You are surpassingly the Selfsame, you who change not, and in you there is rest* [requies], *forgetful of all labor.* For there is none other with you. Nor have you fashioned me to seek after those many other things, which are not what you are, but "you, O Lord, singularly have settled me in hope." This I read, and I burned with ardor. (9.4.11, my italics)

Lastly, book 9 records five baptisms, just as many as it does Christian deaths. Verecundus and Nebridius are baptized upon their conversions; Alypius, Adeodatus, and Augustine after their return from Cassiciacum. As the sacrament of entrance into the Christian life, baptism proves a *figura* to be fulfilled by entrance into God's eternal life, for which it prepares the soul by cleansing it of sin. Christian theology identifies baptism with participation in Christ's death and resurrection, and hence with the resurrection of all the blessed on the last day.

Again, book 9 is unique in Augustine's autobiography in the attention it gives to baptism actually performed. The previous eight books record but two: Victorinus's (8.2.5) and that of the young Augustine's unnamed friend (4.4.8). Only in book 9 is baptism recurrently and emphatically linked with eternal rest in God: with release from anxiety (*sollicitudo*) leading to "wondrous sweetness" (9.6.14), with the "mountain flowing with milk" of God's "paradise" (9.3.5), with endlessly happy inebriation at his fountain (9.3.6). Such unique emphasis further suggests an author's plan linking book 9 to Augustine's allegory on God's ninth act in Genesis.

These are the principle ways in which the allegory of book 13 proves the paradigm for books 1–9. So ends the first stage of my argument. The second and third stages will prove neither so complex nor so highly metaphorical. For just as the *Confessions* turns, in books 10–

12, to a mode largely philosophical and theological from one primarily narrative and metaphorical, so must our discussion. Such a turn to abstract principles may lead, I trust, to a high ground more familiar to Augustine scholars than the thickets of metaphor we have just traversed.

The correspondences traced in this chapter prove useful, it seems to me, beyond the thesis they serve to argue. They focus attention on a number of oddities in books 1–9 and offer a rationale that interprets them. Why, for instance, should Augustine wait until book 2 to draw explicit attention to his reasons for writing? These seem properly to belong in book 1. In book 5, he presents himself as having longed for Faustus to resolve his doubts about Manichaeism for "almost nine years" (5.6.10), his entire period in the sect. Why mention none of this questioning in books 3 and 4? Why should water imagery be so prominent in books 1–4 and 6, yet practically absent from book 5? Why should all mention of God's immutability be absent from book 6, as the young Augustine struggles to conceive of a spiritual substance? Why does the autobiography continue past the conversion account to Monica's death?

Each of these anomalies, to be sure, is open to interpretations other than those I have suggested. Nonetheless, a significant pattern of correspondences does obtain between Augustine's autobiography and the allegory concluding the *Confessions*. Books 1–9 record God's creating the young Augustine as a Christian, and these nine books parallel God's creation of the universe in nine acts, recorded in Genesis. More precisely, the autobiography recapitulates, in great detail, the "divinely inspired" allegory on Genesis as signifying the "creation of the Church." That allegory encompasses not only the scope of all Creation but the sweep and meaning of all time and Scripture, from Genesis to Revelation. For the Church, as Augustine understood it, represents God's Word on earth and continues Christ's saving work by preaching God's Word to humankind. The Church, in its divinely instituted *magisterium*, comprehends the meaning and end of all history and Scripture, for Augustine: leading humankind from time to eternity.

The parallels between autobiography and allegory in the *Confessions* imply a bold labor of self-understanding by Augustine the author. The young Augustine's life recapitulates the scope of the whole cosmos, the sweep of all time, the substance of all Scripture, and the meaning of all history, salvation in God's Church. Autobiography and allegory prove carefully paralleled and, thus, deeply integrated. According to the premise of the *Confessions*, these parallels lie beyond the ken of Augustine the speaker but are central to God's guiding plan for his prayer. For Augustine the author, however, they imply an understanding of himself as fully integrated with the scope, course, and meaning of the cosmos and its history, all of which are encompassed by the Church. In the *Confessions*, Augustine the author envisions himself, in a quite thorough way, as a microcosm, the universe contracted to a span.[36]

Yet this is not simply the microcosm of Neoplatonism, where man stands at the horizon of the physical and the spiritual and so contains, in his being, the principles governing the whole.[37] First, without the allegory at the end of the *Confessions*, the autobiography cannot be understood as microcosmic in the way I have set forth. Nowhere in the volume does Augustine explicitly declare that the course and meaning of the universe can be found in his own life *per speculum in aenigmate*. Such an understanding emerges only when one reads "between the parts" of the work, seeking its informing patterns. Further, the allegory is thoroughly biblical in its texture and ecclesiastical in its subject. This autobiographical microcosm, therefore, should be seen as Augustine's Christian and revisionary use of a Neoplatonist principle.

Second, both autobiography and allegory narrate processes, rather than describe objects. They are histories of a person and the Church being created, not treatments of a cosmos already fashioned for contemplation. And both the autobiography and the allegory occur within the process of the speaker's present and ongoing prayer, itself an event unfolding in history, according to the premise of the volume. The *Confessions*, thus, presents both the young Augustine's history and the allegorical history of the Church as providentially governed, but not only that: the volume presents itself as a providentially guided event within universal, Christian history.

Augustine's autobiography, therefore, is not simply a microcosm of God's creation of the cosmos and the Church. Books 1–9 prove a microhistory unfolding in an order "governed by God." In so doing, the autobiography recapitulates universal history, as envisioned in the allegory: its origins, recorded in Genesis; its end, the "eternal sabbath" revealed at the close of Scripture; its meaning, salvation through the Church; and its mode, governed by Providence. Books 1–9, however, can be understood as a microhistory only in their relations to the allegory that concludes the *Confessions*. Like universal history, the meaning and pattern of the volume can only be understood retrospectively, from the end, when "everything that is hidden shall be revealed."

For Augustine, such retrospective illumination is a pattern fundamental to all communication in language. The speaker's *sermo* unfolds in time. His words continue "by successive departures and advents" until they "make up the universe of which they are parts" (4.10.15). Only at the end may the speaker, and those who heed him, "hear the whole" (*totum audias*, 4.11.17). Only in its "inspired" conclusion does the providential paradigm for the *Confessions* become clear. At the end of the volume we discover its beginning, and the whole work thus traces a pattern fundamental to Augustine's thinking: the return to origins.

4 ✛ Book 13 and Books 10–12

In the previous chapter, we examined Augustine's allegory on God's nine acts at the Creation and its relation to the nine books of his autobiography. Clearly, the allegory on Genesis cannot provide a paradigm for books 10–12 in the same way it does for books 1–9. We must, therefore, reconsider the allegory in terms suitable to Augustine's new projects and methods in the second "part" of his *Confessions*. What might these terms be?

The *Confessions* undergoes an obvious change in book 10, from the narrative of books 1–9 to philosophy and theology. The first nine books do not, of course, lack philosophical and theological reflections, nor the next three a certain narrative progress. On the whole, however, the differences between the two blocks in the volume are quite sharp. In book 10, as Kenneth Burke observes, the *Confessions* turns "from a *narrative of memories* to the *principles of Memory*."[1] This turn to principles continues as Augustine meditates on the "first things" of Scripture in books 11–12. He explores the principle of time, considers the nature of God's eternal "heaven of heavens," and meditates explicitly on the relationship between eternity and time at the Creation.[2]

Hence, to be adequate to books 10–12, this analysis must imitate Augustine's own turn to principles. We have seen how the allegory on Genesis provides a narrative and metaphorical paradigm for the autobiography in books 1–9. If the allegory is to prove a paradigm for books 10–12, it must be reenvisioned in terms of principles. A deeper paradigm, one expressed in abstract and philosophical terms, must be sought in the allegory. If such a paradigm be discovered, it should provide the formal principle that underlies the movement of books 10–12. And as a formal principle of the allegory, it should underlie books 1–9 as well.

Such proves the project for this chapter. First, the allegory on Genesis must be reconsidered: no longer as a narrative of nine acts but as structured, at a deeper level, by a formal principle. Such a principle has been described by A. Solignac. Commenting on the final chapters of the *Confessions*, where Augustine summarizes the days of creation and his allegory, Solignac observes:

> On the other hand, chapters 32–34 of book 13 allow one to understand that the author has considered the *totality* of the creation in its material reality and in its spiritual signification, that is to say, as a figure of the Church and of the spiritual Universe of the saints. The book and the whole work are then concluded in a fitting close through the evocation of the Seventh Day, the peace "of the sabbath that will have no evening" (13.35.50). *The cycle of time is, in that way, dialectically perfected: time is opened for us out of eternity by the fiat of the Creator and it is closed in the eternity of the heavenly rest, without ceasing to be governed by the transcendence of the divine eternity.*[3]

Solignac's statement emphasizes the scope of Augustine's allegory: it takes in the totality of creation, both physically and spiritually. It also encompasses the sweep and direction of all time, which proceeds from God's eternity and returns to it.

The allegory achieves such comprehensive scope, I have argued, by imitating Scripture. The subject of Augustine's treatment, the Church, embraces the scope of God's word in its mission of salvation. The sweep and direction of the allegory imitate the structure of the Bible. For Augustine, the Bible encompasses the whole direction of time by its very structure: from Genesis to Revelation, from creation to the end of time. God governs every moment of time, just as he governs every word of the sacred text. Providentially governed history and divinely inspired Scripture: these are structured homologously. The latter reveals the former. Time is in movement toward eternity, from which it originated. Human life in history proves, analogously, movement toward God, from whom it originates.

Solignac's description, therefore, enables us to see the formal principle of Augustine's allegory, conceived as a whole. Its subject embraces the purpose of Scripture, the salvation of humankind. Its movement imitates the structure of Scripture: the return of humankind in time to God in eternity. Clearly, these are different ways of saying the same thing. We may sum them up, therefore, in a single formula: the return to the Origin. For a Christian, every moment on that return is governed by God, its Origin and End. Thus, a single formal principle may be seen to govern Augustine's allegory, as well as Scripture: progress forward entails return to the Origin, who governs at every moment the whole movement.

This formal principle possesses wide and deep relevance for Christian Platonism, as every Augustine scholar knows. Let us recall briefly some of its resonances and implications. Then this principle can function as the standard rule with which to measure the progress of books 10–12 and 1–9.

First of all, the "return to the Origin" is a fundamental—perhaps the fundamental—Neoplatonist idea. It implies an ontological and metaphysical principle: all things proceed from and return to the One. It expresses an epistemological principle: the cosmic order can be rightly comprehended only by a person who returns, through reason at least, to its Origin. It also expresses a moral principle: one's life should be directed toward, and disciplined for, that journey of return. The "return to the Origin" is, in these senses, fundamental to Augustine's thinking. Regardless of the precise nature of his Christian Platonism at the time he wrote the *Confessions*, this principle explicitly informs the volume at many points.

For a Christian Platonist, as we have seen, it is not only a philosophical principle: it is grounded in the structure of history, as revealed in Scripture. As book 7 of the *Confessions* makes clear, Christianity comprehends and exceeds Neoplatonism, for Augustine. Scripture contains Neoplatonist philosophical truths; it further encompasses them with the historical revelation of the Incarnate Word. For Augustine, therefore, the "return to the Origin" proves an ontological, metaphysical, epistemological, and moral truth that can be discovered in Scripture. Scripture also reveals, however, that the "return to the Origin" can be a *narrative* principle. In the Bible, it proves a principle of literary structure that represents the order of history.

The "return to the Origin," as a literary structure in the Christian Bible, proves formally analogous to the principle of all communication through language. John Freccero has explored this analogy in considerable depth.[4] His treatment is based on Augustine's theory of language in the *Confessions*. He extends the insights of Kenneth Burke, who has examined analogues for "eternity" and "time" in Augustine's language theory.

Burke points to the linguistic analogy in book 4, chapter 10. Augustine is discussing transient things:

> Therefore, when they take their rise and strive to be, the more quickly they grow so that they may be, so much the faster do they hasten towards ceasing to be. This is the law of their being. So much have you given them, because they are parts of things that do not exist all at once, but all of them, by successive departures and advents [*decedendo ac succedendo*], make up the universe of which they are parts. *See, too, how our speech [*sermo*] is accomplished by significant sounds [*per signa sonantia*]. There would be no complete speech unless each word departs [*decedat*], when all its parts have been uttered, so that it may be followed [*succedat*] by another.* (4.10.15, my italics)

Burke points out that the sentence unfolds in time and in the materiality of *signa sonantia*. Its meaning, however, "is not confined to any of the sentence's parts, but rather pervades or inspirits the sentence as a whole." Meaning, thus, proves a kind of essence, analogous to "eternity." Burke sums up the dialectic: "In contrast with the flux of the sentence, where each syllable arises, exists for a moment, and then 'dies' to make room for the next stage of the continuing process, the meaning is 'non-temporal,' though embodied (made incarnate) in a temporal series."[5] The "non-temporal" meaning of the sentence is the origin of its articulation in time. When the listener follows the sentence to its end-point and understands the whole, he arrives at the "non-temporal" origin of that temporal unfolding.[6] Understanding involves a "movement to the origin."

Much of Burke's subsequent analysis of the *Confessions* turns on the dialectical interplay of "eternity" and "time."[7] John Freccero, however, attends to the role of history in Augustine's linguistic analogy: the coming-to-be and passing-away of things in time, like the *signa sonantia* of a *sermo*. Freccero thereby discovers in Augustine's language theory a formal principle common also to conversion, Christian autobiography, biblical allegory, and the Christian vision of history. All share a common structure of understanding: a temporal sequence comes to a close that enables one to apprehend the meaning of the whole, in retrospect. Progress through events in time and words in a sentence entails a return to the origin: one arrives at the meaning that has governed the unfolding sequence.[8]

As a linguistic principle, this should be clear enough. Take, as the simplest model of a *sermo*, a single sentence. As Freccero puts it,

"The perfect act of speech could be imagined as the articulation into time of the intentionality of a speaker until the sentence is completely uttered and, retrospectively, meaning emerges in time when the conclusion exactly matches its point of origin."[9] This is Augustine's own theory, as we have seen.

Augustine explicitly envisions history as structured in the same way. The transient existences of people and things are parts of a universal whole, unfolding in time like the *signa sonantia* of a *sermo* (4.10.15). The meaning of the whole governs the entire sequence, though it is revealed only at the end. And the meaning of history is God in eternity, as Augustine suggests in another linguistic analogy.

In book 4, chapter 11, Augustine is addressing those who pursue the "perverse things" (*perversa*) of their own flesh. They should be converted from the flesh, which perceives things but in part, that they might know the whole through the mind. Conversion, thus, implies apprehension of the whole.

> For by that same fleshly sense you hear what we speak, and you do not want the syllables to stand steady; you want them to fly away, so that others may succeed to them and you may hear the whole statement [*totum audias*]. So it is always with all things out of which some one being is constituted, and the parts out of which it is fashioned do not all exist at once. All things together bring us more delight, if they can all be sensed at once, than do their single parts. But far better than such things is he who has made all things, and he is our God, and he does not depart, for there is none to succeed him. (4.11.17)

History, for the Christian, begins from God's *fiat* and ends with his eternal city. At the end of time, everything that is hidden shall be revealed. What the Christian knows "in part" in time shall be known perfectly in the vision of God face to face. God is, for Augustine, the meaning of history. His eternal Providence governs its temporal unfolding. Only at the end of the *sermo* of history, however, will that Providence be fully understood.

Freccero's analysis of this principle focuses on the Incarnation as "end point" to the Old Testament, rather than the end of all history in the Last Judgment. Thus, he finds in Augustine's linguistic analogy the principle of Biblical allegory:

> Finally, the syntactic model is a basis for understanding biblical allegory and its relationship to confessional structure. The New Testament

should be understood, not as a separate book, but rather as the definitive ending of the Old Testament—its closure. Syntax would be the horizontal axis along which the Old Testament events are unfolded. However, just as the speaker's intentionality must be virtually present at each separate instance of an utterance, providing a vertical or paradigmatic axis, in the same way the New Testament fulfillment of individual Old Testament figures and events subtends the narrative as a "type" or "figure" that is revealed only at the end. Ultimately, like all successful utterances with respect to their intentionality, it is a tautology. The ending is the Word made flesh, but in the beginning was the Word.[10]

For Augustine, as for Saint Paul, the figures and events of the Old Testament reveal those of the New: they reveal Christ. The Word of God stands at the origin of God's word in the Old Testament, is figurally present throughout it, and his Incarnation marks its closure. That closure, like the end point of a sentence, reveals retrospectively the "true meaning," for Augustine, of the Old Testament. Arrival at the end marks a "return to the Origin" through retrospective understanding.

Such retrospective understanding, however, is possible only for those already converted to faith in Christ. As Saint Paul argues in 2 Corinthians 3, conversion to Christ proves essential to reading the Old Testament truly, "in the spirit." Without such conversion, Jewish readers remain blind to the "true meaning" of their Scriptures: "the veil is upon their heart" (3:15). Christian conversion, from the Old Man to the New, is correlative with the faith that the Old Testament is fulfilled in the New.[11]

Hence, biblical allegory and Christian autobiography, the story of conversion, prove formally analogous. Freccero shows that both are characterized by a "turning point" from the old to the new. In both, that turning point marks a closure that enables the "old" to be understood retrospectively in a new and true light. Such understanding reveals the new to have been present throughout the old, however enigmatically: God's Word is figurally present throughout the Old Testament, his Providence governs the young Augustine's *errores*. Hence, conversion, like biblical allegory, marks a "return to the Origin," understood retrospectively to have been present all along.

Freccero summarizes these ideas and relates them explicitly to the linguistic analogy:

Conversion is both the subject matter of his work and the precondition for its existence. Form and content are therefore in some sense analogous, inasmuch as conversion not only is a traditional religious experience, but also has its counterpart in language, where it may be defined as that central syntactic moment in which the ending marks the beginning and the circular identity of the author coincides with the linear evolution of his *persona*.[12]

The moment of conversion, the climax or "end point" of a Christian autobiography, proves the origin of that very narrative. Without conversion, the story of conversion would never be told. This tautology is formally analogous to that of meaning in a sentence. The intentional meaning, made clear at the end, is the precondition of the utterance in the first place. The syntax of events in the young Augustine's life is informed by a providential meaning that is not at all clear to him. The closer he comes to conversion—the end of the sentence—the clearer God's role in his life becomes to him. Yet not until the young Augustine "dies" in conversion—comes to his end point—can the meaning of his life emerge clearly to his resurrected self, the Christian author of the story.

For Augustine, then, the structure of biblical allegory and of Christian autobiography proves formally analogous to that of all linguistic communication. Freccero simply develops the correlations implied in Augustine's own theories of conversion, biblical hermeneutics, language, and history. Conversion from the Old Testament to the New and from the Old Man to the New are like the "turning point" at the end of a sentence, when the meaning of the whole is revealed. For Augustine, surely, these analogies are based on God's word in Scripture. The biblical narrative is a *sermo* structured as a "return to the Origin." It reveals the providential structure of all history, which the history of each Christian imitates, albeit in different ways.

Though Freccero's discussion focuses on the Incarnation as the turning point from old to new, his principles apply equally well to the end, when time turns to eternity. Augustine makes this clear in a famous passage from book 11:

I am about to recite a psalm that I know [*novi*]. Before I begin, my expectation extends over the entire psalm. Once I have begun, my memory extends over as much of it as I shall separate off and assign to the past. The life of this action of mine is distended into memory by reason of the part that I have spoken and into expectation by reason of the part I am about to speak. But attention is actually present and that which was to be is borne along by it so as to become past. The more this is done and done again, so much the more is memory lengthened by a shortening of expectation, until the entire expectation is exhausted. When this is done the whole action is completed and passes into memory. What takes place in the whole psalm takes places also in each of its parts and in each of its syllables. The same thing holds for a longer action, of which perhaps the psalm is a small part. The same thing holds for a man's entire life, the parts of which are all the man's actions. The same thing holds throughout the whole age of the sons of men, the parts of which are the lives of men. (11.28.38)

Here, Augustine draws a detailed analogy between a linguistic act and events in history. The history of a person and the universal history of all persons prove analogous, part for part and whole for whole, to the recitation of a psalm. The analogy points explicitly to the movement of time in recitation, implicitly to the development in an unfolding *sermo*.

Since the psalm has been memorized (*novi*), its recitation progresses by a "return to the origin." The recitation proves analogous to universal history, for Augustine, because both move from "eternity" through "time" to "eternity." In the present of Augustine's intention to recite, memory and expectation are indissolubly one. This is clearly analogous to God's vision of all time, past and future, in his eternal present. Once the recitation begins, however, memory and expectation become radically divided: the more there is to come, the less has passed into memory, and vice versa. This is also true for the temporality of history, for a Christian. God has fixed its limits: the closer one is to the *fiat* of time, the further one is from its *finis*, and vice versa. This antithesis of past and future continues throughout the recitation, throughout the period of history. At the end of the recitation, however, at a single stroke, memory and expectation are abolished in the present of Augustine's knowledge (*novi*) of the whole psalm. Similarly, human history comes to closure in God's eternity. Augustine's knowledge of the psalm is the paradigm governing its syntactical unfolding in speech. It is analogous to God's Providence, which governs the unfolding of history. Partial meaning emerges at many points in both processes, to be sure. But the meaning of the whole emerges only at the closure, when Origin and End are fully revealed as one.[13]

In sum, then, the "return to the Origin" is a principle common to linguistic communication, Christian autobiography, biblical hermeneutics, and universal history. For Augustine, all these analogies are founded in Scripture: God's word representing the structure of all history. The "return to the Origin" proves also an ontological, metaphysical, epistemological, and moral principle. Though these ramifications are treated explicitly in Neoplatonism, Augustine would insist that Scripture comprehends and exceeds them.

Hence, as Solignac suggests, the "return to the Origin" is indeed a formal principle of Augustine's allegory in book 13. But not only there. "Return to the origin" describes the literary form of Augustine's autobiography, at least up to his conversion. It describes conversion itself. It expresses, in a brief formula, a range of ideas central to his philosophy and theology. As a linguistic principle, it expresses the form of the *Confessions* in a general way, even though its writer-speaker is not fully in control of his utterance. Guided by God, according to its premise, the text is governed ultimately by his Providence, and so by his intentions. This paradigm is fully revealed only in the "divinely inspired" final chapters of the volume. The unfolding syntax of Augustine's *sermo* ends, thus, with a return to the origin.

But does "return to the origin" govern, as a formal principle, the narrative progress of books 10–12, as it does the allegory? Can it also describe the narrative development of books 1–9, which move *past* the young Augustine's conversion? The formal coherence of a narrative order is what my argument requires. Other formulas have described thematic "unity" in the *Confessions*: "reading and speech," the "confession" itself, the relationship of time to eternity, and so on. The "return to the Origin" can, surely, join their ranks. But thematic coherence does not necessarily imply a plan to the volume, but rather a single writer with persistent concerns, as Luc Verheijen has observed.[14] Only formal coherence, the union of narrative form and fundamental themes, can argue the *Confessions* as a carefully planned work. Can "return to the origin" describe the narrative progress of the whole volume?

At least two scholars have argued that it does. R. D. Crouse has defined the "pattern" of the *Confessions* as "the itinerary of descent, conversion, and return."[15] The whole work traces a return to the Origin, as his title suggests: "'*Recurrens in te unum.*'" So, equally, does each of its three parts: the autobiography of books 1–9, the introspection in book 10, and the "meditation upon the eternal Word as the *principium* of creation," books 11–13.[16] Crouse outlines a movement from *exteriora* through *interiora* to *superiora* within each part and, more generally, from part to part throughout the volume. The *Confessions*, thus, traces an *itinerarium mentis in Deum* at every level.[17]

Crouse's vision of the whole agrees fundamentally with Knauer's in "*Peregrinatio animae.*" Knauer describes the narrative as a "pilgrimage of the soul," from the "restless heart" of book 1, chapter 1, to its "eternal rest" in book 13, chapter 37. Along the way, the soul encounters the regions of sin: of lack (book 2), death (book 4), distance from the Father (book 6), of unlikeness (book 7). Eventually, Providence leads the soul to conversion (book 8) and to a brief mystical vision of eternal life (book 9). The soul's continued thirst for the vision of God leads to continued journeying, into memory (book 10) and Scripture (books 11–13). Finally, it arrives at a vision of God's eternity and the peace of rest in him. The soul has journeyed to its Origin and End, and the work is concluded.

Basically I agree with these views. The description I offer here, however, differs from them chiefly in two respects. First, as I have argued, the *peregrinatio* proves the journey of Augustine the *speaker*. He does not plan the course of his prayer: it emerges through the dynamic of his dialogue with God, recreated in our reading. Hence, its frequent digressions, its seeming planlessness. At the same time, Augustine repeatedly asserts that God is guiding his prayer. Given this premise, its formal structure as a return to the origin is created providentially. The providential structure of Augustine's *Confessions* thus imitates God's guiding the young Augustine to conversion, which it records. It also imitates the structure of the Christian Bible, a divinely inspired work that traces the providential structure of history as a return to the Origin.

Second, like Crouse, I hope to show that "return to the Origin" describes each part of the *Confessions* as well as the whole. Though the parts I outline here prove slightly different from his, and so does the exposition, our treatments are analogous at many points. They articulate similar visions of the whole with slightly different emphases. Books 1–9, 10–12, and 13, I shall argue, each trace a return to the origin by Augustine the speaker. The *Confessions* thus traces a progressive "ascent to principles" from part to part and over the whole. It culminates with its "divinely inspired" paradigm, the allegory on Genesis, the original or founding structure of the volume.

Kenneth Burke has argued that books 10–12 trace "the kind of dialectical progression that is traditionally, in Neo-Platonist thought, called the Upward Way."[18] The discussion of memory in book 10 marks an "ascent to principles" from books 1–9: "the turn from a *narrative of memories* to the *principles of Memory*."[19] Book 9 investigates the principle of Time at considerable length. Book 12 dwells on God's eternal "heaven of heavens" and on the "formless matter" of creation that is neither wholly temporal nor eternal. In a general way, then, these books progress from memory to time, and from time to eternity. Time is a principle anterior to memory, just as eternity proves anterior to time. Books 10–12 thus progress as an ascent to principles.[20]

That ascent, as Burke notes, does not prove such a "clearly graduated progression" as his summary might indicate.[21] Burke does not understand the *Confessions* as representing a prayer in the process of being spoken. Hence, he has no rationale for the restless surface beneath which he acutely perceives the Upward Way. Yet if he follow the progress of Augustine's *voice*, as well as the topics he treats, a more carefully graduated ascent may come into view. This ascent contains its halts and digressions, to be sure: the *Confessions* is not the *Divine Comedy*. The large digressions themselves, however, become part of the forward "return to origins." Let us follow this movement in greater detail.

Augustine begins book 10 with an explicit meditation on the work he is writing. "*Quo fructu?*" he asks repeatedly in chapters 2–4: with what fruit, benefit, advantage, does he write his *Confessions*? In posing and answering this question, Augustine reveals why he has wanted to write books 1–9 and why he wants to continue writing. Since desires, or *voluntates*, prove the origin of communication, according to his analysis (1.8.13), the writer is considering the origins of what he has written and shall continue to confess. His "turn to principles" in book 10 begins by reflecting on the motives standing at the origin of his whole project.

Augustine also explicitly asks "with what benefit" his readers wish to hear his *Confessions* (10.4.5). He thereby treats the proper attitudes that his readers should bring to the text. These attitudes are, in principle, prior to reading, the origins of "right reading." Augustine's "turn to principles" thus addresses the origins of his readers' motives for reading, as well as his own for writing.[22] Chapters 1–5 of book 10 comprise a coherent unit: Augustine is meditating on the work he is writing. Chapter 1 opens with the issue of knowing oneself in and through God; chapter 5 closes by affirming *confessio* as the means to such knowledge.

Chapter 6 begins a new movement: Augustine turns from the issue of knowing God to loving him. He poses the question, "What is it then that I love when I love you?" (10.6.8), and this initiates a philosophical ascent, an attempt to return to the Origin. Summarized in chapter 40, this *ascensus* governs the rest of book 10. It moves from creatures, *exteriora* (10.6.9–10), to ascend the faculties of the soul, *interiora* (10.7.11). This brings Augustine to the principle of memory and to a lengthy meditation upon it: chapters 8 through 25, eighteen chapters all told.

The philosophical *ascensus*, however, balks on a certain paradox: Augustine is *memor* of God, God dwells in his *memoria* (10.24), yet he must traverse the memory to find God (10.25). This leads the speaker, striving to return to his Origin, to meditate on his relationship with God (10.27–29) and to examine the state of his spiritual continence (10.30–39). Chapters 40 and 41 then summarize the course of the book from chapter 6 onward: the ascent (40) and the "sickness of my sins" that stands between the speaker and God (41).

Still seeking to return to the Origin, Augustine asks, "Whom could I find to reconcile me to you?" (10.42.67). This question leads him to think on Christ, the *verax mediator* (10.43.68), who unites God and man, eternity and time. The failure of his philosophical *ascensus* brings Augustine to consider his faith in the Word of God, whose self-sacrifice redeems and heals him (10.43.69).

Here lies the crucial link between the end of book 10 and the beginning of book 11.[23] Desiring to return to his Origin, Augustine needs the Christ who is revealed in Scripture. God's eternal Word and his written word "that shall not pass away": Augustine often uses *verbum Dei* to refer to both. Book 11 opens by raising the question of how God's eternity is related to human time: "Lord, since eternity is yours, are you ignorant of the things I say to you, or do you see only at a certain time what is done in time?" Only Christ bridges eternity and time; Scripture alone reveals this truth. Only the *verbum Dei* can heal Augustine's moral failings and resolve his intellectual perplexities.

The progress of Augustine's return to the Origin in book 10 thus brings him to God's Word at its close and to God's word in book 11. The progress of his prayer arrives, in this way, at an explicit meditation on the Bible. Scripture, of course, provides the origin of the faith that leads the writer to confess in the first place. And his prayerful seeking brings him to the very beginning of Scripture, the text on origins.

As I argued in chapter 2, Augustine the speaker prays to meditate on all of Scripture, not simply the Hexameron, at the beginning of book 11. Struggling to return to the Origin, he has recognized his need for Christ and so aims to grow closer to God's Word through meditating on God's word. He prays fervently, in a chapter replete with biblical quotations, to undertake an impossible project: to "consider 'the wonderful things of your law,' from that beginning, wherein you made heaven and earth, even to an everlasting kingdom together with you in your holy city" (11.2.3). By the end of book 13, that prayer has been answered, albeit in a manner unforeseen by Augustine the speaker. He is led through grace to the "divinely inspired" exegesis that concludes the volume. The progress of his prayerful, often digressive meditation enacts a return to origins in several different ways.

Augustine begins his investigation of Scripture by a progressive inquiry into different modes of God's speaking. First, in book 11, chapter 3, he points to God's speaking through Moses in Scripture and prays that the truth which inspired Moses may help him to understand the sacred text. Then, in chapters 5 and 6, Augustine meditates upon God's speech at the Creation. This further modulates, in chapters 7–9, to thinking about God's coeternal Word, the *principium* through whom God creates. From chapters 3 to 9 in book 11, thus, the progress of Augustine's meditation upon the *verbum Dei* moves progressively "backward" in time and "higher" in ontological categories: from Scripture to Creation to the eternal Logos.

These thoughts on the eternal *principium* lead directly to the central inquiry of book 11: the nature of time. That inquiry begins properly at chapter 14 and is not concluded until chapter 28. Augustine prays several times for God to aid his search, as he works

130 + Augustine's Prayerful Ascent

through erroneous positions before he finally arrives at a true under-standing.[24] This progress toward truth, of course, functions as a "re-turn to origins" for a Platonist. For Augustine, erroneous understand-ings are all defective images of a truth which is, in principle, both prior in time and higher in dignity. His progress toward understand-ing thus proves an "ascent to truth." It culminates in the passage quoted earlier, where time is treated as analogous to the recitation of a psalm. And that passage culminates with a *gradatio* that asserts the highest, most comprehensive relevance of the inquiry just com-pleted: "What takes place in the whole psalm takes place also in each of its parts and in each of its syllables. The same thing holds for a longer action, of which perhaps the psalm is a small part. The same thing holds for a man's entire life, the parts of which are all the man's actions. The same thing holds throughout the whole age of the sons of men, the parts of which are the lives of all men" (11.28.38). This *gradatio* of synecdoches proves a synecdoche for the greater, more indirect ascent toward understanding of the nature of time, which the speaker is completing.

In the opening chapters of book 12, Augustine returns to the text of Genesis. Having thoroughly considered "In the beginning," in book 11, he begins to treat the meaning of "heaven and earth." This for-ward movement in Genesis 1:1, however, takes Augustine's thought "backward" in time. He first considers the *informis materia* from which God formed the universe (12.3–8). This matter, represented in Scripture as "earth *invisibilis et incomposita*," exists *prior* to time, which begins with the creative *fiat*. Augustine contrasts this "earth" with its counterpart in the verse, "heaven." He argues that this refers to the "heaven of heaven," the *intellectualis creatura* that partici-pates in God's eternity and is beautifully formed thereby (12.9–11). Thus, both "heaven" and "earth" in Genesis 1:1 signify created things that exist prior to the Creation, beyond time yet not properly eternal. Forward movement in the speaker's investigation of Scripture brings him to consider earlier and more fundamental modes of being. He is being led on a return to origins.

After summarizing his understanding of Genesis 1:1 in chapters 12–13 of book 12, Augustine begins to examine several other inter-pretations in some detail. That Christians may legitimately disagree in their understanding of the Bible leads him to meditate upon some principles of scriptural hermeneutics. This discussion makes up the final ten chapters of book 12. Augustine introduces and frames it with this definition of the hermeneutic enterprise:

> May I be united to them, O Lord, in you, and may I rejoice with them who feed upon your truth in breadth of charity. Let us together approach the words of your book, and *let us seek in them for your will by means of the will of your servant, by whose pen you have dispensed these words* [et accedamus simul ad verba libri tui et quaeramus in eis voluntatem tuam per voluntatem famuli tui, cuius calamo dispensasti ea]. (12.23.32, my italics)

Interpreting Scripture involves seeking God's *voluntas*, the intention or desire that stands at the origin of his words, as of all communication (1.8.13). That search is to be conducted by means of the *voluntas* of Moses, the inspired *scriptor* of Genesis, and these related *voluntates* are approached through the *verba* of the sacred text. Interpreting Scripture, thus, clearly involves a return to origins: movement from material signs to the divine *voluntas* at the origin of the text.

Much of Augustine's subsequent discussion springs from this definition. To what extent does Moses' *voluntas* in writing represent God's *voluntas* in inspiring the text? To what extent can Moses' *voluntas*, for that matter, be clearly discerned in the words we read? Augustine finally urges the "rule of charity" in all interpretations of Scripture, that "Amid this diversity of true opinions, let truth itself beget concord" (12.30.41). And he concludes by asserting that however many truths Moses may have understood in the words he wrote, the Holy Spirit who revealed those truths to him understands them completely (12.32.43).

Augustine's discussion of hermeneutic principles in chapters 23–32 of book 12 perhaps seems a digression from his study of Genesis 1. Nonetheless, it functions as yet another stage in the speaker's journey toward origins. These hermeneutic principles, as principles, are logically, if not existentially, prior to Augustine's practice of interpreting. In book 12, chapter 23, the speaker begins to think about the origins of the hermeneutic inquiry he has been engaged in since book 11, chapter 3. Further, he is inquiring into the original principles underlying the biblical text: the nature of "the word of God" and how

Scripture mediates God's *voluntas* to the reader. The principles that Augustine investigates prove prior both to his act of reading and to the sacred text he is reading.

This inquiry into the principles at the origin of a text recalls, even as it exceeds, the chapters on why Augustine is writing his *Confessions*. The investigation concluding book 12 "encompasses" the meditation opening book 10. In the latter, as we saw, Augustine treats the desires that move him to write his *Confessions* and the charitable disposition he hopes his readers will bring to the work. At the close of book 12, he inquires into the *voluntas* at the origin of Scripture and argues for the "rule of charity" in reading it. Just as Scripture stands at the origin of Augustine's faith, and thus of the work he is writing, so the end of book 12 exceeds and comprehends the opening of book 10. Exploring the principles underlying "the word of God" is an intellectual task both higher and more comprehensive than treating the analogous principles of his own text. The differences between the two measure how far the speaker has journeyed toward origins.

This return to the same issues on a higher level proves one reason why I treat books 10–12 as a unified, component "part" of the *Confessions*, even though this division departs from the scholarly tradition. Customarily, books 1–9 and 11–13 are seen as distinctive units within the volume, with book 10 proving either a later addition, an interlude, or a connecting link. However, I have already argued why the last twenty-seven chapters of book 13 should be considered distinct from the treatment of Genesis that begins in book 11: they represent a radical departure in the subject, style, tone, manner, and pace of Augustine's exposition. Since these chapters comprise over two-thirds of book 13, one may consider the whole book as a distinct "part" of the whole.

Books 10–12, I am suggesting, constitute a coherent part of the whole as well. They pursue a kind of spiraling path, such that the end circles around to be aligned with the beginning, but on a higher level. In the course of his prayer, Augustine the speaker is led, beyond his awareness, on a progressive return to origins. He moves from considering the *voluntas* behind its own writing to that at the origin of Scripture. In so doing, he progresses from the principle of memory, which underlies his autobiography in books 1–9, to the principle of revelation, underlying the sacred text that founds his faith and his whole *Confessions*. He progresses to ever-anterior principles by meditating thoroughly on the first two verses of Genesis. From memory, he moves to consider the nature of time in book 11, and then to the nature of the timeless matter of Creation, in book 12. When Augustine is led to meditate on the original principles of Scripture, he progresses even closer to eternity, as it were. He considers the divine origin of the word of God that, unlike heaven and earth, "shall not pass away": "Heaven and earth shall pass, but my words shall not pass" (Matt. 24:35). The divine *voluntas* of Scripture is eternal: it lies in the Holy Spirit, God's *velle* (13.11.12), who directly inspires the text.[25]

The division I am proposing here outlines a trinitarian form for the whole *Confessions*. The volume consists of three parts, composed respectively of nine books, three books, and one book. The latter—a final unity—contains in its final twenty-seven chapters the paradigm for the whole volume. The perfectly trinitarian number of chapters in that concluding allegory ($3 \times 3 \times 3 = 27$) accords with its being "divinely inspired." According to the premise of God's guiding the speaker's *Confessions*, his triune Providence informs the allegory more directly and, hence, more perfectly, than the tripartite unity of the whole volume.

According to this division, the speaker's journey to origins is no more perfectly trinitarian than it proves a perfectly graduated ascent. The first eleven chapters of book 13 constitute a remainder left over from this division. But since the volume presents itself as the unfolding prayer of Augustine the speaker, no such perfect division is necessary or possible. His return to the Origin contains halts for puzzlement and petitions for grace, shifts of direction and longer digressions that sometimes delay, sometimes contribute to his progress. Augustine the speaker, responsive to grace though he is, possesses a will of his own and the need to "work things through" at his own pace. Only in the concluding allegory, according to his premise of the work, does that patient *inquisitio* become thoroughly infused with grace and turn to a confident *expositio*.

I have already argued, in chapter 2, how that "divinely inspired" allegory proves a fitting conclusion to the volume: it fulfills the speaker's prayers (11.3, 12.32) to consider the whole of Scripture. Such inspiration, Augustine asserts, conveys to him the original meaning of Genesis 1: "We have already examined [*inspeximus*] those things in keeping with that mystical purpose [*propter figura-tionem*] whereby you willed them either to be fashioned in such an order or to be described in such order [*ista vel tali ordine fieri vel tali ordine scribi voluisti*]" (13.34.49). Augustine asserts here that his insight (*inspeximus*) has penetrated to the divine will (*voluisti*). Whether God created the universe precisely as recorded in Genesis 1 or simply willed his creating to be so described does not prove a pertinent question. In either case, Augustine the speaker believes that he has penetrated to the divine purpose.

This is an astonishing assertion. The Holy Spirit, God's *velle*, inspires the sacred text; Augustine the speaker claims a divinely inspired understanding such that he apprehends God's *voluntas* there. He believes that he has apprehended, by the grace of its divine origin, the original meaning of the biblical text on origins. Through his allegory, the speaker discovers in Genesis "all of Scripture," from Creation to the "eternal sabbath" after the Last Judgment. He discovers the meaning, for a Christian, of all human history: salvation in Christ through his Church. He discovers all human history, as it were, providentially present in the divine *voluntas* to create the universe.

Hence, the allegory fulfills Augustine the speaker's return to the Origin. Through divine inspiration, he achieves a comprehensive vision of Scripture and of human history. He discovers the end of Scripture in its beginning, the *finis* of all history in its *principium*. A view higher, more comprehensive, or closer to the Origin, it seems to me, can hardly be as articulately conveyed by a pilgrim-searcher in this life. Augustine the speaker thus completes his return to the Origin, and his *Confessions* draws to a close.

In this way, return to the Origin describes the narrative progress of books 10–13. Augustine's "inspired" insight into the original meaning of Scripture, in book 13, transcends his meditation on the principle of divine inspiration, at the end of book 12. The speaker's progress toward ever-prior and, thus, higher principles is steady throughout these books, even though slow and not perfectly graduated. I have suggested why this movement might be divided into two parts, books 10–12 and book 13. Even should one prefer the traditional division—book 10 and books 11–13—the speaker's progressive return to the Origin could still be described in the same way.

"Return to the Origin," let us recall, is the narrative paradigm of the concluding allegory, as it embraces the sweep of Scripture, from Creation to the heavenly city. The narrative movement of the allegory thus proves the clearest model for the "return to the Origin" enacted over the whole *Confessions*. The allegory also represents the highest moment of that return. Thus, it forms a summation of the *Confessions*, even as it does a kind of summary of Scripture. In the allegory of book 13, the speaker arrives at the "origin" of his *confessio*: the clearest and most comprehensive illustration of its informing narrative principle, the return to origins, and the highest realization of its aspiration to be like Scripture. According to the premise of the work, he is led there providentially. Only from the end point of his ongoing *sermo* can Augustine the speaker turn back, as we are doing, to understand how the *voluntas* of Providence has informed the movement of his prayer.

How books 1–9 enact a return to origins remains to be shown. Freccero's analysis of Christian autobiography describes this return in one way, as we have seen: Augustine's autobiography traces the story of his conversion, and without that conversion the story would never be told. Conversion, in Freccero's analysis, proves both the crucial event that enables Christian autobiography and the climactic event of the narrative. Conversion is the *principium* and *finis* of Christian confession.

The *Confessions*, of course, does not end with the narrative of Augustine's conversion, nor does the autobiography of books 1–9. Yet there are several ways in which book 9 recalls book 1 such that one can envision these books as tracing a return to origins. The young Augustine's spiritual progress is concomitant with a return to Christ, in whom he is signed as a newborn: "I was signed with the sign of his cross, and seasoned with his salt, as soon as I issued from my mother's womb" (1.11.17). His physical birth, in book 1, is transcended by his spiritual birth in his conversion. This is perfected in his baptism, in book 9, a sacramental rebirth that orients him wholly toward his Origin.

The chapters on Monica and her death, which conclude book 9, themselves complete a "return to the Origin" in the speaker's meditation. Monica is Augustine's mother both physically and spiritually (9.8.17). In recalling the "vision at Ostia" and her death, Augustine contemplates the return of his origin to her Origin. Thus, the progress of the speaker's text and the spiritual progress of the young Augustine's life both develop, from book 1 to book 9, as a return to origins.

This movement, in fact, proves quite thorough and carefully detailed. My thesis is corroborated by William A. Stephany's "Thematic Structure in Augustine's *Confessions*."[26] Stephany shows that books 1–9 of the *Confessions* are structured as a chiasm. Book 5 proves the physical center of this pattern and the locus of its crucial transitions: from Manichaeism and Faustus in Africa to Italy, Ambrose, and Christianity. Around this center, thematic parallels link books 4 and 6, 3 and 7, 2 and 8, and 1 and 9. This chiastic structure implies a development in books 1–4 that is recapitulated, in reverse order, from books 6–9. That reverse development, I shall argue, constitutes a movement of return to origins.

I should like to summarize Stephany's rich analysis by outlining a few of the parallels he treats. These must serve to illustrate the coherence of his thesis. This outline, then, may provide the basis for further reflection on the significance of the pattern Stephany traces.

Books 1 and 9, according to Stephany, emphasize physical birth and spiritual birth, respectively. Augustine's narrative of his own life begins with his birth (1.6.7) and concludes with his baptism (9.6.14). Book 9 also records the sacramental births of Verecundus, Nebridius, Adeodatus, and Alypius. All except the last are dead when the *Confessions* is written, and Augustine envisions each as born into eternal life. Remembrance of their deaths precedes the vision at Ostia, evoked by a discussion on the nature of eternal life, and Monica's death. These passages resonate against Augustine's wondering whether he had any life before his birth in book 1 (1.6.9). Movement into earthly life (book 1) is counterpointed by movement away from it into the eternal life of heaven (book 9).

Stephany notes that many scholars have observed parallels between books 2 and 8: "both are dominated by a single episode which takes place in a garden with a fruit tree."[27] Both books treat the perversity of human will after the Fall, whether inclined toward evil (book 2) or unable wholly to will good (book 8). Stephany goes on to trace the role of friendship in each. In book 2, the young Augustine's companions lead him to commit acts he would not have otherwise committed. In book 8, the Christian friendship of Simplicianus and Ponticianus leads to his conversion.

In books 3 and 7, the young Augustine discovers crucial texts from pagan philosophy. In book 3, he studies Cicero's *Hortensius* and is inflamed with a love of wisdom. In book 7, he discovers the "books of the Platonists" (7.9.13), which lead to his intellectual conversion. The young Augustine joins the Manichaeans in book 3, partly because they profess to teach the origin of evil and they do not conceive God as "confined within a corporeal form" (3.7.12). These problems are differently solved in book 7. After his intellectual conversion, the young Augustine understands the nature of a spiritual substance and the negative ontological status of evil.

Stephany goes on to trace several parallel details in books 4 and 6. Early in book 4, we are told that the young Augustine has a mistress (4.2.2); late in book 6, he sends her back to Africa (6.15.25). In the former, he is leading others astray, both by converting friends to Manichaeism and by teaching rhetoric for money (4.1.1); in the latter, he seeks a life of *otium*—not *negotium*—to pursue wisdom (6.10.17, 6.14.24) with friends whom he has led *away* from Manichaeism. Most significantly, the two books are counterpointed in their portrayals of friendship. The central event in book 4 is the death of the young Augustine's friend. Theirs is "not a true friendship," which occurs only when cemented by the Holy Spirit in charity (4.4.7). The young man has seduced his friend into Manichaeism and is indignant when the friend affirms that while he was unconscious he was baptized. His death causes Augustine intense and fruitless grief, and this leads to a long meditation against "the love of mortal things" and on the proper object for love (4.6–12). Book 6, in contrast, devotes several chapters to men who helped rectify the young Augustine, Ambrose (6.2–3) and Alypius (6.7–10). For Stephany, this accords with Augustine's portrayal of a different kind of friendship. "In book 6, friendship is moving toward its proper function as Augustine and his friends urge each other, not yet toward Christianity specifically, but at least toward truth and morality." They plan for a life of retirement together in pursuit of wisdom, and Alypius urges the young Augustine away from marriage and toward continence (6.12).

At the center of this pattern of parallels stands book 5. And at the midpoint of its fourteen chapters, Augustine narrates his crucial decision to leave Africa and his departure for Italy. At the end of chapter 7, as Stephany observes, "Faustus's inadequacies have permanently checked [the young] Augustine's enthusiasm for the Manichaean faith." The opening sentences of chapter 8 then describe his decision to go to Rome to teach. Augustine asserts God's Providence in all these developments, his use of "allurements" so that "I would change my residence on earth for the sake of my soul's salvation" (5.8.14). The central chapters of the central book in the autobiography, thus, relate the details of a spiritual and physical movement that lead the young Augustine, beyond his ken, to Ambrose and, eventually, Christianity. Such central placement gives one, as Stephany puts it, "the sense of an imposed balanced structure."

How might one describe the narrative movement within this chiastic structure? Books 1–9 could be seen to trace the young Augustine's spiritual descent and ascent, or movement away from God and return to him. The text conveys a powerful sense of the young Augustine's spiritual progress after he encounters Ambrose in book 5, chapter 13. To be sure, there are details that suggest continuing moral weaknesses, such as taking a concubine after sending his longtime mistress back to Africa (6.15.25). On the whole, however, the young Augustine's moral and intellectual progress seems steady from the time he begins to hear Ambrose preach, in book 5, to his baptism and the vision at Ostia in book 9.

Similarly, books 1–4 seem, at many points, to record gradually increasing perversity in the young Augustine. The bishop criticizes his adolescent behavior, in book 2, far more vehemently than his boyish waywardness in book 1. His attack on his past Manichaean folly in book 3 seems more vituperative still. His intellectual dissatisfaction with Manichaeism, in the first half of book 5, perhaps suggests a nascent amelioration. Yet the bishop sternly criticizes the ruse by which the young Augustine abandons his mother in Carthage and sails alone to Rome (5.8.15). And in the following chapter, the young man's spiritual *dementia* rages as hotly as the fever which nearly takes his life:

> My fever grew worse within me: I was now about to depart and to perish. Where would I have gone, if I had then left this world, except into the fire and torment that were worthy of my deeds, according to the truth of your dispensation? . . . Nor in so great a danger did I desire your baptism: I had been better disposed as a boy, when I had begged for it of my mother's piety, as I have already recorded and confessed. But I had grown in my shame, and, a very madman [*demens*], I scoffed at the healing remedies of you who did not let me as such a man die a twofold death. (5.9.16)

Perilously close to physical as well as spiritual death, the young Augustine is barely preserved from the former that he may be saved from the latter. This refusal of grace *in extremis* represents, arguably, the young man's spiritual nadir. It is narrated in the sixty-seventh of the 134 chapters in books 1–9. Thus, it can be said that the young Augustine is "farthest away from God," at precisely the halfway point of his autobiography. Here is another facet to the mathematical and thematic centrality of book 5. From this moment on, the young Augustine is gradually led to intellectual and moral healing.

In a general way, then, Augustine's autobiography traces a movement of spiritual descent and ascent, movement away from God followed by return to him. The chiastic structure that Stephany details illustrates this movement in formal terms. Representing it algebraically, or in the manner of a rhyme scheme, shows clearly how it progresses as a return to origins: *a b c d e d c b a*. Books 1–4 are thus recapitulated on a higher level in books 6–9: analogous themes, issues, and images are shown in the mode of healing and conversion, rather than disease and perversity. And those parallels, as Stephany shows, are balanced chiastically around the center of the autobiography.

How does the distinction between Augustine the author and Augustine the speaker-writer of his *Confessions* affect our interpretation of this narrative pattern? Its latency, I would argue, suggests that we should not understand it as the speaker's conscious creation.

Augustine the speaker, according to the work's premise, is fully engaged in the process of his unfolding *confessio*. He is praying through and over his past life until it seems appropriate to him to stop. The speaker does not know that this process will continue for nine books. Hence, for example, he cannot have planned the complex centerings that occur in book 5. Engaged in an ongoing prayer that possesses a dynamism of its own, he cannot have planned the chiastic structure of his autobiography. Indeed, that story of his conversion does not end where such stories customarily end, with his conversion. For reasons not made clear in the text, Augustine the speaker continues the record of his past up to the death of his mother. And in the following book, book 10, he embarks on a different kind of project, again with no explicit clarification of his rationale. The design or *ratio* of Augustine's autobiography, as of the whole *Confessions*, does not lie "on its surface." Unlike Dante in the *Commedia*, Augustine does not draw explicit attention to the rational structures or principles of his work. Such structures must be discovered as informing patterns beneath the surface of the speaker's restless prayer.

Augustine the author, of course, has shaped his text so as to embody both the articulations of an "unquiet heart" and deeper, informing structures. According to the premise of the *Confessions*, those structures emerge through God's guiding the speaker's ongoing prayer. The chiastic structure of Augustine's autobiography proves, thus, providential. God's guiding the young Augustine to conversion, the content of the text, proves analogous to God's guiding Augustine's prayerful remembrance of it, the form of the text. Both stand as microcosms or "types" of God's Providence governing all human history.[28]

This, surely, is the message of Scripture, taken as a whole. The seeming chaos of human history is revealed to possess a providential form and meaning, from Creation and Fall to Redemption and eternal life, with the Exodus pattern of exile and return as synecdoche and type of the whole. The pattern of the young Augustine's life recapitulates this providential form, and so does the text that records it. The parable of the prodigal son, as is well known, is the explicit and recurrent model for this pattern of "return" within the text.[29] The pattern, however, occurs throughout Scripture. Indeed, Augustine might well call it the pattern of Scripture, perhaps even the pattern of all human life. As we have seen, it is a linguistic as well as historical pattern for Augustine, one whose progress and fulfillment can be described as a return to the Origin. Books 1–9 trace that movement in detail, as Stephany has shown, in a chiastic structure.

That chiasm reveals the "hand of Providence" in Augustine's text in another way. The simplest chiasm resolves a dyadic parallel structure: *a b b a*. Books 1–9 contain four pairs of parallel books— 1–9, 2–8, 3–7, 4–6—around the center, book 5. Since a double pair creates a single chiasm, a triple pair creates a double chiasm. A quadruple pair, therefore, creates a threefold chiasm. Here is yet another trinitarian structure within the *Confessions*, in the nine books (3 × 3) of the autobiography. According to its premise, here would be yet another sign of God's triune hand in the formation of the text.

Further, a "chiasm" is a rhetorical scheme named after the Greek letter chi. That letter is the first in the name "Christ" when written in Greek. That letter also describes a cross, *X*, whence a "chiasm" is a cross-structure. Since books 1–9 of the *Confessions* are structured chiastically, they contain "the sign of Christ" in their very form. Augustine's autobiography, thus, is "signed with the sign of Christ," as is the infant Augustine at his birth. This is a pattern beyond the ken of Augustine the speaker. According to the premise of the work, it emerges through God's guidance, a sign of its author's hand, a sign of its speaker's vocation and, perhaps, redemption. It is yet one more sign of the parallel between books 1–9 and the "nine acts" of Genesis allegorized in book 13 as "the creation of the Church," Christ's Mystical Body, founded by his redemptive death on the Cross.

5 ✢ Recapitulation

Robert M. Durling treats the pattern of "return to the Origin" in the *Confessions* as a movement of progressive "recapitulation." The Neoplatonic "ascent to principles" progresses to categories of Being ever prior, both temporally and existentially, ever higher in dignity and more comprehensive in scope, until it completes its "return to the One." Each higher mode of contemplation subsumes those beneath it, and so it "recapitulates" them from its encompassing perspective. Durling argues that this principle is fundamental to the poetic form of the *Confessions*. He summarizes his thesis in the following way:

> One must read the beginning in the light of the first principles, which can only be set forth at the end of the entire process. The theme—and the gesture—of *gathering the scattered* inevitably has a central importance. In the *Confessions* one sees this with particular clarity as the nucleus of 7 is expanded to fill 10, expanded again in 11–13, and as, toward the end of 13, all seven days of creation are run through several additional times (first in the longer allegory of the Church, then in two final summaries); the formulae become more and more compressed as the recapitulation approaches its source, the One. The relation to the whole work of the last three books of the *Confessions* gives the pattern for the relation of the *Paradiso* to the rest of the *Commedia*.[1]

Durling's discussion of "recapitulation" in the *Confessions* has been crucial to my thesis. Our descriptions of pattern in the work prove rather different, perhaps due, in part, to his working outward from the center (book 7), while I work retrospectively from the end.

"Recapitulation," however, is not only a Neoplatonic principle but a Christian one. For the early fathers, as John Freccero shows, recapitulation represented both a narrative principle in Scripture and a theory of history:

> *Conversion* is the technical term of the theologians to describe the way the Old Testament was transformed in the light of the New. That trans-

formation is precisely in the form we have been describing, forward motion toward recapitulation. This movement is the essence of the Christian theory of history, referred to by the early Greek fathers of the Church as *anakephalaiosis*, or *recapitulation*. Irenaeus is the Church father most often associated with the theory, which is defined by a modern theologian in words that might equally describe *terza rima*: "It means not just flowing backward to the beginning, but movement forward in time as the integration of the beginning in the end, and this is the significance of the movement itself, insofar as it is at once in time and above time."[2]

Freccero is restating, in slightly different terms, the principle examined in the previous chapter as "return to the Origin." "Recapitulation" describes a forward movement in time that leads back to the beginning: a progress toward principles. The term comes from Ephesians 1:10:

> We are told that the eternal plan of the Father was realized by the Son: "and this His good pleasure He purposed in Him, to be dispensed in the fullness of time: to *re-establish* [recapitulate] all things in Christ, both those in the heavens and those on earth." Thus, Christ is the recapitulation, the fulfillment of the promise and the return to the beginning, as is said in the Gospel of John: "In the beginning was the Word."[3]

Thus, the conversion of the Old Testament to the New reveals the conversion of history: the eternal Word who created the world comes into it in order to bring it back to himself. For Christian-Neoplatonists like Dante and Augustine, Scripture and human history are providentially ordered as a return to the Origin, the recapitulation of all things in Christ, their *principium et finis* (Rev. 22:13).

The language of recapitulation, thus, provides new Christian-Neoplatonist terms to describe the literary form of the *Confessions*. I shall use them to restate and summarize the thesis argued in previous chapters. Here, the narrative structure of the *Confessions* emerges as "a movement forward in time that is simultaneously a recapitulation."[4]

The *Confessions* moves forward in time both in Augustine's life and in its self-presentation as an ongoing prayer. The temporal progress of books 1–9 follows, for the most part, the temporal progress of the young Augustine's life; in book 10, the writer examines the present state of his conscience; in books 11–13, the bishop performs his present and future duty in expounding Scripture; and the final four chapters of the work look forward to the future "sabbath of eternal life" (13.36.51). The *Confessions*, like other literary works, offers itself to be read in a certain temporal order of books and chapters, and these can be said to move forward in time. Further, since the work presents itself as a prayer being made in an ongoing present, it offers itself as composed, as originally occurring, in that temporal order. The *Confessions*, thus, moves forward in time both in its speaker-writer's life and in his prayer-text.

This movement forward in time proves simultaneously a movement "backward," toward origins, as the previous chapter has shown. The salient points of that discussion can now be recapitulated, following the order of the *Confessions*.

In the chiastic structure of Augustine's autobiography, the spiritual regress traced through books 1–4 is reversed, book by book and theme by theme, in the young man's spiritual progress through books 6–9. The young Augustine progresses spiritually by returning to origins: to the Church of his mother, to the Christ whose sign marks him at birth, to an experience of God in the vision at Ostia. And the text of Augustine's autobiography concludes with the death of Monica: the return of his origin to her origin.

In the first five chapters of book 10, Augustine meditates on the origin of the work he is writing. He then begins a return to origins, a philosophical *ascensus*, moving from *exteriora* (10.6) to *interiora* (10.7). This leads him to examine the faculty of memory (10.8–25), the origin of the autobiography he has just completed. In book 11, Augustine begins to examine Scripture, the origin of the faith at the origin of his writing, and he begins at the beginning, with the text on origins. The principle of memory that enables him to write his own history is recapitulated and fulfilled in the text on the origin of all history, inspired by the divine "memory."

Augustine's examination of Genesis begins with his meditating on the "word of God." This meditation itself progresses as a movement toward origins. Augustine first considers the word of God in Scripture (11.3), then God's word creating heaven and earth (11.5–6), and finally God's eternal Word, the *principium* of all things (11.7–9). This forward movement toward "God's Word, the beginning" (11.8.10) leads Augustine to consider the nature of time. Time, of course, is a principle anterior to the text he is writing, to the text he is reading, to the faculty of memory, to the memories recorded in books 1–9. The examination of time in book 11 thus "recapitulates" the previous books of the *Confessions*. Closer to the origin in its object of contemplation, it progresses as a "return to origins" itself by working through inadequate understandings to arrive at the truth.

In book 12, Augustine moves forward in the text of Genesis 1:1 to examine the meaning of "heaven and earth" (12.2–22). Yet this leads him, simultaneously, "backward," to consider objects anterior to time: the matter of Creation and God's "heaven of heaven," both of which stand beyond time.

This movement toward origins then shifts to a hermeneutic meditation: Augustine inquires into the principles that should govern the study of Scripture and into nature of the divine inspiration (12.23–32). Such principles, as principles, are prior to the exegesis Augustine has been engaged in since the beginning of book 11. Even more so is the principle of divine inspiration anterior to the text he is examining. And this shift from considering "heaven and earth" to the principles of Scripture also proves a return to origins. For the Bible is closer to God's eternity than is the timeless matter of creation. "Heaven and earth shall pass" (Matt. 24:35), "the heavens shall vanish like smoke, and the earth shall be worn away like a garment" (Isa. 51:6), but God's "words shall not pass" (Matt. 24:35), "the word of our Lord endureth for ever" (Isa. 40:8). Though the biblical text emerges in time, its Origin and End stand beyond time. According to Augustine, God intends an eternal goal for Scripture: to lead humankind on a return to the Origin, beyond time to his eternity.

Augustine's considering the principles of Scripture subsumes and recapitulates the entire *Confessions* up to that point. Without divine inspiration, the Bible is just another book; studied without the right disposition, it may not lead the Christian to its truth. Scripture founds Augustine's understanding of matter, of creation, and of time. It leads him to consider the faculty of memory in a universal context, the return to origins. It stands at the origin of his conversion, of his Christian faith, and so of his autobiography. The origin of Scripture and the principles of its study, treated at the end of book 12, thus exceed and comprehend Augustine's meditation on the origins of the work he is writing, at the beginning of book 10.

And all these are further recapitulated in the allegory on Genesis

I that concludes the volume. First, that allegory presents itself as "divinely inspired." It purports to scrutinize not simply the biblical text but God's will, the divine intention and Holy Spirit, inspiring it (13.34.49). The allegory thus presents itself as "closer to Scripture" than any other part of the *Confessions*. Equally, its sustained density of biblical quotations also makes it "closer to Scripture" in its very texture. In these ways, it proves nearer to the Origin than the meditation about Scripture that concludes book 12.

The subject of the allegory, the Church, itself comprehends all other subjects in the volume. As the Mystical Body of Christ, it represents the ongoing activity of God's Word in its preaching of God's word in Scripture. Its *magisterium*, for Augustine, comprehends that of the Bible, since the Church is given authority to teach how the text may be understood. Further, like the Word of God it represents and mystically embodies, the Church bridges time and eternity. Though created in time, the Church is an eternal institution, for Augustine: it not only endures past but is perfected by the Last Judgment. It is an institution providentially created and governed for the salvation of humankind, to lead us from time to eternal life.

As an institution with "carnal" as well as "spiritual parts" (13.12.13), the Church comprehends the "heaven and earth" discussed in book 12. It works redemptively amid "the waters" of "this world," transforming material objects into sacramental instruments for salvation (13.20). It labors to bring what is "earthly" and "in time" to heaven and eternity.

Further, since the Church comprehends in its *magisterium* the "memory" recorded in Scripture, it embraces all human memory, including that of its bishop in Hippo (book 10). Likewise, Augustine's personal history has become a part of Church history. The autobiography in books 1–9 record his coming to the Church, where he is a member, a leader, and through which he hopes to attain eternal salvation. Indeed, the young Augustine's creation as a Christian is recapitulated, in great detail, in the allegory on God's creating the Church, as I have shown in chapter 3. The allegory on God's nine acts in the week of Creation parallels, in its progress and central images and themes, the first nine books of the *Confessions*.

The allegory in book 13 offers a vision of such astonishing compass that it could only be "divinely inspired." It envisions the scope of all creation, set forth in Genesis 1, the sweep of all time, from the

Creation to the Last Judgment, and the truths of all Scripture, from Genesis to Revelation, as subsumed in "the creation of the Church." Augustine discovers all of Scripture in its first chapter, and the meaning of all history, for a Christian, in the origin of time. In scrutinizing the origin of the universe in God's intention to create, Augustine discovers the end of Providence: the salvation of humankind through the Church. In the original sabbath, Augustine discovers the final "sabbath of eternal life." In the beginning of Scripture, Augustine discovers its end, and at the end of his *Confessions*, he is led to its beginning: the principles that have informed his prayer as a whole. The return to the origin, revealed in Scripture as the end to universal and individual human history, is completed in the speaker's contemplation of God "forever at rest, for your rest is yourself" (13.38.53). And so the volume comes to a close. The "restless heart" of its very first chapter, the heart that searches so insistently throughout the prayer of the *Confessions*, comes to rest. The *finis* of Augustine's words is joined with their *principium*, and so the work imitates God's word in the whole sweep of Scripture and his eternal Word revealed there.

The *Confessions*, thus, can rightly be considered a microcosm: a literary text embodying patterns fundamental to the universe, as Augustine understood it. Robert M. Durling examines these patterns in some detail, treating the work as "microcosmic in several senses."[5] Here, however, I have considered the *Confessions* more as a process than as a product, more as the prayer of Augustine the speaker, unfolding in an ongoing present, than as the carefully shaped and revised work of Augustine the author. Hence, "microcosm" proves a less appropriate term, in this context. Rather, the "return to the Origin" that unfolds in the speaker's prayer points to the *Confessions* as a type or figure of universal salvation history. For this reason, we might call it a micro-*aion*, from the Greek word for the time of all earthly history.[6]

This micro-aion consists of three parts: Books 1–9, 10–12, and 13. The whole unfolding prayer enacts a return to the Origin, and each part itself enacts a return to origins in different ways. Similarly, the whole of Scripture describes all of history taking place as a return to the Origin, as we have seen. And this process is traditionally said to occur in three stages: the old law, the new law, and their culmination in "future glory." The old law ends with the Incarnation, the conversion of history to its origin, God's Word, as Freccero has shown. The new law ends with his Second Coming, when history "returns to the Origin" in a higher, more perfect way. In "future glory," Augustine believed that God would be "all in all" (1 Cor. 15:28) and the saved would be eternally turned to their origin. Then "everything that is hidden shall be revealed," the mysterious workings of Providence clarified. Analogously, the final part of the *Confessions* contains the scriptural paradigm for the whole prayer: it recapitulates in a "divinely inspired" allegory the whole volume. The trinitarian form of the *Confessions* imitates the trinitarian form of universal history.

And both prove trinitarian because both purport to be providentially governed. The triune God inspires the Scripture that reveals the shape of history. For Augustine, the triune God shapes the course of history, which thus bears a trinitarian stamp. Likewise, according to the premise of the *Confessions*, Augustine's prayer is guided by God. Wander as it often does or leap from one subject to another, its speaker has not planned the course of his *Confessions*, yet he insists that God is leading him. The trinitarian form of this micro-aion thus purports to have been planned by God as it emerges beyond the speaker's ken. Providentially governed, like universal history, it comes to have the same form as universal history: a threefold return to the Origin emerging over time at ever-higher, recapitulatory levels.

In sum, then, Augustine's *Confessions* embodies a fully coherent unity of form and content, of narrative structure and central themes. Our summary formula for this unity is "return to the Origin." For a Neoplatonist, "return to the Origin" describes the Upward Way: a moral imperative and a principle at once ontological, metaphysical, and epistemological in its implications. For a Christian in late antiquity, "return to the Origin" describes the Christian theory of history and of biblical allegory. These two, of course, imply one another; both are suggested in the theological term "recapitulation." "Return to the Origin" also describes the experience of conversion and its ultimate aim, as well as the literary form of the conversion story. Augustine's language theory in the *Confessions* describes the process of communication in a *sermo* as a "return to the origin." "Return to the Origin" thus implies Augustine's central philosophical and theological themes in the *Confessions*; it also describes the formal structure of conversion, conversion-narrative; it even expresses the principle of communication through language, the literary form of the *Confessions* at its most basic level.

"Return to the origin" also describes the narrative progress of the *Confessions* as a whole and over each of its three parts. As a microaion, the work recapitulates the narrative structure of Scripture and of all history, as Augustine understood it. Providentially guided, according to its premise, the volume bears the stamp of the Trinity in its form. In sum, therefore, the *Confessions* recapitulates, on multiple levels and in different ways, the fundamental structures of Being: of the eternal God, of the temporal universe, and of their relationship in the history of salvation. And that recapitulation presents itself as an act of the eternal God, in time, for the salvation of its writer and of all who read him.

Understood in this way, the *Confessions* hardly suffers from the inept planning of which Augustine has so often been accused. And yet lack of plan remains a vital aspect of the work, for Augustine the speaker has little or no plan for his prayer. Indeed, such planlessness is central to Augustine the author's plan: to compose a work whose progress represents, simultaneously yet in different ways, the disorderliness of human history and its deeper, providential structure. The daring scope of Augustine's thinking in the work has long been recognized, but it is nothing second to his equally comprehensive ambition for formal coherence. And such formal coherence demanded a certain obvious lack of form upon a deeper informing order.

Here is the fundamental principle governing the literary form of the *Confessions*: the dialectic between the young Augustine's *errores* and his being led to conversion; between Augustine the speaker's unplanned prayer and the Providence guiding it; ultimately, between the temporary structures and disorderly shiftings of human efforts and God's enduring governance and deeper ordering of history. Augustine's autobiography records the first of these, and the entire *Confessions* presents itself as the second. Both recapitulate—both, for Augustine, are founded in—the Christian vision of history under God's Providence. In this vision, and in the *Confessions*, sin leads to redemption, digressive wanderings become directed movements in an ascent, disorder is founded on and informed by order.

Augustine's genius recapitulates this dialectical vision in the literary form, the narrative structure, of his *Confessions*. The dynamic encounter of Augustine the speaker, in time, with God, in eternity, emerges as a prayer largely planless, on the speaker's part, but deeply ordered by Providence, according to the premise of the work. The

Confessions thus bears the unmistakable stamp of a man, Augustine the speaker, and his God, as Augustine the author understood him. The human experience of difficulty and disorder is represented in the literary form of the work, but equally the triune "return to the Origin" in the Christian vision of history is recapitulated. The fundamental processes of all Being and history, as Augustine understood them, are not only discussed in the *Confessions* but are also recapitulated in its literary form. Augustine the author's conception for his masterpiece proves as sublime as it is daring. For in the surgings and shiftings of events in history, as in those of the *Confessions*, an underlying order is never easily apprehended.

Hence, it would be difficult to discover any literary work more richly unified, more fully coherent, more carefully planned, than Augustine's *Confessions*. In Western literature, perhaps only Dante's *Commedia* can rival it.[7] And yet Dante's poetic fiction of a journey to the other life, unlike Augustine's prose-prayer journey, made in this life, does not so thoroughly embody the dialectic of history and Providence, disorderliness and order. Bold enough to make a seeming formlessness part of his literary form, Augustine the author sustains, on many levels, a rich interplay of content and form, of theme and literary structure, in his *Confessions*, while effacing himself from the work. That such literary unity should present itself as created by the Unity governing the speaker's prayer seems an audacious premise. And yet, perhaps Augustine would say that it signifies only his humble recognition of the truth.

In this book, I have arrived at an understanding of literary form in the *Confessions* by treating the text, for the most part, intrinsically. I have examined certain patterns and relations within the work, though I have treated them as informed by a principle that informs all being and history, as Augustine conceived them. Broadly formalist in method, though not in theory, the foregoing pages have considered the *Confessions* in isolation, as it were, from its author and his readers.

Hence, we might now inquire into the extrinsic relations of literary form in Augustine's masterpiece. How might this form have functioned for its author? How might he have envisioned it functioning for his readers? Granted, response to these questions must needs be speculative. Yet if we fail to entertain such considerations, we abandon the literary form of the *Confessions* to solitary confinement, and our imaginations fail Augustine's grand design.

Such speculation seems warranted by Augustine's explicit treatment, at the beginning of book 10, of his motives for writing and his readers' for reading. That inquiry begins a new movement in the work, one Kenneth Burke rightly calls a "conversion": a turning toward principles.[8] Given the number of chapters in the volume (278), it takes place almost precisely at the mathematical center: occurring between chapters 135 and 139 of the whole, it completes the first half. The inquiry into motives, thus, proves thematically and mathematically central to the *Confessions*. At the core, at the heart of the volume, Augustine regards his intentions and looks toward those of his readers. He answers the implied question Why am I writing? for himself and for them. Phrased by Augustine the writer-speaker regarding the prayer he is setting down, his answers may be reconsidered in terms of Augustine the author and the literary form of the whole *Confessions*.

Briefly put, Augustine avers that he is confessing in order to know God and himself. He begins book 10 with the prayer "May I know you, my knower, may I know you even as I am known" (*Cognoscam te, cognitor meus, cognoscam sicut ut et cognitus sum,* 10.1.1). For Augustine, of course, the self cannot be known apart from God, nor can one know the original to whose "image and likeness" a person is made without thereby knowing oneself. When he considers his readers, he hopes that his *Confessions* may rouse up their hearts (*excitant cor,* 10.3.4) toward God and his merciful love. From these avowals, we may begin to speculate on how Augustine the author envisioned the literary form of his work functioning vis-à-vis himself and his readers.

First, that literary form constitutes an act of self-knowledge: the author understands himself in terms of the most comprehensive categories available to his thinking. This has long been recognized as an explicit theme of the work. Peter Brown observes that the incidents of the young Augustine's life "are always placed in relation to the most profound philosophical concepts available to a Late Antique man: they embodied, for Augustine, the great themes of the Neo-Platonic tradition in its Christian form; they are suffused with a sense of the omnipresence of God, and they illustrate the fatal play of forces in a wandering soul, the tragedy of a man 'disintegrated' by the passing of time."[9] For similar reasons, Solignac finds a "universal value" in the young Augustine's life, "a universality which is not only that of a *type* of existence, but indeed that of a destiny understood in the history of universal Redemption."[10]

This study of literary form in the *Confessions* strengthens these perceptions and takes them even further. For Augustine does not merely understand his destiny within the history of universal Redemption; every Christian, as a Christian, does (or should do) that. Rather, the author creates detailed parallels between his autobiography and the allegory in book 13. That allegory, let us recall, embraces the scope of Creation, the sweep of all time, the substance and course of all Scripture, and the meaning of all history, salvation in the Church. Augustine's self-history thus imitates the scope, sweep, and meaning of all the universe, as both are set forth in the *Confessions*. Augustine does not thereby merely present himself as a microcosm in general or in principle: his autobiography recapitulates the "divinely inspired meaning" of the cosmos and its history stage by stage, with rich interconnections of imagery and theme.

Noverim me, noverim te, in this light, takes on new meaning. To be sure, Augustine the speaker understands God's will for his own life in terms of God's redemptive intention for all history. Augustine the author, however, elaborates a detailed understanding of his own life and text as fully integrated with the scope, sweep, and meaning of the universe. Through the narrative and theological principles implied in "return to the Origin," he provides a thorough account of his own being in terms of all Being, an interpenetration of all levels of meaning.[11] Just as the allegory recapitulates the whole volume in its comprehensive vision, so is the autobiography richly infused by that understanding of God's will in Genesis, the cosmos, Scripture, history, time, and eternity. For Augustine the author, the literary form of the *Confessions* involves a fully integrated vision of himself in terms of everything, and of everything as it informs himself.

Such a thoroughgoing vision should also be understood as an act of worship by its author. The *Confessions* explicitly presents itself as an offering to God, a "sacrifice of praise," by Augustine the speaker. Equally, we may construe the author's latent design for the work as an act of praise and as an intellectual-spiritual exercise of great depth and rigor. Augustine modeled his work on God's work. Composing his micro-aion thus involved the author's sustained consideration of

God's plan in the macro-aion. Elaborating its details, occulting its plan in a seeming planlessness, demanded devotion and study. The aesthetic pleasure that formalism customarily ascribes to the perception of literary form was doubtlessly enjoyed by him. But we may be sure that such pleasure, for Augustine, participated in a nobler aim: the contemplation of God's will, as an act of worship and of praise.

The literary form of the *Confessions* also acts upon its readers. As I argued in chapter 1, its self-presentation as a prayer forces readers to impersonate—to take on the persona of—Augustine the speaker. One cannot read the *Confessions* without praying Augustine's prayer, without addressing God. One cannot read the volume without taking up, in one's own first person, the speaker's *inquisitio veritatis*. Even before Augustine's rhetorical powers begin to "rouse up the hearts" of his readers, the *Confessions* engages them in prayer to God from its very first words. The persuasive force of this literary strategy can hardly be overestimated.

Further, all readers of the whole volume necessarily follow the "return to the Origin" it traces. Readers not only hear Augustine's theories of language and history, of Scripture and Creation, of Being and "return to the Word": they are also led on a narrative progress that recapitulates the principle informing these universal structures. Willy-nilly, the reader of the *Confessions* prays; willy-nilly, he journeys on a "return to the Origin." Such pilgrim's progress is doubtlessly beyond the reader's ken, as it is beyond Augustine the speaker's, but pursue it every reader does.

But what persuasive force can an unperceived literary structure have? Some might argue "little or none," locating the most powerful influence of a work in its explicit meanings. Others would argue that subliminal informing patterns prove rhetorically powerful, even though the explicit "verbal action" of a work remains primary. The rhetorical effectiveness of modern advertising might suggest that rousing subliminal feelings and associations conveys a message quite effectively.

Late antique rhetoric itself recognized a similar principle. Longinus, treating the persuasive force of rhetorical figures, argues that a concealed figure proves more effective than an apparent one:

> The unconscionable use of figures is peculiarly subject to suspicion, and engenders impressions of hidden traps and plots and fallacies. . . . Thus a

rhetorical figure would appear to be most effective when the fact that it is a figure is not apparent.

Sublimity and the expression of strong feelings are, therefore, a wonderfully helpful antidote against the suspicion that attends the use of figures. *The cunning artifice remains out of sight, associated from now on with beauty and sublimity, and all suspicion is put to flight.*[12]

For Longinus, the formal pattern that functions without drawing attention to itself disarms "suspicion" and comes to be felt as "beauty and sublimity."

Longinus is articulating a particular application of a principle widely held in ancient times, if much debated: that the greatest art disguises its artificiality to appear "as nature." *Ars latet sua arte.* Augustine finds a form of this principle functioning in the Bible. In the *Confessions*, he praises the simplicity of Scripture, rich with meaning and wisdom, even as he criticizes the young Augustine's fascination with Ciceronian grandeur (3.5.9). So, too, in the *De doctrina Christiana*, he finds "eloquence" appearing in the Bible not as though through the rules of art but as naturally: "And in those places where by chance eloquence is recognized by the learned, such things are said that the words with which they are said *seem not to have been sought by the speaker but to have been joined to the things spoken about as if spontaneously,* like wisdom coming from her house (that is, from the breast of the wise man) followed by eloquence as if she were an inseparable servant who was not called."[13]

Augustine, therefore, need not have read Longinus's work in order to have encountered his doctrine of the "concealed figure." It may well have been current in the schools where Augustine studied or taught. If not, he surely possessed the abilities to work it out for himself from the principle of "natural [seeming] eloquence." Geoffrey of Vinsauf, in the thirteenth century, treats the superior effectiveness of "covert" to "open" comparison (*collatio*), and he certainly did not read Longinus.[14] Either an oral tradition of the doctrine endured, or Geoffrey rediscovered it for himself. Augustine, closer to Longinus's tradition and a much greater writer than Geoffrey, surely understood the power of hidden patterns in a work.

In the *Confessions*, we see him practicing that doctrine to "rouse up the hearts" of his readers to God. The work's literary form carries its readers "upward," through progressively higher stages, on a "return to the Origin." Augustine understood that return to be profoundly *natural*. The desire to return to God was fundamental to the human heart: at the root of human nature, it flourished in God's design for the cosmos and its history. "Return to the Origin" was a principle that informed everything, for Augustine and his Christian-Neoplatonist contemporaries. They felt deeply the reality, the natural necessity, of that return.

Augustine, therefore, appealed to deep convictions in his audience by informing his work so deeply with that principle. He understood the literary form of his *Confessions* to address not only their deepest conceptions but also their very nature and deepest desire, as souls in exile from the true *patria*. "Return to the Origin" proves a literary form designed to act upon its readers even beyond their ken. High in its aims, both literally and figuratively, grand in its design, which imitates God's, the literary form of the *Confessions* proves essentially sublime, however subliminal, as it seeks to sublimate its readers' hearts for their own journeys to God.

Notes

Introduction

1. Solignac, "Introduction," pp. 19–26, and Trapé, "Introduzione," pp. xvi–xxiv, provide brief introductions to the scholarship. Luongo, "Autobiografia ed esegesi biblica nelle *Confessioni*," offers a fuller, and more recent, treatment.

2. See Courcelle, *Recherches*, p. 21, and O'Meara, *Young Augustine*, pp. 13–17.

3. Verheijen, *Eloquentia pedisequa, observations sur le style des "Confessions" de saint Augustin*, traces Augustine's use of these words throughout the *Confessions*.

4. Solignac, "Introduction," p. 20, his italics. He quotes Landsberg, "La conversion de saint Augustin," p. 33. All translations from works of scholarship in this book are my own unless otherwise noted.

5. See Cooper, "Why Did Augustine Write Books XI–XIII," pp. 42–46; Flores, "Reading and Speech in St. Augustine's *Confessions*." Flores uses the approach developed by Eugene Vance, "Augustine's *Confessions* and the Grammar of Selfhood," and Marcia Colish, *The Mirror of Language*, pp. 18–49.

6. See Landsberg, "La conversion," and Le Blond, *Les Conversions de saint Augustin*, p. 17.

7. See Pfligersdorffer, "Das Bauprincip Von Augustins *Confessions*." See Luongo's response, "Autobiografia ed esegesi," p. 294.

8. Trapé, "Introduzione," p. xxii.

9. This paper was presented at the Eleventh International Conference on Patristic, Mediaeval, and Renaissance Studies held at Villanova University, October 10–12, 1986. In Verheijen's absence, the paper was presented by Frederick Van Fleteren.

10. See Brown, *Augustine of Hippo*.

11. Durling, "The Ascent of Mt. Ventoux and the Crisis of Allegory," pp. 17–25.

12. Consider, for example, O'Meara, *Young Augustine*, pp. 173–85. O'Meara examines the literary relations among the conversion stories in book 8 in order to answer historical questions.

13. Burke expounds the principle that literary form acts upon readers in his early essay, "Lexicon Rhetoricae," in *Counter-Statement*, pp. 123–83; see especially pp. 123–49.

14. See O'Meara, *Young Augustine*, and Brown, *Augustine of Hippo*.

15. Solignac, "Introduction," p. 24.

16. Ibid., p. 14, his italics.

17. Kenneth Burke, *The Rhetoric of Religion*, p. 124, his italics.

18. Solignac, "Introduction," p. 24.

19. Chapter 4 examines this nexus of ideas in some detail; they have been recurrent themes in Freccero's work on Dante. See *Dante*, especially "Medusa: The Letter and the Spirit," pp. 119–35, and "The Significance of Terza Rima," pp. 258–71.
20. Burke, *Rhetoric of Religion*, p. 156.
21. See Burke, *Grammar of Motives*, pp. 420–30. Unfortunately, Burke's highly suggestive remarks have gone largely unnoticed in scholarship on Plato. Charles L. Griswold, Jr., develops a similar position on the *Phaedrus* in his book *Self-Knowledge in Plato's "Phaedrus."* He argues that the dialogue develops through a progress of "palinodes," each successive "section" encompassing and critically reflecting upon the previous one.
22. On this score, I follow the pioneering studies of John Freccero and Robert M. Durling, both of whom have explored the Augustinian literary principles of Dante's poem. Freccero's most important essays have been collected in *Dante*. Durling has articulated his thinking on Platonist poetics in public lectures over many years and in personal conversations with me. One finished statement of his views was presented as a lecture, "Platonism and Poetic Form." I am grateful to Durling for giving me a copy of this talk, which is now in circulation.
23. The Neoplatonist elements in Boethius's *Consolatio* have been widely studied, and Seth Lerer has recently discussed the work's literary form as a *gradus*—an ascent—in *Boethius and Dialogue*. I describe the Platonist principles underlying Burke's book in "Kenneth Burke's Divine Comedy: The Literary Form of *The Rhetoric of Religion*," forthcoming in *PMLA*.
24. See Ferguson, "Saint Augustine's Region of Unlikeness," and Vance, "Augustine's *Confessions* and the Grammar of Selfhood."

Chapter 1: The Self-Presentation of the *Confessions*

1. Brown, *Augustine*, pp. 166–67.
2. Ibid., p. 167.
3. Solignac, "Introduction," pp. 12–13, his italics.
4. G. Bouissou, "Le Style," chapter 7 in Solignac's "Introduction," p. 223.
5. Oroz Reta, "Priere et Recherche de Dieu," p. 118.
6. Christine Mohrmann, "Considerazioni sulle *Confessioni* di Santi Agostino," part 1, "Le *Confessioni* come opera letteraria," in *Etudes sur le latin des Chretiens*, 2:282.
7. O'Meara, *Young Augustine*, p. 13.
8. Ibid., p. 13. Courcelle also finds the work poorly planned; see his *Recherches*, p. 21. See also O'Meara's reply, *Young Augustine*, pp. 14–17.
9. See James J. O'Donnell's judicious remarks on the differences between private prayer and prayer as a public literary form in the *Confessions*, in *Augustine*, pp. 82–83.
10. 1.1.1; all translations from the work are by John K. Ryan in *The Confessions of St. Augustine*.
11. All Latin quotations from the *Confessions* are taken from the Skutella-Verheijen edition in the Corpus Christianorum Series Latina, vol. 27.

12. Bouissou points to this text as a sign of God's action on Augustine's prayer, in "Le Style," p. 223.
13. O'Meara, *Young Augustine*, p. 13.
14. For a general treatment of the differences between "textuality" and orality in culture, see Ong, *Orality and Literacy*.
15. Its compositional stages do not, however, lie beyond scholarly speculation. E. Williger has argued that book 10 of the *Confessions* was interpolated into an original version in which the present book 11 followed immediately after book 9. See Williger, "Der Aufbau der *Konfessionen* Augustins," especially pp. 103–6. He has been followed by Courcelle (*Recherches*, p. 25) and others. See Luongo's critique of this view, "Autobiografia ed esegesi," pp. 296–301.
16. See William E. Mann, "Theft of the Pears," especially pp. 54–57.
17. See, for example, Jaroslav Pelikan: "Even though he might not have done it without the company of his peer group who egged him on, it was not their companionship but the theft itself that he loved" (*Jesus through the Centuries*, p. 78).
18. Courcelle, *Recherches*, p. 23.
19. O'Meara, *Young Augustine*, p. 16; Courcelle's theory is discussed on pp. 14–17 of O'Meara's book.

Chapter 2: The Conclusion of the *Confessions*

1. The problem is clearly seen by Max Zepf, *Augustins Confessiones*, p. 14, and by Courcelle, *Recherches*, pp. 23–24.
2. Flores, "Reading and Speech in St. Augustine's *Confessions*," p. 12.
3. Vance, "Augustine's *Confessions* and the Grammar of Selfhood," p. 6, sees this clearly.
4. See Mohrmann, "Le *Confessioni* come opera letteraria," in *Etudes sur le latin des Cretiens*, 2:282. See Henri-Irenee Marrou's judicious discussion of the problem in *Saint Augustin et la fin de la culture antique*, 1:59–76.
5. Solignac, "Notes," 14:622–29.
6. F. Cayré, "Le livre XIII des *Confessions*," pp. 144 and 146.
7. Solignac, "Introduction," pp. 13–14, his italics.
8. Pellegrino, Le *"Confessioni"* di Sant'Agostino, p. 198.
9. See the Skutella-Verheijen edition of *Confessionum Libri XIII*, their notes on sources for book 7.9.15.
10. First noted by Flores, "Reading and Speech in St. Augustine's *Confessions*," p. 12.
11. Solignac, "Introduction," p. 24.
12. See Augustine's *De civitate Dei* 16.3, *Patrologia Latina* 41, 479. I am grateful to Irven M. Resnick for these references on the significance of the number seventy-two.

Chapter 3: Book 13 and Books 1–9

1. The Hebrew Bible and the Vulgate do not record that God saw his second act, the creation of the firmament, as good. Augustine's Old Latin version follows the

Septuagint in adding to Gen. 1:8 the words "And God saw that it was good." See Augustine's *De Genesi ad litteram*, 2.1. See also his *The Literal Meaning of Genesis*, translated by John Hammond Taylor, S.J., and Taylor's note on 2.1.

2. See Pizzolato, *Le "Confessioni" di Sant'Agostino*, and his *Le fondazioni dello stile delle "Confessioni" di Sant'Agostino*, where he deepens his earlier analysis.

3. See Luongo, "Autobiografia ed esegesi biblica nelle *Confessioni* di Agostino," pp. 290–92, for his evaluation of Pizzolato and for a bibliography on other reviews of the thesis.

4. Durling, "Platonism and Poetic Form." Durling has been thinking about these issues for many years and informs me that his thesis has been presented in different forms, at several institutions.

5. The work of Leo C. Ferrari is one significant exception to the generalization made above. His essays attend to patterns of imagery in the *Confessions* in a way that is informed by, and that informs, the historical and philosophical study of Augustine. His essays are cited in the bibliography. Readers unfamiliar with this approach might well begin with "Pear-Theft" and "Barren Field."

6. The allegory in book 13 deserves more careful study than it has received. Cayré's "Le livre XIII des *Confessions*" remains a fine introduction to its structure and to its role in the work.

7. In presenting the biblical text, I quote from Augustine's Latin version as it appears in his *Confessions* and from John K. Ryan's translation of Augustine. Ryan notes that in his translation "Biblical quotations in English are adaptations of the traditional Rheims-Douai version." See his introduction, p. 38. My own quotations from Scripture are all taken from the Douai-Rheims translation, unless otherwise noted.

8. Durling, "Platonism and Poetic Form."

9. Because Durling's paper was presented as a public lecture, it does not fully elaborate his thinking on Gen. 1 in books 1–7. It treats, and that briefly, only days (and books) 1, 4, and 7. Undoubtedly, Durling's thinking could have informed my treatment of books 2 and 3, as well as book 1. In book 4, however, I look for correspondences with God's fourth *act*, which occurs on the *third* day. From that point on, our theses diverge.

10. See Solignac's discussion of *creatio-formatio* in his "Notes," 14:613–17.

11. Freccero, "Logology," pp. 58–59, my italics.

12. Burke, *Rhetoric of Religion*, p. 94, his italics. See also Ferrari, "Pear-Theft." Ferrari's other studies of book 2 deserve attention not only for their insights but for the ways he employs a literary methodology in conjunction with philosophical and theological concerns; see "Symbols of Sinfulness" and "Arboreal Polarization."

13. For sea imagery generally in Augustine, see Rondet, "Le symbolisme de la mer chez saint Augustine." Pizzolato points to sea imagery throughout books 2–6 and links it to the instability of *adolescentia*, in *Le "Confessioni" di Sant'Agostino*.

14. The text implies that the Manichaean "waters" are "stolen" from the pure fountain of Scripture. Drinking the "bitter waters" of Manichaean doctrine, however, is like drinking seawater: it increases thirst and makes one ill.

15. See Ferrari, "Monica on the Wooden Ruler," for a rich treatment of this image.
16. The autobiography begins in chapter 6 of book 1. The paean to God's eternal transcendence in 1.4.4, thus, is excluded from my generalization.
17. Ferrari traces this strand of imagery in "Barren Field"; he cites this passage on pp. 62–63.
18. This is given as the first definition of *infelix* in the *Oxford Latin Dictionary*, ed. P. G. W. Glare (Oxford: Clarendon Press, 1982).
19. See Ferrari, "Barren Field," p. 67.
20. The distinction between the "natural order" of narration in the historical sequence of "events" and an "artificial order" that manipulates sequence is standard in medieval *artes poetriae*. E. R. Curtius notes that Macrobius, Augustine's contemporary, makes a similar distinction between history and poetry in *Saturnalia* 5.2.9 and 5.14.11. See Curtius, *European Literature and the Latin Middle Ages*, p. 455. Another significant exception to the "natural order" of the *Confessions* is treated in section VII of this chapter. Consider also the report of Adeodatus's death in 9.6.14. Monica dies earlier than her grandson in history but later in the text of the *Confessions*. I am grateful to Robert M. Durling for pointing this out to me.
21. William A. Stephany emphasizes this point in an unpublished paper, "Thematic Structure in Augustine's *Confessions*." I am grateful to him for sending me a copy of it. I discuss his thesis in chapter 4.
22. Out of the nine "gifts of the Spirit" named in 1 Cor. 12:7–11, Augustine lists eight, dropping off "interpretation of speeches" (12:10). Augustine states that these gifts "have been narrated in order, like the stars" (*donorum, quae deinceps tamquam stellae commemmorata sunt*, 13.18.23). "Stars," here, clearly means the planets of the geocentric cosmology. Such is the primary meaning of *stella*, and only such "stars," revolving in their concentric spheres, could be "narrated in order." Augustine explicitly links "wisdom" to the sun, and "knowledge" to the moon. His text implies, by its narrated order, these other correlations: "faith"—Mercury; "healing"—Venus; "miracles"—Mars; "prophecy"—Jupiter; "discerning of spirits"—Saturn; "divers tongues"—the fixed stars. Some of these correlations possess an obvious logic: the diversity of "tongues" to the multitude of stars; Mercury, the "messenger of the gods," to "faith"; perhaps Saturn, the planet associated with probing thought, to the "discerning of spirits." The logic governing the others is by no means so clear, though not beyond speculation. It would seem that Augustine is implying a Christian revision of astrological theories of "heavenly influence."
23. Stephany touches on these points, treating Ambrose and Faustus as "mirror images," in "Thematic Structure in Augustine's *Confessions*."
24. Equally, the "waters of the sea" here can be read as a metaphor for the young Augustine's Manichaeism. Since it occurs while the writer describes slipping away from Monica to sail alone to Italy, its explicit reference seems historical, with allegorical resonances.
25. The imagery is also used for Alypius. His love for gladiatorial contests arises from "the maelstrom of Carthaginian customs" (*gurges morum Carthaginiensum*) that "suck him down" (*absorbuerat*, 6.7.11). Also his love for the young Augustine

leads him to become "involved in that superstition" of Manichaeism (*illa mecum superstitione involutus est*, 6.7.12). *Involutus* implies being "rolled about in" the stormy sea of heresy.

26. 6.7.12; see the end of 6.8.13 and the second sentence of 6.9.14 for other assertions that the young Alypius is learning lessons useful to the future bishop. Note also, in the above passage, that God is the *gubernator*, the steersman at the helm (*gubernaculum*) of all things: another nautical image in book 6.

27. *Confessions* 6.8 contains Augustine's dramatic portrayal of Alypius's fascination with gladiatorial contests. The passage has received a trenchant stylistic analysis by Eric Auerbach in *Mimesis*, pp. 66–76. Lawrence Rothfield explores the relations between the passage in book 6 and the young Augustine's conversion in book 8. See his "Autobiography and Perspective in the *Confessions* of St. Augustine."

28. As is well known, ancient physiology understood semen to be "perfect blood," i.e., made from blood by a special process of "digestion" that gives it the formative power to impregnate a mother's blood. See Aristotle's *The Generation of Animals*, 720a, 726a–b, 737, 765–66, and passim. Hence the male orgasm involves the "loss of blood." The popular correlation between orgasm and death is quite ancient. It governs the "die pun" in English literature, late in its history, as well as the patristic and monastic critique of sexual intercourse. Orgasm is "a little death," and for Augustine that understanding has moral connotations as well as physical.

29. Augustine recurrently yet subtly links the etymons of *forma* and *firma* paronomastically. The *forma* of Christian doctrine is closely related to the firmament of Scripture and to the "dry land" of the faithful. In books 1–9 true *formatio* is always linked with Christianity and its eternal truths, with "solid faith" and continence. *Formatio* after the values of "this world," in contrast, is always portrayed as *deformatio*, "conformity to this world" of unstable, temporal cares, chaotic and "watery." Such *deformatio* leads to the young Augustine's *infirmitas*. He can only be made firm by turning away from the watery desires of the flesh so as to "be reformed in newness of mind" (13.22.32; Rom. 12:2).

30. Durling, "Platonism and Poetic Form."

31. Ibid., my italics.

32. Ibid.

33. Nor is the theme featured in book 5, though it is mentioned there briefly in 5.3.5, quoting Rom. 1:20, and 5.12.22.

34. See O'Connell, *St. Augustine's "Confessions,"* pp. 29–30, where this rich strand of imagery is treated as a "Lexicon of Happiness" derived from the *De beata vita.*

35. Marcia Colish makes a similar point in *The Mirror of Language*, p. 32; O'Meara suggests it in *Young Augustine*, p. 178. I do not wish to argue that the historical Augustine came to belief in the Incarnation and dedicated himself to continence at the same moment. That is a separate issue. See Courcelle, *Les Confessions*, pp. 59–67, and more recently, Anton C. Pegis, "The Second Conversion of St. Augustine."

36. Augustine's vision of his life as integrated with the meaning of the cosmos in history suggests that we revise our current understanding of his self-representa-

tion in the *Confessions*. Recent work in the history and theory of autobiography has paid considerable attention to this issue. See, among others, Weintraub, *Value of the Individual*; Spengemann, *Forms of Autobiography*; and Gunn, *Autobiography*.

37. For a rich discussion of microcosmic patterns in the *Confessions* in Neoplatonist terms, see Durling, "Platonism and Poetic Form." I quote Durling's summary statement of his argument at the beginning of chapter 5.

Chapter 4: Book 13 and Books 10–12

1. Burke, *Rhetoric of Religion*, p. 124, his italics.
2. See ibid., pp. 123–24, and 141–57, especially 155–57, for a summary statement. I treat Burke's argument in greater detail later in this chapter.
3. Solignac, "Introduction," pp. 23–24.
4. See especially the essays collected in *Dante*. His ideas are discussed in some detail, below.
5. Burke, *Rhetoric of Religion*, p. 27.
6. See also Eugene Vance's discussion of this principle in "Augustine's *Confessions*," pp. 11–13, and "Saint Augustine."
7. See Burke, *Rhetoric of Religion*, pp. 50–51, 81, 141–55, especially 141–43.
8. I capitalize "Origin" when the term obviously refers to God but write "return to the origin" (lowercase letters) when the phrase refers primarily to a linguistic or literary structure. Clearly, however, Augustine's use of the linguistic analogy derives from his theological beliefs. Hence, "return to the origin" often modulates toward "return to the Origin," much as Augustine's use of the phrase *verbum Dei* often shifts its primary reference from God's word in Scripture to God's Word, Christ.
9. Freccero, "Logology," p. 61.
10. Ibid., pp. 62–63.
11. Freccero discusses this text in "Medusa: The Letter and the Spirit," in *Dante*, pp. 119–35. This article, first published in 1972, marks his first full statement of the formal analogies I am setting forth here. These principles have proven the basis of his recent Dante criticism. They are also set forth in "The Significance of Terza Rima," in *Dante*, pp. 258–71, and in other essays in that volume.
12. Freccero, "Logology," p. 64.
13. Freccero examines this passage in "Logology," pp. 63–64, and in "Terza Rima," in *Dante*, pp. 270–71.
14. Verheijen, "The *Confessions*"; see my introduction for a brief summary of Verheijen's thesis.
15. Crouse, "'Recurrens in te unum,'" p. 392.
16. Ibid., p. 391.
17. Ibid., p. 389, 392.
18. Burke, *Rhetoric of Religion*, p. 156.
19. Ibid., p. 124, his italics.
20. Burke summarizes this argument on pp. 155–57; he first outlines it on pp. 123–24.

21. Ibid., p. 124.
22. For a detailed discussion of the chapters opening book 10, see O'Donnell, "Augustine, *Confessions* 10.1.1–10.4.6."
23. Luongo emphasizes the point, "Autobiografia," pp. 299–300.
24. Paul Ricoeur offers a careful exposition of the progress of this inquiry in *Time and Narrative*, 1:5–30.
25. William C. Spengemann divides the volume into the same three parts for different, though often analogous, reasons; see *Forms of Autobiography*, pp. 1–6.
26. I am grateful to Prof. Stephany for permission to report his argument in some detail. This does not, of course, imply that he agrees with the way I go on to describe the narrative movement in the pattern he traces or the use to which I put his insights.
27. See Burke, *Rhetoric of Religion*, pp. 93–117, and Ferrari, "Pear-Theft" for more extensive treatments of these relations.
28. Stephany introduces and concludes his paper by exploring Augustine's rationale in the order he imposes on his autobiography. In closing he argues that the literary order that Augustine the author crafts into his narrative "helps his readers to perceive the hand of the Craftsman who truly did impose order upon the experiences of his life."
29. See Ferrari, "Theme of the Prodigal Son."

Chapter 5: Recapitulation

1. Durling, "Platonism and Poetic Form," his italics. I would argue that only the allegory in book 13 proves analogous to the *Paradiso*.
2. Freccero, "The Significance of *Terza Rima*," in *Dante*, p. 266, his italics; he is quoting Hans Urs von Balthasar, *Man in History*, p. 116.
3. Freccero, *Dante*, p. 267, his italics. For the doctrine, Freccero refers to E. Scharl, *Recapitulatio mundi*.
4. Freccero, *Dante*, p. 265.
5. Durling, "Platonism and Poetic Form."
6. I have preferred *aion* to the normal English version of the word, "aeon," precisely because "aeon" does not have connotations of salvation history. Edward Schillebeeckx defines the Greek *aion* as "time, time of life, period of time; hence, the time of the world's existence as the time of the whole of earthly history; finally also eternity" (*Christ*, p. 899).
7. James J. O'Donnell makes a similar judgment from different criteria: "No other work of Christian literature does what Augustine accomplishes in this volume; only Dante's *Commedia* even rivals it" (*Augustine*, p. 82).
8. Burke, *Rhetoric of Religion*, pp. 123 and 155.
9. Brown, *Augustine of Hippo*, p. 168.
10. Solignac, "Introduction," p. 14, his italics.
11. My language, here, draws on that of Durling to describe Dante's use of microcosmic form in his *rime petrose*; see "'Io son venuto,'" p. 114. Durling's treatment of the *Confessions* implies the understanding I am arguing here.

12. Longinus, *On the Sublime*, p. 127, chap. 17, my italics. I am grateful to Robert M. Durling for directing me to Longinus's doctrine.
13. Saint Augustine, *On Christian Doctrine*, p. 124 (4.6.10), my italics; Augustine illustrates his point in the following chapter.
14. See Geoffrey of Vinsauf, *Poetria Nova*, lines 241–63. I have used the edition and translation of Ernest Gallo, *The Poetria Nova and Its Sources in Early Rhetorical Doctrine*. Gallo does not treat the source, if any, for "covert comparison."

Bibliography

Aristotle. *Generation of Animals.* Translated by A. Platt. In *The Complete Works of Aristotle,* Vol. 1. Edited by Jonathan Barnes. Bollingen Series 71. Princeton: Princeton University Press, 1984.

Auerbach, Eric. *Mimesis: The Representation of Reality in Western Literature.* Translated by Willard R. Trask. Princeton: Princeton University Press, 1953.

Augustine. *The Confessions of St. Augustine.* Translated by John K. Ryan. New York: Image, 1960.

_____. *Confessionum Libri XIII.* Edited by Martin Skutella. Revised by Lucas Verheijen, O.S.A. Corpus Christianorum Series Latina, 27. Turnholt: Brepols, 1981.

_____. *De civitate Dei.* Edited by Migne. Patrologia Latina, 41.

_____. *On Christian Doctrine.* Translated, with an introduction, by D. W. Robertson, Jr. Indianapolis: Bobbs-Merrill, 1980.

Augustine, St. *The Literal Meaning of Genesis.* Translated and annotated by John Hammond Taylor, S.J. Ancient Christian Writers, no. 41. New York: Newman Press, 1982.

Bouissou, G. "Le Style des *Confessions.*" In A. Solignac, "Introduction." *Les Confessions,* pp. 207–35. Bibliotheque Augustinienne, vol. 13. Paris: Descleé De Brouwer, 1962.

Brown, Peter. *Augustine of Hippo.* Berkeley: University of California Press, 1967.

Burke, Kenneth. *A Grammar of Motives.* Berkeley: University of California Press, 1969.

_____. *Counter-Statement.* 2d ed. Berkeley: University of California Press, 1968.

_____. *The Rhetoric of Religion: Studies in Logology.* Berkeley: University of California Press, 1970.

Cayré, F. "Le livre XIII des *Confessions.*" *Revue des Etudes Augustiniennes* 2 (1956): 143–61.

Colish, Marcia. *The Mirror of Language: A Study in the Medieval Theory of Language.* Rev. ed. Lincoln, Nebr.: University of Nebraska Press, 1983.

Cooper, John C. "Why Did Augustine Write Books XI–XIII of the *Confessions?*" *Augustinian Studies* 2 (1971): 37–46.

Courcelle, Pierre. *Les "Confessions" de saint Augustin dans la tradition littéraire, antécédents et posterité.* Paris: Etudes Augustiniennes, 1963.

_____. *Recherches sur les Confessions de saint Augustin.* Paris: De Boccard, 1950.

Crouse, R. D. "'*Recurrens in te unum*': The Pattern of St. Augustine's *Confessions.*" *Studia Patristica* 14 (Texte und Untersuchungen, 117), pp. 389–92. Berlin: Akademie Verlag, 1976.

Curtius, Ernst Robert. *European Literature and the Latin Middle Ages*. Translated by Willard R. Trask. Bollingen Series 36. Princeton: Princeton University Press, 1973.

Durling, Robert M. "The Ascent of Mt. Ventoux and the Crisis of Allegory." *Italian Quarterly* 18 no. 69 (1974): 7–28.

_____. "'Io son venuto': Plato, Seneca, and the Microcosm." *Dante Studies* 93 (1975): 95–129.

_____. "Platonism and Poetic Form: Augustine's *Confessions*." Public lecture delivered at Princeton University, March 1982.

Ferguson, Margaret W. "Saint Augustine's Region of Unlikeness: The Crossing of Exile and Language," *Georgia Review* 29 (1975): 842–64.

Ferrari, Leo C. "The Arboreal Polarization in Augustine's *Confessions*." *Revue des Etudes Augustiniennes* 25 (1979): 35–46.

_____. "The Barren Field in Augustine's *Confessions*." *Augustinian Studies* 8 (1977): 55–70.

_____. "Monica on the Wooden Ruler (*Conf.* 3.11.19)." *Augustinian Studies* 6 (1975): 193–205.

_____. "The Pear-Theft in Augustine's *Confessions*." *Revue des Etudes Augustiniennes* 16 (1970): 233–41.

_____. "Symbols of Sinfulness in Book II of Augustine's *Confessions*." *Augustinian Studies* 2 (1971): 93–104.

_____. "The Theme of the Prodigal Son in Augustine's *Confessions*." *Recherches Augustiniennes* 12 (1977): 105–18.

Flores, Ralph. "Reading and Speech in St. Augustine's *Confessions*." *Augustinian Studies* 6 (1975): 1–13.

Freccero, John. *Dante: The Poetics of Conversion*. Edited, with an introduction, by Rachel Jacoff. Cambridge, Mass.: Harvard University Press, 1986.

_____. "Logology: Burke on St. Augustine." In *Representing Kenneth Burke*, edited by Hayden White and Margaret Brose. Selected papers from the English Institute; n.s., no. 6. Baltimore: Johns Hopkins University Press, 1982.

Gallo, Ernest. *The Poetria Nova and Its Sources in Early Rhetorical Doctrine*. Paris: Mouton, 1971.

Griswold, Charles L., Jr. *Self-Knowledge in Plato's Phaedrus*. New Haven: Yale University Press, 1986.

Gunn, Janet Varner. *Autobiography: Toward a Poetics of Experience*. Philadelphia: University of Pennsylvania Press, 1982.

Knauer, G. N. "*Peregrinatio animae*. Zur Frage der Einheit der augustinischen *Konfessionen*." *Hermes* 85 (1957): 216–48.

Landsberg, Paul Louis. "La conversion de saint Augustin." *La Vie Spirituelle* 48 (1936, supplement): 31–56.

Le Blond, J. M. *Les conversions de saint Augustin*. Paris: Aubier, 1950.

Lerer, Seth. *Boethius and Dialogue: Literary Method in the Consolation of Philosophy*. Princeton: Princeton University Press, 1985.

Longinus. *On the Sublime*. In *Classical Literary Criticism*, translated, with an introduction, by T. S. Dorsch. Baltimore: Penguin, 1965.

Luongo, Gennaro. "Autobiografia ed esegesi biblica nelle *Confessioni* di Agostino." *Parola del Passato* 31 (1976): 286–306.

Mann, William E. "The Theft of the Pears." *Apeiron* 12 (1978): 51–58.

Marrou, Henri-Ireneé. *Saint Augustin et la fin de la culture antique.* Vol. 1. *Retractio.* Vol. 2. Paris: De Boccard, 1938, 1949.

Mohrmann, Christine. *Etudes sur le latin des Chretiens.* Vol. 2. Rome: Edizioni di storia e letteratura, 1961.

O'Connell, Robert J. *St. Augustine's Confessions: The Odyssey of Soul.* Cambridge, Mass.: Harvard University Press, 1969.

O'Donnell, James J. *Augustine.* Boston: Twayne, 1985.

———. "Augustine, *Confessions* 10.1.1–10.4.6." *Augustiniana* 29 (1979): 280–303.

O'Meara, John J. *The Young Augustine: An Introduction to the Confessions of St. Augustine.* New York: Longman, 1980.

Ong, Walter J. *Orality and Literacy: The Technologizing of the Word.* London: Methuen, 1982.

Oroz Reta, José. "Priere et Recherche de Dieu dans les *Confessions* de saint Augustin." *Augustinian Studies* 7 (1976): 99–118.

Pegis, Anton C. "The Second Conversion of St. Augustine." *Gesellschaft, Kultur, Literatur: Beitrage Luitpold Wallach gewidmet.* Edited by Karl Bosl. Stuttgart: Anton Hiersemann, 1975.

Pelikan, Jaroslav. *Jesus through the Centuries: His Place in the History of Culture.* New Haven: Yale University Press, 1985.

Pellegrino, Michele. *Le "Confessioni" di Sant'Agostino. Studio introduttivo.* Rome: Editrice Studium, 1956.

Pfligersdorffer, Georg. "Das Bauprincip von Augustins *Confessiones.*" *Festschrift Karl Kretska zum 70 Geburgstag,* pp. 124–47. Heidelberg, 1970.

Pizzolato, Luigi Franco. *Le "Confessioni" di Sant'Agostino. Da biografia a "confessio."* Saggi e ricerche, serie 3: Scienze filologiche e letteratura, 7. Milan: Universitá Cattolica del S. Cuore, 1968.

———. *Le fondazioni dello stile delle "Confessioni" di Sant'Agostino.* Saggi e ricerche, serie 3: Scienze filologiche e letteratura, 12. Milan: Universitá Cattolica del S. Cuore, 1972.

Ricoeur, Paul. *Time and Narrative.* Vol. 1. Translated by Kathleen McLaughlin and David Pellauer. Chicago: University of Chicago Press, 1984.

Rondet, H. "La Symbolisme de la mer chez saint Augustin." *Augustinus Magister* 2 (1954): 691–701.

Rothfield, Lawrence. "Autobiography and Perspective in the *Confessions* of St. Augustine." *Comparative Literature* 33 (1981): 209–23.

Scharl, E. *Recapitulatio mundi.* Freiburger Theologische Studien, 60. Freiburg im Breisgau: Herder, 1941.

Schillebeeckx, Edward. *Christ: The Experience of Jesus as Lord.* Translated by John Bowden. New York: Crossroad, 1986.

Solignac, A. "Introduction." *Les Confessions.* Bibliothèque Augustinienne, vol. 13. Paris: Descleé De Brouwer, 1962.

———. "Notes." *Les Confessions.* Bibliothèque Augustinienne, vols. 13 and 14. Paris: Descleé De Brouwer, 1962.

Spengemann, William C. *The Forms of Autobiography: Episodes in the History of a Literary Genre.* New Haven: Yale University Press, 1980.

Stephany, William A. "Thematic Structure in Augustine's *Confessions*." Paper presented at the 1982 Patristics, Medieval, and Renaissance Conference held at Villanova University, November 1982.

Trapé, Agostino. "Introduzione." *Le Confessioni*. Nuova Biblioteca Agostiniana, vol. 1. 4th ed. Rome: Cittá Nuova, 1982.

Urs von Balthasar, Hans. *Man in History*. London: Sheed and Ward, 1968.

Vance, Eugene. "Augustine's *Confessions* and the Grammar of Selfhood." *Genre* 6 (1973): 1–28.

————. "Saint Augustine: Language as Temporality." *Mimesis: From Mirror to Method, Augustine to Descartes*. Edited by John D. Lyons and Stephen G. Nichols, pp. 20–35. Hanover, N.H.: University Press of New England, 1982.

Verheijen, Luc. "The *Confessions*: Two Grids of Composition and of Reading." *Augustinian Studies*, forthcoming.

————. *Eloquentia pedisequa, observations sur le style des "Confessions" de saint Augustin*. Latinitas Christianorum primaeva, vol. 10. Nimwegen: Dekker and van de Vegt, 1949.

Weintraub, Karl Joachim. *The Value of the Individual: Self and Circumstance in Autobiography*. Chicago: University of Chicago Press, 1978.

Williger, E. "Der Aufbau der *Konfessionen* Augustins." *Zeitschrift für die neutestamentliche Wissenschaft* 28 (1929): 81–106.

Zepf, Max. *Augustins Confessiones*. Tübingen: J. C. B. Mohr, 1926.

Index